# A CHILD IN MIND:
# PROTECTION OF CHILDREN
# IN A RESPONSIBLE SOCIETY

## THE REPORT
of the Commission of Inquiry
into the circumstances surrounding the death of
## KIMBERLEY CARLILE

Presented to the
London Borough of Greenwich and the Greenwich Health Authority
by members of the Commission of Inquiry.

D1347598

London Borough of Greenwich
December 1987

0181 854 8888

# A CHILD IN MIND

Copies of the report are on sale at the following addresses, price £12 each.

**By Personal collection**

London Borough of Greenwich, 29-37 Wellington Street, Woolwich, London, SE18. Between the hours of 9.30 a.m. – 4 p.m. Monday-Friday.

National Society for the Prevention of Cruelty to Children, 67 Saffron Hill, London, EC1. Between the hours of 9 a.m. – 5 p.m. Monday-Friday.

National Institute for Social Work, Mary Ward House, 5-7 Tavistock Place, London, WC1. Between the hours of 9.30 a.m. – 5 p.m. Monday-Friday.

**By Post**

London Borough of Greenwich The Printing Manager, The Town Hall, Wellington Street, Woolwich, London, SE18 6PW. Telephone: 01-854 8888 Ext. 2245.

Price £12.50 (including postage and packing.

ISBN 0 904399 06 0

Cover design and illustrations by the
Printing Unit of the London Borough of Greenwich

Base grid of Percentile charts reproduced by
permission of Castlemead Publications

Published by the London Borough of Greenwich,
Town Hall, Woolwich, London SE18. December 1987

Printed in Great Britain by
Bemrose Security Printing, Derby

# MEMBERS OF THE COMMISSION OF INQUIRY

———————

Mr. Louis Blom-Cooper  Q.C.

Mr. Jim Harding

Miss Elizabeth McC. Milton

The death of a child
is never easy to come to terms with,
even in the abstract: the death of a child
for whom one has had responsibility
leaves its own special mark.

*from the preface to the written
statement made by Mr. Martin Ruddock,
to the Commission of Inquiry
on 29 July 1987.*

# CONTENTS

| Chapter | | | Page |
|---|---|---|---|

## PART IV

### GENERAL ISSUES

## PART V

### CONCLUSIONS AND RECOMMENDATIONS

## APPENDICES

# PREFACE

On 28 May 1987 the London Borough of Greenwich and Greenwich Health Authority jointly appointed a Commission of Inquiry into the circumstances surrounding the death of Kimberley Carlile, who was born on 3 November 1981 and died on 8 June 1986. The Commission of Inquiry was composed of Mr. Louis Blom-Cooper QC, Mr. Jim Harding and Miss Elizabeth Milton.

## Terms of Reference

The Commission's terms of reference were as follows :-

"(a) To investigate the events leading up to, and the circumstances surrounding the death of Kimberley Carlile on 8 June 1986.

(b) To determine what steps were taken by the two authorities and their respective staff during the period from October 1985 to June 1986 in relation to the welfare of Kimberley Carlile, and the adequacy of any such steps.

(c) to inquire into the structure and co-ordination of services to the family of Kimberley Carlile by the two authorities and any other persons or agencies (statutory or voluntary) and the liaison between them.

(d) To examine the legal and statutory framework within which the services and other relevant agencies were empowered to act in the protection of Kimberley Carlile against abuse within her family, and to consider what (if any) change in the law and practice relating to child abuse is necessary.

(e) To inquire into any matter relating thereto, as the Commission may think fit.

(f) To make such recommendations arising out of the above, as the Commission may deem appropriate, including the nature of child abuse inquiries.

The two authorities further direct that:-

1. The Commission of Inquiry is to be held at such place(s) within the London Borough of Greenwich, as the Commission may determine.

2. The Commission may, if it thinks fit, hold its Inquiry, or part of it, in private.

3. The Report of the Commission of Inquiry, which the two authorities undertake to publish in due course, is to be rendered to the authorities by the thirtieth day of September 1987, or at such later date as may be directed at the request of the Commission."

## Circumstances leading to the Commission of inquiry

Kimberley Carlile died, aged $4\frac{1}{2}$, at 49 Cambert Way, Ferrier Estate, Kidbrooke, London SE3 in the Borough of Greenwich, where she had lived since 4 October 1985 with her step-father, Mr. Nigel Hall,[1] her mother, Mrs. Pauline Carlile and three siblings, identified only as X (a boy aged 9), Y (a girl aged 7) and Z (a girl aged 19 months). Her death was due to a traumatic subdural haemorrhage caused by an injury to the left temple, consistent with having been caused by a blow, such as a kick. At the post-mortem it was discovered that she had multiple bruising and scarring on various parts of her body, some of them obvious to even the most casual observer; those not visible would have been obvious to the family whenever she was bathing or undressed. These wounds were consistent with repeated episodes of physical abuse. At death she was dehydrated and severely undernourished. Between the age of 2 years and her death she had gained only 2.5 lbs (1.26Kgs). Mr. Hall was convicted of Kimberley's death at the Central Criminal Court on 15 May 1987 before Mr. Justice Steyn and a jury; he was sentenced to life imprisonment. He was also convicted of causing Kimberley grievous bodily harm, for which he received a concurrent sentence of 18 years' imprisonment. No application for leave to appeal against either conviction or sentence has been lodged. Mrs. Carlile was convicted of causing Kimberley grievous bodily harm, and sentenced to 12 years' imprisonment. She has applied for leave to appeal against sentence only.

The Commission of Inquiry sat in private session on 25 days, between 29 June and 6 August 1987, at Shrewsbury House Community Centre, Bushmoor Crescent, Shooters Hill, London SE18, and for a further three days - on 1, 2, and 3 September - to hear oral submissions. This break in the Inquiry facilitated the lodging of final written submissions preparatory to the oral submissions. The Commission had earlier sat in public on 8 and 15 June 1987 to deal with preliminary matters relating to the procedure to be adopted, including the decision to hold the Inquiry in private. It heard 63 witnesses, including taking evidence from Mrs. Carlile at H.M. Prison, Holloway on 3 July, and from Mr. Hall at H.M. Prison, Wormwood Scrubs on 8 July.

## Acknowledgements

The role of counsel in a child abuse inquiry is crucial to the accomplishment of the assigned task, whatever kind of procedure is adopted for conducting the hearings. That role was made more arduous in our Commission of Inquiry by the tight time-table imposed on us by our terms of reference. (We are acutely conscious that we have overrun our deadline). Given the speed with which we started the Inquiry, and which continued to have its impact during, and after the conclusion of the hearings, we owe a special indebtedness to our counsel, Miss Presiley Baxendale and Miss Monica Carss-Frisk. They assimilated the documentation at an astonishing rate, presented the material in a palatable form with efficiency, and conducted their questioning of the witnesses in an exemplary fashion. We are also aware that their liaison with the legal representatives of the parties before the Inquiry was a model of courtesy and helpfulness. It proved to be invaluable when we encountered one or two bumpy passages in the course of the hearings. Their contribution

---

[1] We have treated Mr. Hall throughout this report as Kimberley's step-father, although he had co-habited with Mrs. Carlile only since early 1985.

to the conclusion of the Inquiry cannot be overestimated; without it we would have felt gravely handicapped.

Members of a Commission of Inquiry and counsel to the Commission inevitably depend heavily on the administrative back-up they receive. In this respect we have been fortunate. Mr. Peter Bailey, a committee secretary with Greenwich Borough Council, came to his unique task of serving the Commission as its secretary, displaying evident relish. In a quiet, unassuming and unobtrusive manner he performed every task that we set him, and more. He organised our meetings, during and after the oral hearings, and processed the seemingly ceaseless drafts of our report with consummate ease. Our thanks to him are sincere, and go beyond the gratitude usually and politely expressed by committees to their secretariats.

While the burden of administration was at its heaviest, before and during the oral hearings, Mr. Bailey was supported by Mrs. Anne Curr, also in ordinary life a committee secretary with the local authority. She too was a model of efficiency. We felt her loss, when she was pulled back to her regular duties.

Throughout June and July we were supplied with a succession of typists, too numerous for us to name them. Our thanks are due to them, collectively and anonymously. As soon as we began to draft our report we were supplied with two IBM word-processors and two splendid secretaries, Miss Nicola Clayton and Miss Christine Surin, who transferred our variable handwriting on to the word-processors and tick-tacked on the print-out. Their cheerfulness in the face of demanding commissioners was welcome relief from the torpor of draftmanship.

We should add that we are grateful to the sponsoring authorities for having ensured that there was always the appropriate and reliable administrative support to the Commission. We wish also to acknowledge the manner in which the two authorities set up the Inquiry. Once they had laid the foundations of our Inquiry - selecting the membership, framing the terms of reference, and providing the venue for the hearings - they distanced themselves from our task and thus preserved both the fact and the appearance of our independence.

Shrewsbury House Community Centre proved to be an ideal spot for our hearings. It is situated in a leafier part of suburban London, perched at the southern end of the Borough with a fine panoramic view of central London. Its seclusion from the hubbub of Woolwich and Greenwich gave us a sense of quiet contemplation, over and above the privacy of our proceedings. We are grateful to the manager and his staff at the Centre for smoothing our daily routine. Our occupancy of the main meeting room was never disturbed, save for an occasional, not unwelcome, accompanying music emanating from dancers down below.

Our final thanks are reserved for those who had a hand in the actual preparation of our report and its handsome appearance. Mr. Colin Martin, Printing Manager for Greenwich Borough Council, was introduced to us at an early stage. His advice on matters of design, lay-out and method of presentation was offered with gentleness and deference to our wishes. If the report finds favour with the reader, it will be in no little measure due to Mr. Martin's efforts on our behalf to produce a readable and indestructible work.

Dr. John Gibson, a retired medical practitioner and now a professional indexer, was selected to compile the index, which we regard as an essential feature of any report. Dr. Gibson produced an excellent index timeously and without bother. We are grateful to him.

A CHILD IN MIND:
PROTECTION OF CHILDREN IN A
RESPONSIBLE SOCIETY

# PART I

## THE INQUIRY

# Tasks of a child abuse inquiry

The task of Commissioners of Inquiry is akin to that of historians: To reconstruct events of the past and understand how they happened. Yet, as John Lewis Gaddis pointed out in a recent review in the Times Literary Supplement:[1] "Writing history is an oddly schizoid activity. It involves imposing upon the past, but also stripping away from it, layers of retrospective interpretation. It aims to reconstruct 'what actually happened', but it goes about this in apparently contradictory ways: by allowing preoccupations of the present to determine what we find relevant from the past, so that history becomes a device for explaining how we got to where we are; but also by rejecting such 'presentism' on grounds that those who made history can hardly have had our concerns uppermost in their minds when they did so. To say that the past affects the present but that the present affects only our perception of the past is to point out an obvious asymmetry. But the corollary principle that time, so far as we know, flows only in one direction... has not impressed itself upon historians as much as one might think"; nor, despite a recognition of the seductive appeal of hindsight, has the principle impinged itself on those who conduct public inquiries.

Our uninhibited ambition to serve the children of the future justifies our using any information we can obtain to serve their cause. It is the historian, Michael Sturmer[2] whose claim for history best relates to the aspirations of inquiries: "Whoever supplies memory, shapes concepts, and interprets the past...will win the future". We want to win the future for children. We can make allowances. We can recognise that the specialist focus of the Inquiry, the significance of events under scrutiny, especially when viewed through that most accurate of diagnostic instruments, the 'retrospectivescope', are far removed from the hectic, demanding and fleeting days as they were lived at work in the welfare services. Any hour from our life will seem odd, if moved across months and studied at a different intensity to the way it was lived. As the Third Priest comments in T.S. Eliot's "Murder in the Cathedral":

> "... One moment
> Weighs like another. Only in retrospection, selection,
> We say, that was the day. The critical moment".

Our Inquiry is about what went wrong in the failed efforts of a few people attempting to protect one little girl from abuse at the hands of her parents. It isolates a slice of time - some few months in early 1986. It does not alight on one single moment of time. It surveys the spectrum of that time and relates it to the backcloth of the system and the fallible human beings that inhabit it. Our findings, and the recommendations that flow from them, will inevitably have been influenced by hindsight. In making our judgments about past conduct, we cannot escape our conditioning by the present and the

---

[1] "A time of confrontation and confusion". A Modern History Review in the Times Literary Supplement, 8 May 1987.
[2] Quoted in "The Battle of the Historians", Encounter, June 1987.

instant knowledge it brings. In recognising the danger of substituting to-day's view of events for the operative factors of yesteryear, we have kept in the forefront of our deliberations the overriding demands of thoroughness and fairness.

# CHAPTER 1

# PROCEDURE

## Public or private?

Whether a child abuse inquiry should be conducted in public or in private remains the subject of acute controversy, both in professional circles and in public debate. It is, therefore, encumbent upon us to add our voice, in the hope that an acceptable solution will soon be arrived at.

The consultative paper, issued by the DHSS in September 1985, states that the "inquiry should normally be conducted in private", while requiring that the report of the inquiry should be published in full. We understand that no one who responded to that consultative paper has argued to the contrary, so that we expect the final version on child abuse procedure will echo that statement. We endorse that approach. Our experience supports it.

In framing the terms of reference for the Commission of Inquiry, the two sponsoring authorities left it to us to decide whether our Inquiry should be conducted in public or in private. We noted that Lambeth Borough Council, in setting up the Tyra Henry Inquiry, under the chairmanship of Mr. Stephen Sedley Q.C., had directed that inquiry to be held in public, although a slight amendment to that direction was subsequently made. It is our view that the question ought invariably to be left to the inquiring body, because it is only after a provisional view of the documentation and the issues raised by the particular case has been taken, together with an assessment of the degree of public disquiet about the case, that it is possible to gauge whether the presumption of a private inquiry is or is not rebutted.

Conscious of our task to determine the issue speedily, we called a preliminary meeting on 8 June 1987 - only ten days after our appointment - to decide what procedure we should adopt. Even after a hearing lasting three hours we remained undecided. We invited the parties to supplement their oral submissions by written submissions, and a few did. (We note, parenthetically, that Wirral Borough Council which was represented by its Borough Solicitor, Mr Goodacre, did not oppose a hearing in private; and Mr Goodacre specifically supported the quasi-judicial procedure we employed for conducting the Inquiry). On 15 June 1987 we announced publicly that we had unanimously come to the conclusion that we should hear the Inquiry in private. We indicated, however, that there would be a daily transcript of the evidence and that after the report was published, anyone interested in reading the evidence could apply to Greenwich Borough Council and to Greenwich Health Authority for permission to see the transcript. (Our reasoned decision for going into private session is reproduced at Appendix F to this report).

Nothing that has happened during the hearings, or while we were writing this report, has in any way altered our view that it was right to conduct the Inquiry in private. If anything, we are fortified by our experience, to which we shall allude hereafter. We state here shortly why we decided as we did.

We began our consideration of the issue by asking ourselves the question: Just who is the Inquiry into the death of Kimberley Carlile supposed to help? It was necessary to pose such a question, simply because, listening to the various submissions, the purpose of the Inquiry had been forgotten in the welter of controversy surrounding the issue, whether it should be conducted in private or in public. The Inquiry is not primarily for the benefit of public consumption, via media reportage, however legitimate and understandable may be the public's interests in the case: which is not the same as saying that the case is one of public interest. Its purpose is to ascertain the sequence of events that led up to the death of a child; and by establishing what happened, to draw lessons that would help prevent other children from becoming the victims of abuse by their parents. In short, the Inquiry is about protecting the lives of children at risk. Against that, the other important principles must generally take second place. That includes the holding of inquiries, in which the public has a legitimate interest in ensuring a thorough and independent report, in full sight of the public.

We attach the highest importance to the principle of open justice, but there is a danger of elevating it to a position of paramountcy. It does not even have that position invariably in the courts of law: proceedings relating to children are commonly heard behind closed doors. The Cleveland Inquiry on 17 August 1987 went into private session when the parents of children, taken into care after alleged sexual abuse, gave their evidence. Even if in our society there are far too many instances of proceedings being conducted in secret, that does not mean that there are not cases which warrant the cloak of privacy. Child abuse inquiries - we mean to say nothing that could or could not apply to any other type of inquiry - normally fall into the category of cases deserving of privacy.

Always remembering that the inquiry is to learn the optimum lessons for the benefit of child protection, we think it imperative that everything calculated to make the inquiry as thorough in its investigation as is humanly possible should be done. It was clear to us that if we were to sit in public, a number of important witnesses (mainly social workers) would decline to give oral evidence (even if they might submit written statements) partly because of their fear that they would be hounded by insensitive journalists, criticised prematurely and out of context in the media long before the Inquiry reported, and be unfairly prejudiced in their present employment or in obtaining employment elsewhere in the future. Not being a statutory inquiry we had no power to compel witnesses to come forward. (We deal with this aspect of child abuse inquiries in chapter 3). Without the evidence of crucial participants in the development of the tragic events leading up to Kimberley Carlile's death, there would be a gaping hole in our investigation. Vital questions would remain unanswered, bits of the story would be missing, and we would have had to engage in surmise and conjecture on some important issues. Appropriate lessons might not be fully learned, due to the insufficiency of the material upon which to construct our recommendations. Who, we ask rhetorically, would be helped by such an incomplete Inquiry? The sponsoring authorities which set up the Inquiry would think that they had got less than full value for the costly exercise. The public, whose justified disquiet over child abuse prompted the two authorities to order the Inquiry, would receive naught for their comfort in a report that was incomplete. Most of all we would be failing the children whose interests we are all trying to protect.

We are aware that at the time of our decision the media were generally hostile to the notion of a private inquiry. A leader in *The Guardian* of 8 June 1987 said, truly, that social workers, health visitors, doctors and other professionals are public servants who must be publicly accountable for their actions; and concluded, tendentiously, that "a *secret* inquiry will look like a cover up - and may even be one." (Emphasis supplied). We are confident that our Inquiry has been neither a witchhunt nor a whitewash. But what we do feel is that, apart from the considerations mentioned above and those contained in our reasoned decision of 15 June 1987, social workers are entitled to some special treatment when it comes to public accountability. As a class of public servants they are patronised by professionals in the law and in medicine; they are vilified by the popular press; they are disliked by sections of the public who misunderstand, or are ignorant of what social work is about; their failings are constantly highlighted, while similar or worse acts of negligence by professionals go unremarked. Until the public is prepared to accord social workers the status granted to others who have to perform difficult tasks for the public benefit, some redress of public opprobrium is not out of place. We were motivated, to some extent, to allow privacy to the social workers for just those very reasons. The Director of Social Services, Mr. Martin Manby, conscious of the pressures on us at the time to sit in public, was appreciative of our decision to hold the Inquiry in private. We ourselves are aware that the Director was telling us that during a very difficult time for his staff, it was possible, as a result of our decision to sit in private, for social workers in Area 4 (and in other Area Offices) to continue to function during the weeks of our Inquiry, with a degree of normality.

## Method of inquiry

We adopted a quasi-judicial process for the conduct of the Inquiry, although a number of the parties represented before us argued that we should employ a simpler and cheaper method of collecting the facts, by calling witnesses and questioning them in the absence of anyone other than the Commission and its Counsel. We think that there are cases where such a procedure is inappropriate for a thorough investigation, and is unfair to those who might be the subject of criticism from whatever source, not to be directly confronted with any allegation about their conduct. We refer to this matter again, in chapter 4, where we deal with the vexed question of the mounting costs of child abuse inquiries conducted quasi-judicially.

Part of the antipathy towards the quasi-judicial procedure stems from attitudes towards the concepts of "inquisitorial" and "adversarial" proceedings. Few words are more misleading as a description of a legal procedure than "adversarial", with its overtones of hostility, antagonism and confrontation. In reality the word simply connotes one of the two main ways, familiar in civilised legal systems, of conducting the legal process. Under the adversarial system the tribunal sits to hear and determine the issues raised by the parties who bring their dispute forward for adjudication, not to conduct an investigation or examination on behalf of society at large. It has distinct advantages. It is based in part on the traditional dialectical approach that the truth will most likely emerge if each interested party is allowed to put his or her own case, from their own perspective. Truth will emerge, so it is claimed, from the opposing thesis and antithesis. There is much to be said for this approach, although it should not be overlooked that neither party may wish for the truth to emerge but only to ensure victory by clouding the issues in dispute. After all, truth, as Francis Bacon wrote, emerges more readily from error than from confusion.

The inquisitorial approach requires the tribunal to define the issues and to call such witnesses as it thinks appropriate to elicit the truth. Thus control lies in the hands of the tribunal and not the parties. Necessarily, the tribunal is more a participant in the fact-finding process, although by the use of counsel for the commission this feature can be much less prominent. The procedure, thereby, can remove any source of hostility that may be evoked by questioning for the tribunal.

A child abuse inquiry is basically an inquisition, and not a trial. But in the conduct of the inquisition, aspects of the adversarial style are introduced usefully, both to assist in examining every facet of the matters under inquiry and to ensure fairness to those who may come in for criticism. Thus we permitted 14 individuals, seven public authorities, three professional associations and two trade unions to be represented. They were legally represented by 16 barristers and solicitors (see Appendix A). All the parties who were granted legal representation were automatically invited to be present throughout the hearings, but it was obvious that for many, indeed most of them, it was unnecessary to attend throughout. The Commission did its best to provide ahead of a day's hearings, as complete a list of witnesses as possible, with an indication when they would be called. This was not always possible. If there were not such an urgency to hold the inquiry and report with all due speed, it might have been possible to give longer warnings of the attendance of witnesses, and thus save costs.

With one exception - and that of an expert witness - no witness was called without first having given a written statement for circulation. This again frequently did not provide a reasonable opportunity for others to know on what issues they would need to question the witness. Too often, written statements came too late in the day. Only a much more elongated procedure can accommodate the delay, sometimes inevitable, in the production of written statements.

## Nature and order of questioning

All legal representatives were invited to question every witness called before the Inquiry. But we indicated that they would be restricted to asking questions on issues that directly affected their own client's involvement in the case under inquiry. So long as the question could be said to touch on the party's case it should be possible to limit the extent of questioning and thus reduce the time taken to complete the inquiry. Much of the success in restricting the ambit of questioning depends on the lawyers exercising self-restraint, by satisfying themselves that the questions they ask (and the length of time it takes to ask them) are really necessary. It is difficult for the inquiring body always to judge, in advance of a particular line of questioning, the propriety of any questions, without engaging in an oral exchange between tribunal and advocate, an exercise which in itself can be very time-consuming and sometimes can arouse feelings of unfairness if the questioning is curtailed or even stopped altogether.

We indicated, however, that we would allow one modification to the strict rule of adherence to questioning on issues directly affecting the party involved in the questioning. If the questioner noticed some point in the Inquiry that had been overlooked in the course of questioning by the others, or recognised that some issue relevant to the Inquiry had not been touched on, questioning on such matters would be allowed.

By and large, our experience has been that the advocates adhered to the principle of self-restraint. We are not conscious that the time taken in eliciting all the evidence we needed to hear was appreciably lengthened by unnecessary questioning. That there was some duplication and overlap of evidence was inevitable. But even then it was kept in bounds, with only minimal intervention from the Chair.

## Salmon letters

Every child abuse inquiry assumes intense concern among those who may be the subject of criticism for their conduct in the handling of the particular case. This unhappily has particular relevance to social workers who, by contemporary experience, are likely to be more than ordinarily castigated by a press that is often ill-motivated towards social work, such as the treatment by the media of this case when it came before the Central Criminal Court in May 1987. A popular newspaper went so far as to equate the social worker, in the front page lead story, with the step-father who murdered Kimberley Carlile. The use of photographs, accompanied by bitter verbal invective, must have been hard to bear, made worse by the fact that the individual so treated was prevented from making his own comment, partly because the case was *sub judice* and partly because he properly reserved his answers for the formal Inquiry that was announced at the conclusion of the trial.

That apart, some of those who would be giving evidence have their professional reputation at stake. Some may even have their careers in social work in jeopardy; they may have to face disciplinary proceedings at the instance of their employing local authority. It cannot be over-emphasised that the consequences of criticism in the report are as serious as if they were facing civil proceedings for negligence or breach of duty.

The duty of any inquiring body is to be fully alive to the need for scrupulous fairness to those who may be affected. The received wisdom of those conducting inquiries is that if at any time an individual's conduct, on the basis of the documentary material or statements from witnesses, *might* give rise to criticism, the allegations must be reduced into writing and communicated to the individual, so that there is the earliest opportunity to meet the specific allegations. The emphasis is on the word "might", for the inquiring body does not, by administering the letter, commit itself to the criticism. But the individual is made aware that a provisional, even tentative view has been formed that the criticism may ultimately stand. Such letters are known as "Salmon letters," named as such as a result of a main recommendation of the Royal Commission on Tribunals of Inquiry (1966) under the chairmanship of Lord Justice (later Lord) Salmon.

The inquiring body has a difficult task to perform, requiring skill and judgment in the evaluation of the material before it has all been unfolded at the inquiry. Either way, by sending or refraining from sending a Salmon letter, damage may be done. There is no doubt - and we made it clear at the preliminary meeting of 8 June and again at an early stage (in fact, on Day 6) - that a Salmon letter may be issued at any time during the Inquiry, although preferably it should be issued before the hearings begin. Harm may be done by not sending a letter at the outset, because an individual is entitled to prepare his or her case on the basis of potential criticism. To issue the letter in mid-stream, of course, may be unexpected, and have led the individual to conduct his or her case on a false basis. In view of an incident in this Inquiry, we think it desirable to state what we think is good practice.

The inquiring body's duty is to peruse all the documentation available and decide who (if anyone) should be sent a Salmon letter. We issued a number of Salmon letters on 2 July 1987, the fourth day into the Inquiry (by then we had heard an opening by our counsel and only one or two peripheral witnesses.) We now think that we failed to do one thing. Every person who is granted the right to be legally represented should instantly receive a letter, confirming legal representation and informing them that the inquiring body may issue a Salmon letter at any stage. They ought to be warned that the grant of legal representation is itself an acknowledgement that they have a legitimate interest that calls for protection, and that they should prepare their cases with the possibility in mind that, although no Salmon letter is sent to them at the outset, it may be necessary to do so later. In this way no party before the Inquiry, who does not receive a Salmon letter, should be under any illusion that he or she is beyond ultimate criticism.

A problem arose in our Inquiry. Two witnesses were sent Salmon letters immediately following their oral evidence, at an advanced stage of the hearings. We thought that we were doing the only fair thing. But the two witnesses' advocates let us know, in no uncertain terms, that they regarded the delivery of the Salmon letters *after* their clients had given evidence, as grossly unfair. We thought then, and still think, that it is a paradox that we should be accused of unfairness in respect of what was the only fair thing to do. One can imagine the outrage if our report did criticise them without them having had any prior warning, or even a warning at the time of oral submissions. We offered the two advocates the opportunity of recalling their clients, if necessary just before oral submissions at the beginning of September when the Commission was due to re-assemble. We appreciated the point made, with restraint but nevertheless forcefully, that something had gone wrong that should not have happened. It was argued that there was nothing in the oral evidence that could have changed our minds on a proper assessment of the material available before the oral evidence. Either the Salmon letter was issuable at the beginning, or not at all. We disagree. We think that there was a significant difference in the evidence before, and after, the two witnesses gave evidence. All three of us did get a very distinct and quite different picture after hearing the oral testimony. Members of an Inquiry must also start as far as possible, with an open mind. Judgments form as the evidence unfolds. Opinions about issues and events may change, not only as a result of oral testimony but also because events can be placed in an increasingly better-informed context. At the end of the day it must be a matter of judgment. We hope that those affected by the incident will accept that any reasonable tribunal might well have made precisely the judgments we made, and when we made them.

## Delay in Inquiry

The Beckford Panel of Inquiry (page 4) made a strong recommendation that in all child abuse prosecutions involving children in care of a local authority, the criminal trial of the parents should usually take place within 3-4 months of the homicidal event. This recommendation was motivated by the desire that there should be minimal amount of delay between the death of a child and the inquiry into the responsibility (if any) of Social Services and other agencies in their handling of the case. (No completely comprehensive inquiry can be undertaken until the trial process has been completed, although we recognise - and deal with in Chapter 4 - that a worthwhile inquiry can take place before any criminal proceedings.)[1] **We make the like recommendation in respect of child abuse prosecutions where there is no statutory responsibility towards the child, but Social Services (as in this case) or other agencies have been working with the family in circumstances where child abuse is suspected.**

In this case the period of time elapsing from death (8 June 1986) to trial (5 May 1987) was almost a year. We have not felt it necessary to examine why it took so long for Mr. Hall and Mrs. Carlile to be brought to trial; we cannot think that such a delay was reasonable. The arrests were made instantaneously; there were damning admissions made by Mrs. Carlile, and Mr. Hall's silence on interrogation was eloquent testimony of his complicity; the post-mortem report detailing the multiple bruising and scarring could hardly be explained away by those who alone had the care of Kimberley Carlile; and the prosecution evidence was contained within a narrow compass of witnesses in and around the Ferrier Estate. On the face of it the delay appears inexcusable. Child abuse cases represent a classic type of criminal event where a limit should be placed on the time within which a trial must take place. A power to impose a time limit on a criminal trial exists in the Prosecution of Offenders Act 1985. **We recommend that the Secretary of State for Home Affairs should consider exercising that power in relation to child abuse cases. That apart, we recommend that the Director of Public Prosecutions should set up an internal inquiry as to why the prosecution of Mr. Hall and Mrs. Carlile was so long delayed.**

---

[1] cf. The inquiry by the Standing Panel of Inquiry of Nottinghamshire Area Review Committee into the circumstances surrounding the death of Reuben Carthy (September 1985).

Although some of our witnesses from Social Services had already given evidence at the Central Criminal Court, it is no part of our function to consider any aspect of the criminal trial of Mr. Hall and Mrs. Carlile. Were it not for the fact that the media quoted a remark made by Mr Justice Steyn in his summing up to the jury, wrenched out of its context, we would have observed faithfully that self-denying ordinance. The judge told the jurors that they might be forgiven for thinking that Greenwich Social Services had "abandoned" Kimberley Carlile. This judgment on the social workers concerned was headlined by the newspapers and given prominence in the media generally, to the dismay and hurt of the persons concerned. The Director of Social Services told us that it had made life in the Social Services Department, already difficult because of the impact of the tragedy, that much more difficult. The press, ever-ready to pillory social workers, was quick to seize the opportunity of apparent judicial support. We wish to say only this: having conducted a thorough investigation of the events surrounding Kimberley Carlile's death we have come emphatically to the conclusion that there never was any question of the Greenwich Social Services abandoning Kimberley Carlile, other than in a colloquial sense.

# CHAPTER 2

# EVIDENCE

## Disclosure of Confidential Documents

The Inquiry was sponsored by Greenwich Borough Council and Greenwich Health Authority jointly. Wirral Borough Council and Kensington and Chelsea Borough Council declined invitations to join in as co-sponsors, but both readily supplied the Inquiry with all relevant documentation.

From the outset of our Inquiry the Social Services Department of Greenwich Borough Council handed over all the documentation from its files relevant to the Carlile family. Greenwich Health Authority, on the other hand, expressed a reluctance to allow its files containing such confidential material to be seen other than by the members of the Commission of Inquiry. Accordingly, on 15 June 1987, Mr. Alan Hannah, the solicitor representing the Authority, to whom the Commission is indebted, delivered to the Commission's secretariat the file, but limited its disclosure to the members of the Commission, unless and until the Commission had obtained the consent of the mother of the children. Confidentiality about the health of the Carlile family required, it was claimed, such limitation upon disclosure. Unavoidable delay in obtaining the requisite consents led the Commission to request Greenwich Borough Council to obtain a declaration from the High Court that it would not be unlawful for Greenwich Health Authority to override confidentiality in the circumstances of the case. (We deal elsewhere with the precise status of local authorities which set up an independent inquiry in a child abuse case, and with the sequential points of disclosure of documentary material and the Commission's ruling on the admissibility of evidence).

To be fair, Greenwich Health Authority was just as keen as its co-sponsor of the Inquiry to obtain the sanction of the Court. What it was not prepared to do was to release the documents generally for the purpose of the Inquiry without a court order. It sought, in effect, a judicial fig-leaf to protect itself against a possible charge that it was ignoring the claims of confidentiality.

At the outset, the Commission was aware that it would be necessary to obtain the permission of the Family Division of the High Court to use the records relating to the siblings of Kimberley Carlile, who had been made wards of court in May 1987. With the helpful assistance of the Official Solicitor, such permission was obtained from Judge Phelan on 17 June 1987. Whereas the High Court had jurisdiction over wards of court, no such power, however, existed over adults who would be entitled to claim confidentiality. Greenwich Borough Council felt obliged to take the matter to court, for a ruling that would allow Greenwich Health Authority to disclose documents for which confidentiality had not been waived by Kimberley Carlile's mother.

The matter came before Mr. Justice Mann on the afternoon of Wednesday 24 June, when both authorities were represented by counsel. The judge was apprehensive about the Court's jurisdiction, since he presumed that the Court was being asked to order disclosure. In fact the Court was being asked only to say that Greenwich Health Authority had misdirected itself in law in concluding that, without parental consent, the claim of confidentiality of the family's medical and health records debarred disclosure, at least beyond the eyes of the Commission.

Whether or not the judge fully understood the precise nature of the application for judicial review of Greenwich Health Authority's decision about disclosure, the question of the extent to which the undoubted claim to confidentiality could be lawfully overridden was clearly one that was legally arguable.

Mr Justice Mann granted Greenwich Borough Council leave to serve short notice of motion and ordered that a Divisional Court (composed of a Lord Justice and a puisne judge) be convened on Friday 26 June. He also asked that the Attorney-General should appoint an *amicus curiae* (friend of the court) to assist the Court at the adjoured hearing. Although there was some exasperation at the legalistic approach adopted by the judge, it was felt nevertheless, that there would be a great value in having a ruling by the High Court on the status of confidential material in the hands of either an authority which has ordered a public inquiry, or one whose conduct fell within the inquiry's terms of reference (without itself being a party to the setting up of the inquiry). Predictably, the effect of the service of the notice of motion on Mrs. Carlile was to prompt an immediate consent to the waiver of confidentiality. Thus the Court proceedings were rendered futile. We think, however, that the question is of sufficient general interest to those concerned with the administration of child abuse inquiries for us to describe the legal framework of such inquiries, other than by the Secretary of State under the statutory powers relating to child care.

## The power to disclose

We examined the issue initially from the point of view of a Health Authority. Claims to confidentiality over the files of a Social Services Department of a local authority would require examination of the statutory provisions relating to Social Services.

*Prima facie*, a Health Authority is under an obligation not to disclose information obtained from families whom it assists, without their consent. An action for breach of confidence may be brought to restrain the disclosure or use of information which is not publicly known and which has been entrusted to a person in circumstances imposing an obligation not to disclose or use that information, without the authority of the person who imparted it. There is some complication in the fact that information is received by a host of medical, paramedical and administrative personnel in a treatment context. Absolute confidentiality between doctor and patient has not been possible for some time now. It is based on the myth, dear to the hearts of many doctors, of the one-to-one doctor/patient relationship. This can be maintained only for minor ailments. For anything more complicated, patients come to teams of health care professionals, of whom the doctor is one of those in the frontline. Confidentiality is thus shared by all the members of the team, consisting, among others, of pathologists, radiologists, nurses, physiotherapists, occupational and speech therapists, health visitors and hospital social workers. The team needs to know all the problems presented, in the interests of protecting the patient. The solution may be to regard all the accumulated information as supplied to the employing authorities. Confidentiality rests in the authority, and its employees are bound to accept non-disclosure as a term of their contracts.

The action for breach of confidence is independent of statute or contract, resting on an equitable obligation not to disclose or use information confided in good faith.

Although the courts have yet to establish firmly a rule of confidentiality, the case law up-to-date suggests that the obligation arises whenever a reasonable person in the position of the recipient of information knows or ought to know that what is being imparted is in strict confidence.[1] A third party may also be restrained from disclosing information which he or she knows or ought to know was subject to an obligation of confidence.[2] Only the person to whom the obligation is held may, however, enforce it.[3] An obligation of confidence needs to be distinguished from a privilege from disclosing information. Thus a local authority Social Services Department, or the National Society for the Prevention of Cruelty to Children, may be able to protect from disclosure any information in their possession, by claiming that it is in the public interest not to disclose it.[4] In such cases the court considers the balance in the particular case, between the public interest in preventing disclosure to ensure a public service can function properly, and the public interest in disclosure to achieve justice to the litigating parties. The public interest immunity from disclosure is thus qualified. But it is also distinguishable from an obligation of confidence: an authority may be able to withhold information in the public interest without necessarily being under an obligation not to disclose it.

The extent of any obligation of confidence will depend also on the precise nature of the particular relationship involved. In some cases the recipient of information may not disclose it to anyone else; in others there may be an implicit power to disclose the information to a limited class of persons. This is the case of a Health Authority, whose doctors, officers and other employees may receive confidences in the course of performing the Authority's functions. It should normally be the case that confidential information, acquired in order that services can be provided, should be available without breach of any obligation to those who need to know it for the purpose of providing the service.

It follows from this analysis of the law relating to confidential information, that a public authority's documents will be the subject of an obligation of confidence, even if they are not otherwise privileged from production. Only those documents containing information which the authority is obliged not to disclose would, *prima facie*, be unlawful to produce. On this assumption, therefore, the files of Greenwich Health Authority were subject to an

---

[1] See Megarry J in *Coco v A N Clark (Engineers)* [1969] R.P.C. 41, 48.
[2] *Prince Albert v Strange* (1849), 1 Mac and G 25; *Duchess of Argyll v Duke of Argyll* [1967] Ch. 302.
[3] *Fraser v Evans* [1969] 1QB 349.
[4] In *Re D (infants)* [1970] 1 W.L.R. 599; *D v N.S.P.C.C.* [1978] A.C. 171; *Campbell v Tameside Borough Council* [1982] 2 Q.B. 1065.

obligation of confidence, and hence not to be disclosed without consent. Two separate bases exist for the exercise of a discretion to disclose:

(a) production of the documents to the Commission of Inquiry was required to enable Greenwich Health Authority to perform its own statutory functions and was, therefore, authorised, by the law (the statutory function);

(b) production of the documents was required in the public interest; in such circumstances there is no absolute obligation of confidence (the public interest function).

## (a) The Statutory Function

An obligation of confidence may be overridden by statutory provisions which require the disclosure of information.[1] Section 22 (1) of the National Health Services Act 1977 provides that "in exercising their respective functions health authorities and local authorities shall co-operate with one another to secure and advance the health and welfare of the people of England and Wales". Implied in that duty is the notion that it may be necessary for the two types of authority to pool information. In pursuance of that duty, both Greenwich Borough Council and Greenwich Health Authority decided jointly to set up an independent Commission of Inquiry, with terms of reference that call for investigation into how the relevant statutory authorities performed, or failed to perform their respective functions in relation to Kimberley Carlile.

As our terms of reference made clear, both Authorities considered that in order that the Commission of Inquiry might discharge its task, and thereby both to assist the Authorities in the performance of their own separate functions and their general duty, the Commission of Inquiry must examine in detail what the Authorities knew, or failed to discover about the Carlile family, in addition to what the Authorities did, or failed to do in the light of what they knew.

Without such documents the Commission of Inquiry could not perform its task, or at least could do so only under a considerable handicap. The disclosure of Greenwich Health Authority's records was, therefore, required to enable it to discharge its statutory duty that it performed in setting up the Inquiry, and to enable it to acquire the information it needed to perform its statutory functions properly in future : cf.*Prest v Secretary of State for Wales* [1983] 82 L.G.R. 193, where it was held that there was a duty on a public authority to acquire information necessary to perform its statutory functions. A statutory authority, moreover, cannot lawfully act so as to withhold or frustrate what it reasonably considers to be necessary to enable it to perform its statutory functions. Hence, any obligation of confidence must properly yield to the need to disclose the information. It would be irrational for an authority to set up an inquiry and then proceed to shackle the inquirers by a denial of access to information required to perform the assigned task.

---

[1] *Parry - Jones v Law Society* [1969] 1 Ch. 1.

16

## (b) The Public Interest Function

There is a wider basis to the assertion that Greenwich Health Authority was empowered to override any obligation of confidence, where the public interest required disclosure. It has been thought in the past that the requisite public interest was limited to the disclosure of iniquitous behaviour: *Initial Services Ltd v Putterill* [1968] 1.Q.B. 396. But in *Fraser v Evans* [1969] 1.Q.B. 349, 362 A-D, cited approvingly by Stephenson L.J. and Griffiths L.J. in *Lion Laboratories v Evans* [1985] 1.Q.B. 526, 838A and 550B respectively, Lord Denning, MR considered that there was no such limitation: "There are some things which may be required to be disclosed in the public interest, in which event no confidence can be prayed in aid to keep them secret, and [iniquity] is mostly an instance of just cause or excuse for breaking confidence".

The welfare of children is a public interest which the courts have always acknowleged in considering the disclosure or non-disclosure of information. In *Gillick v West Norfolk Area Health Authority* [1986] 1.A.C. 112, 149H, Lord Justice Eveleigh in the Court of Appeal said that "there is no law of confidentiality which would command silence when the welfare of the child is concerned". (Although the House of Lords overturned the decision of the Court of Appeal, the statement indicates the great weight properly attached in the public interest to the protection of members of the public who cannot protect themselves, even if the statement may be too sweeping).

The public interest in serving the sound mangement of the child abuse system and to reduce, if not eliminate the risk of other children being abused, required that the Commission of Inquiry should have full access to all relevant information in order that its findings should be based on a thorough examination of all the facts, and its recommendations should be soundly-based. Confidentiality must in the public interest yield to disclosure.

## Conclusions

The Commission of Inquiry had throughout considered that it was entitled to call upon Greenwich Health Authority to disclose all its records on the Carlile family, irrespective of any consent from the parents. Since the Commission decided to conduct its Inquiry in private it was possible to ensure that the documentary evidence would not be disclosed outside the Inquiry hearings. Legally represented parties were specifically requested not to reveal the contents of documents to anyone not directly involved in this Inquiry. Had the Commission decided to hold the Inquiry in public, it would still have maintained the right to full access to the records of Greenwich Health Authority. Had the Commission entertained any doubt about full disclosure of the Health Authority's documents, it would have accepted, with extreme reluctance, the offer of the documents for sight and use exclusively of the Commission.

Rather than forego the potentially valuable evidence in the records, the Commission would have sacrificed the demands of fairness to the participants in the Inquiry that they too should be privy to the documentary material. **We recommend that in its forthcoming circular on procedures for** child abuse inquiries the Department of Health and Social Security should include a paragraph indicating that local authorities and health authorities will not be in breach of confidence if they decide to disclose the relevant records to an independent review body.

As far as we are aware, the problem of withholding by a local authority of its documents from disclosure has not arisen in any of the child abuse inquiries of recent years. Even if it does arise in the future, we are of the view that precisely the same considerations apply to Social Services as we have found applies to Health Authorities.

## Disclosure of documents by other public bodies

If a panel of inquiry requires documents from a public authority which is not a sponsor of that inquiry, there is always the question whether, and to what extent it would be lawful for such authority to handover documents that contain confidential material, or are otherwise statutorily privileged from disclosure. The problem arose in the course of our Inquiry in relation to the files of the Court Welfare Officer, who was a member of the Inner London Probation Service. Fortunately, the problem was readily overcome, because none of the records concerning the Carlile family contained any confidential discussion with any of the family. Furthermore, on 7 July 1987 Mrs Justice Butler-Sloss had granted the Inner London Probation Service liberty to disclose to the Commission of Inquiry all notes, records, correspondence and reports in its possession or control relating to Kimberley and to the three other children who had become wards of court. Similar leave to disclose was sought and obtained from the resident judge at Wigan County Court which had initiated in mid-February 1986 a request for a court welfare report on the family, for the purpose of determining a dispute over paternal access to the child, Z.

The obstacles to disclosure of such evidential material may not be so easily overcome in other cases where confidentiality prevails. We think, therefore, it would be helpful if we describe shortly the nature of the problem, and how it may be overcome. It is clear from Rule 31 of Probation Rules 1984 that probation records should be regarded as private documents. As with records kept in accordance with the Boarding-Out of Children Regulations 1955, these records are privileged from disclosure in the ordinary course of events.[1]

In *Re M(minors)*,[2] a case in which a subpoena was served upon a probation officer requiring him to attend wardship proceedings, bringing with him the probation records, Mrs Justice Booth held that probation records were privileged and access thereto was allowed only to authorised persons. The basis of such privilege was not the fact that the documents were of a private and confidential nature - there could be no contractual relationship between the probation officer and the probationer - but that Parliament had decreed that it was in the public interest that they should be immune from disclosure. The judge indicated, however, that non-disclosure was not absolute. There was always a discretion whether there should be disclosure. Thus the

---

[1] *Re D (Infants)* [1970] 1.W.L.R. 599.
[2] (1986) 16 Fam. Law 336.

Probation Committee for the relevant area is empowered to allow certain persons access to the records.

There seems to us to be no reason in principle why access to documents should not be offered to members of an independent review body set up to investigate the circumstances surrounding the death of a child. Even more so would that be where the Probation Committee was itself one of the bodies setting up the inquiry.

Two considerations arise, however, in the exerise of any decision to disclose or not to disclose. First, the Probation Committee would have to pay due regard to the matters which caused the records to become privileged. The ability of the probation service to perform its statutory and professional tasks as a court-based service ought not to be in jeopardy if there is a geniune expectation of confidentiality between probation officer and probationer. One could imagine that delicate personal matters might be noted in the records relating to a person who is being supervised while on parole licence on release from prison, under a sentence of life imprisonment for murder. In principle, we do not see that kind of situation differs from the case of a family revealing personal details to Social Services or to a Health Authority.

Second, under the terms of the Probation Rules, access can be afforded only to certain persons authorised by the Probation Committee. There is no power generally to authorise publication of records in the public domain. A Probation Committee might, therefore, be in breach of its statutory duty if it were to release probation records in circumstances where there was any risk that the documents would circulate among the public, whether through the media or by some other form of publication. If the inquiry sits in private, there should be no inhibition upon full disclosure. Since there may be a justified reluctance to escape the statutory prohibition on disclosure where the inquiry is in public, **we recommend that there should be a statutory power in the Secretary of State, on application by the inquiring body, to authorise the disclosure of probation records by the relevant Probation Committee**.

## Admissibility of Evidence

Not all the available relevant material was admitted in evidence before the Inquiry. It was well-known that Greenwich Area Review Committee had set up an inquiry which had submitted an interim report. The Commission decided that the report, and also Greenwich Social Services Management Review Report, together with a similar report prepared by Greenwich Health Authority, should not become part of the documentary material before the Inquiry.

There was little doubt that there would be some value in the Commission knowing the views expressed in the three reports, but whatever advantage might be gained from that knowledge was, in the Commission's view, heavily outweighed by other considerations. First, the members of the Commission would have had to put out of their minds any of the preconceptions that they might have formed from reading the views expressed in the reports. While it is true that to have an open mind is not to have an empty mind, nevertheless it is better that the mind should not be cluttered up with other people's opinions, and that there should be no hint of influence from those others who had conducted their own investigations on issues central to the Inquiry, but on perhaps different and incomplete evidence. If this Inquiry's findings did so happen to mirror those contained in those other reports, it would be difficult to disabuse any critic of the claim that this Inquiry had been less than wholly independent.

Second, the Commission anticipated another problem in admitting the three reports into evidence. A real risk might have existed of transforming this Inquiry into an inquiry as to the correctness of the earlier reports. There might be endless argument about precisely what material had been placed before the members of the earlier inquiry. In short, we might have found ourselves engaged in conducting an inquiry within an inquiry. That would be a futile and expensive exercise.

To ensure that nothing of evidential value in the earlier reports was lost to the Inquiry, the Commission asked its counsel to read the three reports and note any relevant material, drawing anything to the Commission's attention that was considered necessary. Counsel told the Commission that she had read the three reports and had found nothing additional that needed to be revealed. Had the Commission been referred to any such material it would have made it available to the parties and their legal representatives.

## Publicity relating to wards of court

We have already noted that on 17 June 1987 Judge Phelan in the Family Division of the High Court gave leave for the records relating to X,Y, and Z, as wards of court, to be seen and used by the Commission for the purposes of the Inquiry. The Commission had already expunged the names of the three children from the documentation, but was aware that their identities were already known to the press. Since we had decided to hold our Inquiry in private, it was necessary only to warn the parties represented before the Inquiry to respect the anonymity of the children. And this they have complied with. But the safeguard could not apply with like force to those who will doubtless be commenting on our report.

On 28 August 1987, therefore, the London Borough of Greenwich, on the Commission's behalf, applied for, and obtained an Order from Mr. Justice Ewbank in the following terms: "And it is further ordered that no information of any kind (including photographs and correspondence) be published by any person or organisation which relates to the Commission of Inquiry's Report which identifies the above-named minors referred to as X, Y and Z in the said report, or their present whereabouts". **We recommend that the precaution of protecting the identity of vulnerable individuals (particularly children) should be adopted in all future child abuse inquiries**.

CHAPTER 3

# WITNESSES

All those who handled the case of the Carlile family from the time that the family came to Greenwich in the Autumn of 1985 have given evidence before the Commission of Inquiry. We are grateful to all of them for having submitted themselves to the ordeal of having to wait anxiously for their day in the witness chair and then to undergo the unnerving (even to the most stoical individuals) experience of cross-questioning. For those who had already received Salmon letters, the experience was particularly onerous, if only because they knew that their conduct was under special scrutiny; many may not perform at their best in such circumstances.

None of the persons in Wirral Social Services who was concerned with the Carlile family in the years, 1982-1985, when the family lived in the Wirral, was willing to assist the Commission. Their absence was not justified, and indeed their refusal to assist was inconsistent with the attitude of their employer, Wirral Borough Council, which was represented before the Commission throughout the hearings by an assistant solicitor, Mr David Park. His written submissions to the Commission, in which he was at pains to point out were not made on behalf of the Council's employees, were extremely helpful. We were enabled thereby to come to conclusions as to the responsibility of Wirral Social Services for the events leading up to the death of Kimberley Carlile, without the undoubted benefit we would have had in hearing from personnel of the Wirral Social Services Department. Wirral Health Authority did not appear before us, but we received (very late in the day) a written statement and answers to a questionnaire administered by the Commission, from Miss Jean Rowlands, Director of Nursing Services.

## Main participants

Before we deal with the Wirral absentees, we wish to make specific mention of the four main witnesses from Greenwich who were in the front line of potential criticism.

*Miss Marilyn Reader, health visitor*

Miss Reader was the health visitor throughout the whole of the relevant period, from October 1985 to June 1986. She gave her evidence under evident strain and stress. She explained her involvement with the Carliles in a thoroughly analytical way. She conceded, with commendable candour, that she could properly be criticised for bad practice. We feel confident that the experience of contributory failure to protect a child at risk of abuse will have been a lesson that will stand her in good stead. In short, her evidence, both written and oral, and the submissions made on her behalf by Mr. Nigel Pitt, revealed a compelling explanation of how things went wrong in the management of the case. She accepted fully her public accountability. In so far as we criticise her work in the Carlile case, such criticism should not hamper her future in her career as a health visitor or nursing officer.

## Mr. Martin Ruddock, team leader, Area 4

All that, and more, can be applied to Mr Ruddock. He was the prime candidate for blameworthiness in failing to prevent Kimberley Carlile's death at the hands of her step-father. In the middle of the Inquiry he demonstrated his professionalism, even before he submitted his written statement and gave oral evidence, by writing a letter to us in response to a Salmon letter which we had sent to him. This letter, which was distributed to all the parties represented before us, accepted the allegations of fault attributed to him. It requires a high sense of public duty and personal courage to admit that one has fallen well below professional standards that one sets for oneself and are imposed by one's professional bodies.

Mr Ruddock's behaviour before us and his general professionalism lead us to say that, in spite of the criticism that attaches to his handling of the Carlile case, we regard him as an intelligent social worker, conscientious and hard-working, although **we recommend that he should not in the future perform any of the statutory functions in relation to child protection.** We suspect that part of the problem was that he over-worked, to the detriment of his professionalism. Our view was more than amply confirmed by the receipt of his written statement. It is not only an outstanding document of insight into the nature of a social worker's tasks. But it was also well written, movingly reflective and self-critically analytical. It avoids casting blame on others, in circumstances where it might have been expected. Our appreciation of its work can be reflected in **our recommendation that Greenwich Borough Council, Mr Ruddock's employing authority, should make the document available as an educational tool for the training of social workers generally, and for those involved in child abuse particularly.**

## Mrs. Ruby Henlin, Nursing Officer (Health Visiting)

Mrs. Henlin was responsible for the work of Miss Reader. In that capacity she must bear criticism for the fact that Miss Reader failed to perform her routine duties in relation to the Carlile family, and in particular her responsibility for Kimberley Carlile. Mrs. Henlin's lack of understanding of the function of a supervisor in a child abuse case was a serious failure. But she is entitled to some allowance for the fact that she was new in the post, was overwhelmed by her workload, and lacked preparedness for the task of supervising a health visitor in a child abuse case.

## Mr. Don Neill, Area 4 Manager

As Area Manager, Mr. Neill had overall responsibility for the standards of practice provided by the three teams in the Area. He cannot escape some criticism for the fact that one of his teams mishandled a child abuse case. We were aware in the course of our Inquiry that the Area was under considerable strain, including during the relevant period, a complete turnover of team managers, and that Mr. Neill himself received little support from his own line management. We have, however, heard evidence, which we readily accept, that he is a conscientious, caring and approachable manager.

In addition to his general responsibility, Mr. Neill was, exceptionally Mr. Ruddock's supervisor. In that capacity he shares the blame for the failure to make sure that Kimberley Carlile was safe. Since we anticipate he will never again be in a position of having to supervise directly a fieldworker carrying a child abuse case (because we recommend later that Team Managers should never carry a child abuse case), we do not think that our criticism of him in this case should in itself be a factor in any assessment of his competence as an Area Manager.

## Wirral absentees

As soon as the Commission had perused the documentation on the Carlile family during the time that the family lived in Wallasey from 1982-1985, readily supplied by Wirral Borough Council, it was apparent that at least four of the officers of the Wirral Social Services Department, who were directly involved with the family, could materially assist the Commission in its task. The four were Mr. Jim Surridge, Area Officer, Wirral Social Services Department, who chaired the two case conferences in May and August 1984; Mrs. Nicola Madeley and Mrs D.M. Stuart, team leader and social worker respectively in Wirral Social Services Department; and Mr. Robert Ewbank, a social worker who was appointed the key worker at the case conference on 15 August 1984 and was the person who conducted the preparations during the summer and autumn of 1985 leading up to the hand-over of the three children on 4 October 1985. All four of them were at some stage directly concerned with the Carlile children who were in voluntary care in May and in July 1984 and from 13 August 1984 to 4 October 1985.

Mr. Surridge has, since the events of 1982 - 1985, retired. From the outset of the approaches made to all four social workers, Mr. Surridge alone had indicated firmly his continued unwillingness to come and assist the Inquiry. He was one of those who still bear the psychological scars of the Paul Brown Inquiry in 1980. That was the third investigation into that case which reflected both the politically-charged atmosphere surrounding the case and the unhappy relationships among and between the staff of a Social Services Department and local Councillors. That experience, moreover, was undergone in the full glare of publicity. Although it was known by June 15 that our Inquiry was to be conducted in private, that proved to be an insufficient persuader to Mr. Surridge to come and give evidence. Although he was no longer in the local authority's employ, and on that account under no duty to come forward, his sense of professional obligation should have prevailed over a natural desire to be left alone in contented retirement. His attitude, while understandable, was disappointing.

The other three social workers initially showed no disinclination to come forward (as we shall describe) but naturally wanted to take advice from their trade union, NALGO, and from their legal advisers. In fact, before the Commission began its hearings they had provided our counsel with draft statements, and had agreed to attend to give their evidence on 1, 2 or 3 July. Subsequently a problem arose as to the funding of any legal representation. We were not privy to any of those discussions, but we learned that the relevant Committee of Wirral Borough Council would be considering the matter in the evening of June 29, the first day of the Inquiry's hearings. On the morning of June 29 there appeared in *The Guardian* an article which claimed that Wirral Social Services had provided wholly insufficient information on the Carlile family to their counterparts in Greenwich. This publicised allegation of lack of co-operation in the supply of information as between local authority Social Services Departments at first sight appeared, not to put too fine a point on it, unhelpful in persuading employees of Wirral Social Services to expose themselves to inquiry and potential criticism.

If anyone had thought that that was the effect, he would have been wrong. On 30 June we were told that Wirral Borough Council had voted to support funding legal representation of the three social workers, limited to their legal representative attending before the Inquiry only when the three were giving evidence. We were given to understand that this appropriate decision by the local authority found a ready acceptance by the three social workers, and that Mr. R.H.Dawson, of Morecroft, Dawson & Garnetts, Liverpool solicitors, had been instructed and was hurriedly preparing their case. In fact he immediately came to London on Wednesday 1 July and contacted the Commission for documentation and other guidance. He was cautiously optimistic that he would be ready to call his clients by Thursday, 9 July, although originally it had been planned for the evidence of the Wirral witnesses to be taken at the begining of the Inquiry (as we indicated above), since chronologically that was the appropriate stage. The Commission accordingly made arrangements to hear the Wirral social workers.

On Friday, 3 July the Commission was told informally, however, that the three social workers were not intending to assist the Inquiry. A letter was sent on 6 July giving their reasons for declining the invitation to appear before the Commission of Inquiry. Correspondence, which we reproduce at Appendix E, ensued, to no effect.

Following the social workers' refusal to assist, the Commisson invited the Director of Social Services, Mr. David Rickard, to attend the Inquiry (two legal officers, Mr P Mousdale and Mr Maddox, were also invited, but declined). He indicated that he would consult with members of the Wirral Borough Council's Social Services Committee. The result was that the members who were consulted thought that it was inappropriate for the Director to attend, and so instructed him. We find this inconsistent with the local authority's own stance to assist the Inquiry. We would have thought that the matter was for the Director to decide, and that his professionalism would have dictated his appearance before us. Our correspondence with him is similarly reproduced in Appendix E.

To return to the three social workers represented by Mr Dawson, from the points made by Mr Dawson in the correspondence, we deduce three main arguments seeking to justify withdrawal from the Inquiry. First, the social workers believed that the Inquiry should have been set up by the Secretary of State for Social Services, and not by the two authorities in Greenwich. To have done the latter was to give the Inquiry a London-based local authority bias. (We in fact offered to sit in Wirral to take their evidence). Wirral Borough Council knew that the Secretary of State did not think it appropriate to set up an inquiry under his statutory powers, and was encouraging the relevant authorities to do so. Wirral Borough Council, although invited to do so, declined to join in sponsoring the Inquiry, but took part in the proceedings. The form and nature of a child abuse inquiry does not detract from the duty of those involved in the case from giving every assistance. It is not good enough for social workers to refuse to appear before an inquiry simply on the grounds that they do not like the procedure adopted. Some social workers and health authority employees, who *did* appear before us, would have much preferred a different procedure for the Inquiry.

Second, the Wirral social workers felt concerned that not all the relevant witnesses from the Wirral had been invited to attend, and they had no confidence in the comprehensiveness of the Inquiry's ultimate report. At no time did the three social workers suggest further names of persons who might assist. We identified the main workers involved. If it was desired that others should come, we would have welcomed suggestions.

Third, the three social workers wanted to limit the procedure of questioning to counsel for the Commission, and not be extended to legal representatives of other parties. It was open to those social workers to argue for such a limited procedure when we held our preliminary meetings. They did not do so, and Mr Goodacre, the solicitor for Wirral Borough Council, did not support others who did argue for a similar procedure to be adopted. We have given elsewhere our reasons for having rejected such a procedure.

It is hard to think of a more serious breach of a social worker's obligations to - (a) the public he or she serves; (b) the profession of which he or she is a member; and (c) to their colleagues in other authorities.

We recognise that social workers as a whole are weary of the succession of inquiries and the attendant adverse publicity. But the media have been specifically excluded from our Inquiry, with the feelings of social workers in mind. Yet these social workers argued in favour of a public inquiry under central government auspices. Hence publicity was not at the root of their objections. Whatever objection there may be to these inquiries - and we sympathise with some of the objections - there is no excuse for the non-attendance of the Wirral social workers and their Director. It was not in the public interest - nor in their interests - to remain silent. While the effect of their absenteeism is that we have thought it unfair to criticise, by name, their individual conduct of the Carlile case, we can, and do reserve criticism for their refusal to assist the Inquiry. Their employer must bear the brunt of blameworthiness - in our view, that involves not inconsiderable blame for failure to prevent the tragedy of Kimberley Carlile's death.

## Subpoena powers

If ours had been an inquiry set up by the Secretary of State under the powers vested in him by Section 26, Child Care Act 1980, we would have been able to compel attendance of the Wirral social workers. It has been respresented to us that child abuse inquiries set up by local authorities should be granted such subpoena powers. We examine this question briefly.

Order 38, Rule 19 of the Rules of the Supreme Court empowers the Crown Office to issue subpoenas in aid of an inferior court or tribunals. A subpoena may be issued to compel the attendance of witnesses only when the tribunal is a) recognised by law; b) acts judicially or quasi-judicially in the exercise of its functions; c) acts on evidence, whether or not on oath; and d) has no, or insufficient powers of its own to secure the attendance of witnesses or the production of documents. These Rules are at present not wide enough to include non-statutory child abuse inquiries, if only because they are not "recognised by law".

We think that there is some virtue in the situation where all the witnessess appear voluntarily. Compulsion is never a good starting point for uninhibited testimony. The subpoenaed witness may feel bound to tell the truth, but may feel inclined to be economical with it and not reveal the whole truth. And it goes without saying that those who are public servants or professionals, who must account for their actions or omissions publicly, ought to do so without judicial compulsion. It might be different for ordinary members of the public who do not owe any special obligation to come forward and assist an inquiry. But they are rarely, if ever, vital witnessess in a child abuse inquiry.

Nevertheless **we recommend that consideration should be given to enlarging the scope of Order 38, Rule 19**. We think that if at anytime an inquiry cannot get before it an important witness, it should be provided that it can apply to the Secretary of State for a certificate that there shall be legal recognition of the inquiry for the purpose of invoking Order 38, Rule 19. We would expect that the Secretary of State would need to satisfy himself that the inquiry was acting properly.

## Immunity from disciplinary action

We are aware that much of the current hostility among social workers towards child abuse inquiries stems directly from the manner in which Brent Borough Council responded in December 1985 to the report of the Panel of Inquiry into the Beckford Case. Within 48 hours of that report being published, Brent Borough Council purported to dismiss summarily from their employment three members of its Social Services Department,[1] even though the criticisms in the report varied in each of the three cases. It is not for us to comment, one way or another, as to the propriety of that action. What we do say is that, unfortunately, inquiries such as ours are seen by some local authorities as a part of a disciplinary process. Even though the two are properly unconnected, it cannot be gainsaid that criticism in a public report may be used as a springboard for taking disciplinary action. We are of the view that, so far as possible, such inquiries should be conducted without the threat of discipinary action hanging over the heads of social workers and others involved in the case. In order to achieve the objective of finding ways of protecting children, there should be no hindrance in the path of the inquiry. Disciplinary proceedings which lurk in the background can only hamper, and not help that process.

Mr. Alan Hannah, on behalf of Greenwich Health Authority, told us that his client gave every one of its employees who were due to appear as witnesses at the Inquiry an immunity from disciplinary action in respect of their

---

[1] *Dietmann v Brent London Borough Council* [1987] I.C.R.737.

conduct under inquiry. We think that the immunity conferred on the Health Authority's employees was highly commendable, and no doubt justified in respect of those individuals in the light of what was then known to the Authority. But we are uncertain as to how far a public authority can properly forego its duty to discipline staff who have committed a serious breach of the relevant disciplinary code.

Greenwich Borough Council, on the other hand, considered that it would not be proper to give any final or binding undertaking in advance of the Commission of Inquiry. Its reasoning seems to us to be sound in law and in practice. First, it is of the essence of a Commission of Inquiry's function to investigate in depth the detailed facts, and performing that task in a way that has not been undertaken before by some internal management review, or even some informal inquiry conducted independently. Second, the workers' employer is a public authority. It must make appropriate decisions about disciplining its staff on the basis of all evidence and material to hand. It may, of course, approach its decisions on the basis of a disposition not to take disciplinary proceedings, but what it cannot do is to bind itself in advance to ignore whatever findings the Commission makes. Third, the analogy with the immunity from criminal prosecution is false. That immunity is given in order to remove the privilege of self-incrimination before the inquiry. The local authority has a statutory duty to ensure the carrying out of the functions of Social Services. It is bound statutorily to employ appropriate staff to perform those functions, and it cannot bind itself to continue employing staff who may have demonstrated their unfitness to remain in employment.

We think that the approach adopted by Greenwich Borough Council is legally the correct one. In stating that no immunity from disciplinary proceedings can properly be granted, we do not wish to be understood as being unsympathetic to an employing authority which seeks full co-operation from its staff in assisting the Inquiry. It may be that such co-operation with a non-statutory Inquiry should be a factor in any decision subsequently to take disciplinary proceedings.

# CHAPTER 4

# FUTURE OF CHILD ABUSE INQUIRIES

Whenever a local authority (with or without the direct participation of another local authority or health authority) contemplates the commissioning of an independent inquiry into a case of child abuse, the factor of costs inevitably looms large in the decision to set one up. The size of the ultimate bill is dictated intrinsically by the need for an inquisition; it will not be substantially lowered if the inquiry is held wholly or partly in private. It is true that the costs can be lessened if the inquiry adopts a technique that does not involve a quasi-judicial procedure, but instead adopts the interviewing mode of investigation. This latter method, employed by some earlier panels of inquiry, questions each witness individually who is entitled to have his or her legal representative present only during that questioning. In so far as the evidence relates to the actions or inactions of other persons involved in the case, that evidence has to be relayed to the later witnesses. If necessary, the earlier witnesses can be recalled. Thus, confrontation by all other interested parties is avoided. Each one of us at the outset of our Inquiry rejected such a process in principle, as providing neither a guarantee of a thorough investigation of the facts nor, more particularly, a fair way to treat individuals who may face criticism ultimately in the report. There is no eluding the principle that all interested parties should be represented throughout the inquiry, so as to ensure a thorough investigation and scrupulous fairness to those directly affected. Furthermore, public confidence in a comprehensive and accurate report from a demonstrably independent panel of inquiry is sustainable only if the full panoply of the quasi-judicial process is observed. This is particularly so, where the inquiry is heard in private (as ours was) and the public has to take the proper conduct of the inquiry on trust.

Time and the presence of all parties given representation is a very expensive commodity. The large expense of an inquiry can be justified only if the report of the panel of inquiry is of lasting benefit to the future management of the child protection service. And that benefit is achievable only if some general issues that arise in the particular case are fully explored. If all that is required by the sponsoring authorities, on the other hand, is the ascertainment of the facts of the particular case, some simpler method of inquiry, such as by a standing panel of inquiry under the auspices of the relevant Area Review Committee will clearly suffice. Occasionally, as in this case, the public concern, as expressed in the media, will demand a more thorough investigation. That is how we have interpreted our task under the terms of reference given to us.

Inquiries such as ours are, of course, designed to focus primarily upon the detailed examination of the activities of specific individuals in the particular case. That involves at least a two-fold approach: the ascertainment of the true facts of the case and a critical analysis of the role and functions of the relevant agencies, including a close study of the nature and quality of their work and collaborative effort in the particular management of the child abuse system. Like earlier inquiries - and we have particularly in mind the Beckford report - we felt impelled to go further and, in making our recommendations for future legislation, governmental guidelines and professional action, to examine a number of general issues thrown up by the particular case. To that end, there is the temptation, hard to resist, to canvass with the individual witnesses directly involved in the case, supplemented by opinion evidence from expert witnesses, some general issues relating to child abuse. That process, too, calls for the amplest exploration by way of questioning by parties with diversified interests and expertise.

We are, however, acutely conscious that such an approach has provoked criticism from academic and professional sources. It was made attractively, and with emphasis before us, by Mrs. Christine Hallett. She is uniquely qualified as an informed critic. She was the secretary to the Maria Colwell Inquiry in 1983; she has been one of the private secretaries to the Secretary of State for Social Services. She is currently a lecturer in social policy at the University of Leicester. In 1978 she was engaged in a major study of local authority area social service teams, published under the title, *Social Service Teams: The Practitioner's view* (HMSO) and she has written a standard textbook, *The Personal Social Services in Local Government* (Allen and Unwin, 1982). She was able to study the bulk of the documentation before us, and prior to giving evidence had attended many of our sittings. We regard ourselves as having been fortunate to have had the benefit of Mrs. Hallett's expertise and not to have yielded to the temptation to avoid tackling issues of general policy in the field of child abuse. Yet that indulgence on our part forms the substance of the very criticism launched by Mrs. Hallett and other commentators.

The criticism is that when inquiries extend beyond the limited function of reporting on the particular case, they have laid themselves open to the charge that their views on general issues are often under-studied, partially researched and incompletely expressed. We concede that there is no doubt some validity in such criticism. We cannot speak for earlier inquiries. We can only hope that our views on general policy considerations are well-founded and find ready acceptance. If we have arrived at them in an inexpert and incomplete fashion, such as to invalidate them, we shall bear such criticism with as much fortitude as we can muster.

The criticism, as we understand it, is that any recommendations for changes in policy relating to child abuse which are based on the specific details of a single case which, by definition, will have had an unsatisfactory - not to say, tragically fatal - outcome, is to argue the general from the particular of one. (We remind ourselves of the wise remark that every generalisation needs at least two examples). Any recommendations, therefore, cannot be founded on a wide-ranging examination of general issues, which is what the critic demands. Our answer to that is, true, important lessons can be learned only from an examination of at least a cluster of child abuse cases, in particular where some of the cases did not end in tragedy. Where, however, the single case points up, for example, deficiencies in social work or lack of training that have been observed in other reports, studies by the DHSS and in expert testimony of a general kind, the one-off inquiry may permissibly use the single occasion to make generalisations. So long as one is alive to the danger of drawing broad conclusions from the individual case, we see no objection to statements about general policy. Given that cautionary note, and observing its precept, we still think that the individual case permits recommendations for uniform change in the management of the system.

Procedures in child abuse provide a good instance, and they cropped up during this Inquiry. Arrangements for the transfer of records both between local authorities and between health authorities, when families move from one part of the country to another, can undoubtedly be improved.

The way in which anonymous calls from neighbours should be handled provides another instance. The need for a new type of Order requiring parents to produce children for medical examination is a further useful outcrop of our Inquiry. These are just a few of the examples.

Even if it is permissible for a committee of inquiry to address some general issues arising out of the particular case - and we think it is not only permissible but also imperative not to forego the opportunity of saying something on issues of social policy - there is another aspect to the problem. Focusing on general issues relating to the protection of children at risk may, we recognise, divert attention from macro-concerns with the structure, organisation, staffing, training and resources of the agencies involved in providing the sources of child care.

Behind issues relating to a protection service lie chronic resource implications that go way beyond the remit of any child abuse inquiry. Such a task is appropriate only for a Royal Commission and not for the partial investigation of a single child abuse case, however amply its terms of reference are interpreted. The effect of a single child abuse inquiry is often to thrust front-line social workers into the glare of publicity - so often ill-motivated and grossly unfair - while others up the line of management and in government, both central and local, seem immune from the real responsibility for lack of resources that in turn are needed to provide a full-blown child protection service. If society is demanding well-staffed, well-resourced and well-trained services in child protection, it must supply the means by way of adequate financing. It may even have to accept the consequence of tilting the balance in favour of official intervention with family life. If the policy is one of safety first for children at risk, that shift is inevitable. But that shift should not be part of a constant pendulum-swinging between the protection of children's interests to that of parental rights. The policy needs to be consistently stated after a national debate, possibly following a Royal Commission. That is a matter outside our competence. But we advert to it, if only to demonstrate that we are not distracted from an underlying issue that has to be faced.

We have identified and isolated a fundamental aspect of professional response to child abuse that has figured (or rather disfigured) contemporary work by Social Services, Health Authorities and the associated agencies. In Chapter 24 we have concluded that the time is ripe for a choice between a single authority as the provider of a child protection service and a thorough-going shared responsibility. The long-promised legislation in the field of child care will, we earnestly hope, resolve that fundamental issue of policy. When the requisite provisions are on the statute-book, it should be possible thereafter to deal with the occasional tragic death of a child through parental abuse by much less costly inquiries that do no more than elicit the facts of the particular case and expose the particular weaknesses and deficiencies. Our Inquiry and the statutory inquiry at Cleveland, conducted by Mrs. Justice Butler-Sloss and her three assessors, should mark the end of an era of child abuse inquiries, stretching from Maria Colwell to Kimberley Carlile. There have been 34 such inquiries in just under fifteen years. (We list each of them in tabular form in Appendix H). Two a year is too many. We consider below how we see the development of machinery for handling future inquiries in the field of child abuse.

## Procedure

We have had very full and sustained submissions that the quasi-judicial procedure that we adopted was wrong and had very serious disadvantages over and above the one factor of enormous financial cost to the sponsoring authorities, of which we have been very conscious throughout the Inquiry. (We have already dealt with some of the procedural issues that cropped up during the Inquiry). At first, we did not think that this was the place to parade the interesting arguments for and against rival procedures. We were persuaded, however, principally by Mr. Richardson, on behalf of the TGWU, that this was not a stance that we could appropriately adopt. Our terms of reference specifically called on us to consider matters relating to child abuse inquiries. We were reminded that in the autumn of 1985 the DHSS had issued a consultative paper on child abuse inquiries, and that although the period of consultation has long since passed, there has been no publication of the guidelines to local authorities about how they should respond to public demands for inquiries into cases of child abuse.

We strongly suspect that such publication is being delayed until our report appears, along with contemporaneous publication of the Tyra Henry report and the conclusions of the statutory inquiry in Cleveland, conducted by Mrs. Justice Butler-Sloss. Accordingly, we felt impelled to accede to the submission that we should indicate our views. We do so in the context of the larger issues, what kind of inquiry should be set up.

The thrust of the argument for a fundamentally different approach from that employed in the Beckford Inquiry and in ours, came primarily from the TGWU, BASW and Wirral Borough Council. Some of those represented before us, we have assumed, would echo that approach. There are others before us, however, who at the preliminary meeting of the Inquiry endorsed our indicated approach. They have, moreover, not deviated from their support, in substance, of our procedure. Indeed in her final submission on behalf of Mr. Ruddock, Ms Dodson told us that her client changed his stance - he now strongly favoured the procedure which we had used in the Inquiry. Had there been, at the outset of our Inquiry, unanimity among the represented parties in favour of a non-judicial (not an injudicial or injudicious) approach, we might have bowed to popular demand. But we had to choose. And we chose to follow the model that was adopted in the Beckford Inquiry, without too much demur from the participants. In that Inquiry, the Director of Social Services in Brent, Miss Valerie Howarth, specifically commended the management of the Inquiry, its thoroughness and scrupulous fairness. We hoped we could emulate our predecessor in that regard at least.

But that Inquiry was held in public, with only minor exceptions. It is conceded by Mr. Richardson that once it is decided to hold the hearings in the full glare of the public, there is no escape from a procedure at least akin to the ordinary legal process that the public is used to. Whether the process is described as "inquisitorial" or "adversarial" matters not for this purpose. The public merely demands the precepts of due process of the legal system, with variations to accommodate the particular form of eliciting the truth.

It is said, contrariwise, that once the inquiry goes behind closed doors there is no such compulsion to adopt the quasi-judicial process. Indeed, the factor of costs and the pressing need to reduce the level of stress and strain on the actors in the inquiry dictate a simplified, less costly and less cumbersome mode of procedure. In essence the alternative method of conducting the inquiry is as follows : On appointment, the panellists should call for all relevant documentation from the sponsoring authorities and other affected parties, to be disclosed within 14 days. (How that would be enforced without subpoena powers is a little difficult to imagine. It is argued, not very compellingly, that the inquiry body will carry enough prestige to prompt instant obedience to its call for documents and witnesses). Once the documentation has been thoroughly digested, the panel would select the witnesses it needed to hear, and ask them for witness statements within a stipulated timescale. Once these were to hand, the panel, aided by its own counsel, would interview the witnesses singly (probably with their legal representative) but with none of the other interested parties present. A transcript of the interview would be available and immediately made accessible to the interested parties waiting in the wings. This mode of inquiry, it is claimed, can be as thorough and as fair to everyone as the full panoply of the legal process provides. And it will be much cheaper and less stressful for those affected.

Attractive as the argument is for reducing the costs - we are not so confident that the saving in costs will be all that great - we think that the case for simplifying the process and for reducing the heightened public attention on dedicated social workers is a strong one.

We conclude that two principles are in play. First, there is the requirement that the inquiry shall be focused on the protection of children in this country. The management of the system and the handling of the case must be subjected to close scrutiny, so that all the relevant lessons can be learned. That calls for a thoroughness in the process of inquiry. On the whole we think that either approach should achieve that objective, although there is a feeling that the more ample procedure is more likely to uncover the nugget buried in the documentation.

The other principle is that of public confidence, to which we attach great importance. The fact that our Inquiry has been in private makes it more, not less important that the process maintains the confidence of the public. Holding the inquiry in private always arouses suspicion that there is a cover-up. If the public knows that the ordinary legal process is abandoned for some other, less confrontational, less probing examination of witnesses by all the other interested parties, they may assume the worst. The ultimate, published report may not serve to overcome that impression, however unjustified the charge is that there has been a whitewash or a cover-up.

Our view is that there are cases - and this is one - where to hold the inquiry in public or private is highly arguable. We considered, on balance, that as things stood we were right to concede to social workers their strong desire to be protected from a largely hostile press. By the same token we feel the public was nevertheless entitled to expect of us a mode of inquiry that was to be neither a whitewash nor a witchhunt. We think that the public, deprived of its surveillance of our work, was entitled to know that we operated on exactly the same basis as if we had performed in full face of the public. We restrict that observation to *this* case, in the knowledge that the degree of public interest has been such as to make this case exceptional.

## Future inquiries

We consider what form child abuse inquiries might take in the future. We proceed to examine a range of possible choices that are open to local authorities faced with the decision how best to respond to a public demand for an independent inquiry. (We omit from this discussion the cases which can safely be handled internally by management).

The first, immediate body that would be suitable for the task is the Area Review Committee. Each Area Review Committee should take to itself the power to appoint a Standing Inquiry Panel to whom cases for investigation could be referred as and when necessary. The Panel can be set in motion without the delay involved in approaching individuals to serve on a panel. It would operate on an informal basis. Because it would be feasible for the Panel to embark on its task immediately following the incident to be investigated, it will not need to wait for a response to the public clamour for an inquiry that is usually aroused by the revelations in the criminal trial against the abusers. There is some virtue in the Panel's report being prepared in advance of the trial and published immediately following the criminal proceedings. In this way it may be possible to forestall the more ample and protracted investigation.

If it is considered, for whatever reason, that the Area Review Committee is an unsuitable inquiring body, there could be ready-to-hand, an alternative in the form of the Commission for Local Administration in England (The Local Ombudsmen). We say "could be" because the suggestions that we proffer for consideration would require an amendment to Part III of the Local Government Act 1974 providing that, without a formal complaint, the Local Ombudsmen should be empowered to initiate investigations. The objection to such a power has been that it would be inappropriate for a Local Ombudsman to form a provisional judgment of an injustice caused by the maladministration of a local authority. This does not seem to us to be a valid objection, since that is what happens now when a decision is made to investigate a complaint received from an individual. The power to take the initiative should extend the same powers only to cover cases where an individual cannot, or does not make the complaint. The Widdicombe Committee of Inquiry into the Conduct of Local Authority Business recommended (para 9.76) that the power to investigate individual cases on their initiative should be given : "Again, we see advantage in removing this limitation on the Ombudsman's remit. Research undertaken by JUSTICE in 1976-77 showed a very strong middle class bias among complainants, with over 70% of complaints being made by non-manual households. A power to take the initiative in an investigation could help towards redressing this imbalance. The Ombudsman should not pursue a case except where there was good ground for concern, nor conduct an investigation into the general procedures of an authority rather than an individual case where there was reason to suppose that injustice has occurred. Subject to those provisos, we consider that a power to initiate investigations would be a useful addition to the Ombudsman's powers".

We would add that in the field of child abuse cases, local authorities might well welcome the investigation by the Local Ombudsmen, as it would provide the statutory machinery for a thorough and independent inquiry, at no cost to the local authorities.

We noted that the Local Ombudsmen in their evidence to the Widdicombe Committee made specific mention of child abuse cases. They said that they were "aware of some examples of possible maladministration where a citizen is unavailable to claim injustice. In the former category are complaints about children who are injured or sometimes killed whilst in the care or under the supervision of the local authority". (Para 18, Local Ombudsmen's report for year ended 31 March 1986). The Local Ombudsmen noted that the Beckford inquiry was, at the time of submitting their evidence, proceeding without a statutory power to obtain evidence, and pointed out, by contrast, their extensive powers to compel disclosure of documents and the attendance of witnesses.

There are two qualifications that we would make to any wholehearted acceptance of this mode of inquiry. First, the law entitles the Local Commissioner for Administration to investigate a complaint of injustice as a result of inefficient or improper administration. On the face of it, that would not permit the Local Ombudsmen to look at professional standards. And, although there are powers of liaison and collaboration with the Parliamentory Commissioner or the Health Commissioner, the investigative power could not extend to the duties of doctors exercising clinical judgments or even the police. But there may be many cases where the inquiry is within the statutory powers, and we know of one recent instance of such an inquiry (so far unpublished) which is said to have been entirely satisfactory.

The second qualification is, in our view, more serious. While the Local Ombudsmen have acquired enormous expertise in the administration of local authorities, cases of child abuse tend to involve issues that go way beyond acts of maladministration. That is reflected in the composition of the panels of inquiry ever since Maria Colwell in 1974. There is usually a member with direct experience of Social Services and another such member from Health Services. Additionally, doctors and others in the voluntary sector of child care are often asked to serve on such inquiries. Such diversified, specialist knowledge and experience is missing from the Local Ombudsmen system.

While we think that the Local Ombudsmen system is an option that should be available for child abuse inquiries, we think it has limited application.

Given the various options that we have mentioned we think that, quite exceptionally, there will be a need for the kind of inquiry set up in the case of Kimberley Carlile. It is argued that if the degree of public disquiet is such that there is a demand for the full panoply of a public inquiry, then the Secretary of State for Social Services must activate his statutory powers: as he did in the case of the Cleveland Inquiry. Short of that demand, it is urged, there is no place for the half-way house of a local authority inquiry in the manner adopted in our Inquiry. While we see the force of this argument, we do not think that our mode of Inquiry should be excluded from the range of options, although it may, and perhaps ought to be invoked very sparingly.

We noted that at the end of the Crown Agents Inquiry Report[1] the members of that Inquiry firmly recommended that, bearing in mind the variety of circumstances that give rise to public inquiries, "the more flexibility that is possessed, the better". We agree. In deciding what kind of body should investigate a case of child abuse and what procedures that body should adopt, flexibility should always be the watchword.

We think it may be helpful if we list the types of inquiry from which to choose:

1. Where there has been a serious case of child abuse, such that only a full inquiry in public will assuage public disquiet, we anticipate that the inquiry will be set up by the Secretary of State under his statutory powers.

2. Where the Secretary of State declines to invoke the powers of central government, but the case has nevertheless aroused considerable public concern, there should be, exceptionally, a fully independent panel of inquiry. The panel should be left to decide a) whether the hearings are to be in public or in private; and b) what procedure it should adopt for the conduct of the inquiry.

3. Where the case arouses no particular public concern, the investigation should be conducted by the Local Ombudsmen or the Area Review Committee's standing panel of inquiry. This third choice should be the main forum for future child abuse inquiries until the relevant professional bodies working in collaboration can take over the task of holding child abuse inquiries. For that to happen, a General Council of Social Work will have to be established. We hope it will be in the near future.

---

[1] Parliamentary Paper HL149, HC364, at pp 569-574.

# A CHILD IN MIND:
## PROTECTION OF CHILDREN IN A
## RESPONSIBLE SOCIETY

# PART II

## KIMBERLEY CARLILE AND HER FAMILY
*3 November 1981 – 4 October 1985*

# KIMBERLEY'S MEDICAL HISTORY

Kimberley Carlile was born at St. Catherine's Hospital, Birkenhead, eight weeks prematurely on 3 November 1981. At birth her weight was 1970 grams (4lbs 5oz), her length 43 centimetres and her head circumference 32 centimetres. This placed her only just below the 50th centile for length and weight, and above the 97th centile for her head circumference. Kimberley's prematurity was a factor which required more frequent developmental assessments than for a full term infant. Careful plotting of her measurements on a percentile chart was an immediate requirement.

Head circumference is a good indicator of the size of the skeletal bone structure. Kimberley's head was measured again at 3 and 6 weeks and, for the last time, at 28 weeks; she remained on the 97th centile. On these measurements alone, there would be an expectation that she would be of average length, as indeed she was for the first 3 months of life. She certainly should not have dropped below that level. There has to be a persistent falling away from the child's normal weight centile before there is a drop from the child's normal height centile.

The continuous use of percentile charts had long been recognised within the field of child health as a simple, but vital tool in the continuing assessment of a child's development. This was especially true in the case of a vulnerable child, such as one who had been born prematurely, or one who was suspected of being at risk from intermittent physical and/or emotional abuse. The use of such charts had, moreover, been established well before the early 1980s when the assessment and care of Kimberley became the responsibility of health care workers. It was one cardinal feature of the failure in standards of care as provided for Kimberley that such charts were not properly used in her case. Had they been used and interpreted properly, the outcome for this ill-fated child might so easily have been different. We stress this aspect of our Inquiry, not so much to point the finger of blame at the health care services in both Wirral and Greenwich, but because we earnestly hope that those entrusted with the training of health care workers will in the future recognise the value of percentile charts in the service of child protection. **We recommend that all Health Authorities ensure that there is a ready supply of appropriate percentile charts and that they are used for all children up to the age of 2, and for other children whose development gives rise to concern.**

By the time Kimberley was 4½ months old, her weight had dropped to just above the 10th centile; her length was not recorded until 2 months later, when it was found to be consistent with her previous measurements. The next recordings were when she was 2 years old - her weight had dropped below the 3rd centile, and her height, which had dropped below the 10th centile, was by this time reflecting a long-standing failure to grow.

We have reconstructed Kimberley's percentile chart in two parts.

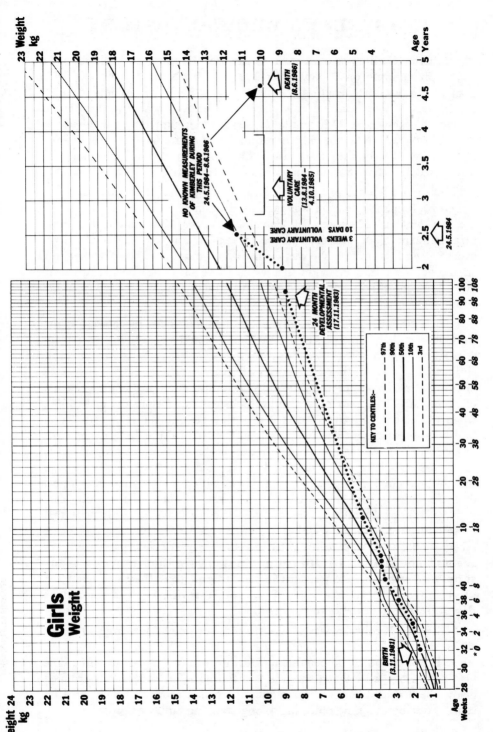

*Kimberley's actual age

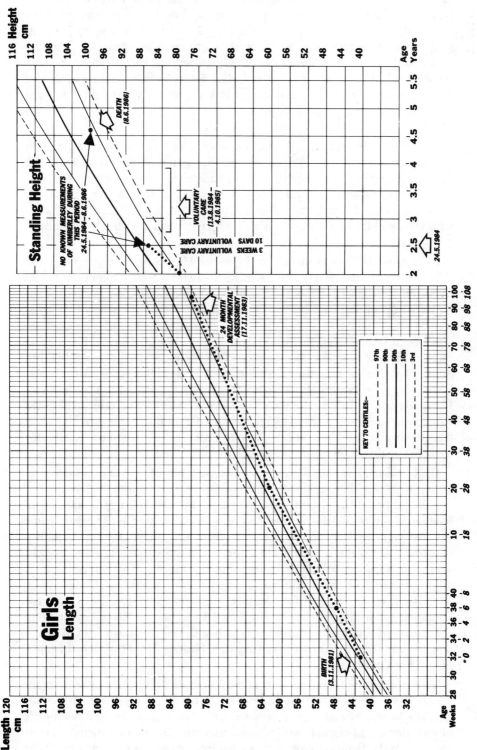

Length 120
cm
116
112
108
104
100
96
92
88
84
80
76
72
68
64
60
56
52
48
44
40
36
32

**Girls**
Length

BIRTH
(3.11.1981)

24 MONTH
DEVELOPMENTAL
ASSESSMENT
(17.11.1983)

KEY TO CENTILES:-
97th
90th
50th
10th
3rd

Age
Weeks
28  30  32  34  36  38  40        10       20       30   40  50  60  70  80  90 100
        *0  2  4  6  8                    18      28      38   48  58  68  78  88  98 108

*Kimberley's actual age

116 Height
cm
112
108
104
100
96
92
88
84
80
76
72
68
64
60
56
52
48
44
40

Age
Years

**Standing Height**

NO KNOWN MEASUREMENTS
OF KIMBERLEY DURING
THIS PERIOD
24.5.1984–8.6.1986

DEATH
(8.6.1986)

VOLUNTARY
CARE
(13.8.1984 –
4.10.1985)

3 WEEKS VOLUNTARY CARE
10 DAYS VOLUNTARY CARE

24.5.1984

2   2.5   3   3.5   4   4.5   5   5.5

41

We reject the explanation given to us in a written statement by Miss Rowlands, Director of Nursing Services, Wirral Health Authority, with regard to Kimberley's weight, as recorded at her 2-year assessment. Miss Rowlands said: "The previous weight gain had been steady and was commensurate with that of a low birthweight baby of 32 weeks' gestation and also the stature of both parents, particularly the father who was small for a male". Kimberley's mother is in fact 5 feet $7\frac{1}{2}''$ tall, and her deceased father was the same height. Kimberley was not, and never should have been regarded as a small child. She ought, moreover, never to have *become* a small child.

Once a baby has reached the age of 6 months and has established a pattern of growth, the child should remain on the same centile. If at any time thereafter the child's weight or height falls below the centile formerly followed by the readings on the percentile chart, alarm bells should start ringing. If there is no obvious explanation for the drop below the 3rd centile, there is a strong possibility that the child is suffering from either a physical disease or deprivation.

On 4 May 1982 the health visitor in Wirral Health Authority reported the baby "off-colour"; she described Kimberley (who was then 6 months old) as having a "very small, thin body, but pushes up on extended arms and stands on feet with support - looks alert, though pale". This description of the child astonishingly failed to attract any particular attention and provoked no effective supervision in the weeks and months ahead. During the coming months the health visitor rarely obtained access to the Carlile household, but did see Kimberley three times in June 1982. Following a report from Wirral Social Services regarding "recent family upset", the health visitor saw Kimberley on 30 July 1982. She was observed to be "well". (Her father died a fortnight later). On 3 May 1983 it was noted that Kimberley was attending day nursery at the Under-Fives Resource Centre in Seacombe. Kimberley was seen again on 18 August 1983; all appeared well.

On 17 November 1983 Kimberley underwent her 24-month developmental assessment. She then weighed 9.1 kilograms and was plotted below the 3rd centile. Although her height was recorded, the significant drop appears to have gone unnoticed, in contrast to the note about her weight being below the 3rd centile. The clinical medical officer for Wirral Health Authority described Kimberley's history since the last examination as: "feeds herself; very poor appetite; will sit on potty - but not use it". The clinical medical officer reported to the health visitor, that Kimberley was a "Small child. Very negativistic. Mother says she talks - but only 'bye-bye' heard. No co-operation for testing hearing". The Child Examination Record, containing the names of the family doctor and the health visitor, showed the doctor's diagnosis as: "Delay in expressive language: Hearing Doubtful: Small Child - below 3rd Centile".

The medical officer who conducted the 24-month developmental assessment should have considered all the findings in the light of the earlier birth weight, changes in weight and height, social circumstances and the health visitor's observations, and should have ensured that the Child Examination Record was sent to the family doctor, with a clear indication that there was cause for concern and a need for active follow-up and supervision. (Perhaps it was, but we have no evidence of that). There should have been active consideration given to Kimberley's obvious failure to thrive at that time. Instead, the doctor asked to see Kimberley again in 2 months time. The appointment was not arranged to take place until 4 months later, and was not kept. No further action was taken by way of another appointment, or by the health visitor following up with home visits; a clear failure of any system of child care that should have been operative.

So far as we have been able to discover, Kimberley was weighed only once more in her truncated life, on 24 May 1984, although on two further occasions she was examined by a general practitioner. These two occasions were on 24 August 1984 and on the day of discharge from voluntary care on 4 October 1985.

On 1 May 1984 Kimberley and her elder brother and sister were the subject of a police Place of Safety Order and were received into voluntary care on 4 May 1984. On the day before her discharge from voluntary care and return to her mother, on 24 May 1984, Kimberley was medically examined. Her weight then was 11.5 kilograms and her height 2 feet 10 inches. Neither recording was plotted on any percentile chart. Had they been plotted, the percentile chart would have shown her weight to be just above the 10th centile and her height virtually on the 25th centile. This would have indicated a very welcome and dramatic improvement in Kimberley's development, but also would have thrown light on her lack of proper development while in the care of her mother. (See the above reconstructed percentile chart). The failure to correlate these measurements with previous data indicates an absence of any system or person effectively monitoring Kimberley's disordered progress.

From the time that Kimberley was taken into voluntary care in August 1984 until her discharge on 4 October 1985 she was, to outward appearances, a perfectly healthy child. The foster-parents' general practitioner saw Kimberley on 24 August 1984 and reported to Wirral Social Services that her general physical condition was "good". His comment was: "A happy child". His partner saw Kimberley fourteen months later, on the day of discharge into her mother's care. He reported to Social Services likewise, adding that she was "happy, clean, well-nourished, well-dressed".

Mr. Gordon Whiteley, Kimberley's and Y's foster-father over the 14 months from August 1984 to October 1985 gave evidence before us. He said that when the two children arrived they were "well-mannered and they were well cared for". He described Kimberley during her fostering as "a total extrovert. She was boisterous, aware of what was going on around her. She was conscientious in everything she did". He said she was a chatterbox, with no problem of speech: "She had quite a remarkable vocabulary" for her age. This description was in marked contrast to that of the clinical medical officer, 9 months earlier. From the improvement in her height and weight at the medical examination of May 1984, it is reasonable to assume that during fostering Kimberley never fell below the 3rd centile, and that indeed she almost certainly made further physical improvements; and that she was having no difficulties in her speech and was developing emotionally.

We regard it as highly significant that on 11 November 1985, within six weeks of her return to her mother in the reconstituted family living in the strange environment of the Ferrier Estate, Kimberley was taken by her mother to the general practitioner, Dr. Mahesh (who practised with colleagues at 31 Telemann Square on the Ferrier Estate). Mrs. Carlile complained that the child was experiencing difficulties with her language. She told Dr. Mahesh that Kimberley was not speaking properly. Without examining the child, Dr. Mahesh gave Mrs. Carlile a letter of referral to the Brook Hospital "for speech therapy". We assume that Mrs. Carlile was telling Dr. Mahesh of a real worry about Kimberley's speech, although she took no action on the doctor's letter.

Dr. Mahesh is no ordinary general practitioner. When he first came to this country in 1967 he started working in children's hospitals. He had qualified in Varanasi, India in 1966; and in 1970 he received a diploma in child health from the University of London. Prior to starting in general practice in 1977 on the Ferrier Estate, he had 3 years' experience of work in psychiatry. He told us that he had "a lot of experience with children's diseases. I also do baby clinics in the district", a reference to Plumstead in the Borough of Greenwich.

Dr. Mahesh's failure to examine Kimberley to ensure that there were no other indices of developmental failure represents a kind of press-button response which is unacceptable as a standard of medical care. In his evidence before us, Dr. Mahesh could not elaborate on the visit to his surgery. Not having seen Kimberley before, he should have made efforts to find information about her history and previous development. He clearly took no further action himself by way of checking with the hospital authorities. We think that he should at least have contacted the health visitor.

Dr. Mahesh's note - "For speech therapy: Brook Hosp.; no problem" - is reproduced opposite.

In the light of his considerable experience in child care, the brevity of his "examination" and prescription was all the more difficult to comprehend. To send a child to a general hospital for speech therapy, without more ado, is inadequate. The doctor should have been alert to the fact that there might have been other problems, and that the language "delay" was a symptom.

Just as a child's physical growth requires assessment, so too does the functional development. We know that at the age of two Kimberley barely spoke, when she should have had a vocabulary of two hundred words. For most of the next two years Kimberley is described as a child "chattering nineteen to the dozen", and then within weeks of reunion with her mother, after a long absence in a foster-home, she appeared to have lapsed in the use of language, to the point where speech therapy was being medically prescribed.

While the assessment of language development is a highly complex matter, an explanation for any delay in language development should be sought, as with any other developmental deviation. No assessment of other aspects of Kimberley's development are recorded after November 1983, with the marginal exception of the weighing on 25 May 1984. At death Kimberley weighed 10.26 kilograms (22.5lbs), height 3 feet 3 inches (0.99 metres) and

MEDICAL RECORD TO FOLLOW

**FEMALE**   Surname
†
Forenames

Kimberley marie

Date of Birth
3-11-81

National Health Service Number

Address
49 Cambert Way Kidbrooke

Dr. Mahesh 43045

Included in Your List on _____

| Date | * | Clinical notes |
|------|---|----------------|
| ~~///////~~ | | |
| 11/11/85 | | for speech therapy brush troop. |
| | | as Brtk |
| | | |
| | | |
| | | |
| | | |
| | | |
| | | |
| | | |
| | | |
| | | |
| | | |
| | | |

\* This column has been provided for doctors to enter A, V or C at their discretion.

00983 Dd8218479 1600M 1/81 MFP

FORM FP8B

†The surname has been deleted by the Commission of Inquiry in order to conceal the identity of Kimberley's siblings.

head circumference 50 centimetres. This was only 1.26 kilograms (2.5lbs) more than her weight at the age of 2. Had she remained on the 3rd centile, she would have weighed 14.0 kilograms (30lbs) and if she had followed her original 50th centile, she would have reached 17.4 kilograms. The failure to plot her physical development at any time after November 1983, and to observe her language development after November 1985 represent a serious failure in the child health service, and consequentially in child care.

We conclude that until she left the Wirral, Kimberley had intermittently failed to thrive, and this was not diagnosed by those who had the opportunity to do so. This failure, undiscovered after November 1983, was masked during the period of foster-care by the obvious affection and care bestowed on her by the Whiteleys. Kimberley's susceptibility to failure to thrive was accentuated post-October 1985 by the incapacity of the reconstituted Carlile family to form a relationship with her.

Whatever she suffered in the Carlile household until the summer of 1984, Kimberley's emotional deprivation, reflected in the 24-month developmental assessment, was exacerbated and accelerated after October 1985, leading to the physical abuse that she undoubtedly suffered, with increasing frequency and severity, almost from the moment that she arrived in Greenwich, until her tragic death on 8 June 1986. We interpret the visit to Dr. Mahesh on 11 November 1985 as a sign that all was far from well in the Carlile household.

Dr. Michael Heath, who conducted the post-mortem on Kimberley on 9 June 1986, gave the cause of Kimberley's death as "traumatic subdural haemorrhage", due to an injury to the left temple, consistent with having been struck a blow, such as a kick. Kimberley's body disclosed multiple injuries inflicted over the weeks and months prior to death. Bruises had occurred within weeks of her death. There was evidence of yellowing over the whole of her body, a colouring of the skin that fitted the description recorded by Mr. Ruddock when he saw Kimberley at Area 4's office at the Mini-Town Hall on 12 March 1986 : "withdrawn, *sallow*, pasty and still" (emphasis supplied). The discolouration indicated an anaemia and many old confluent bruises that could not easily be defined, which had faded, leaving widespread discolouration over the body, and giving the jaundiced appearance.

There were also three very recent injuries around the area of the ears, consistent with someone holding the ears and lifting the child upwards, thus causing that stress to tear the tissue behind the ears. Dr. Heath also found Kimberley's hymen to be inflamed, together with an inflammation to the left of the vaginal opening on the vulva. Although this suggested sexual interference, it was not possible to draw the conclusion that there had been any sexual abuse. Kimberley's body also revealed multiple scarring. Some of the abrasions were fresh, some occurred within the 24 hours before death. Others were of older age, indicating infliction sustained up to six months or more before death.

Kimberley's general, very ill appearance, together with a number of old and recent superficial injuries, would have been visible to anyone who saw her at least up to two months before she died. There was one internal injury which also would have been detected by anyone seeing Kimberley shortly before she died. She had an abdominal injury which caused a rare complication. Dr. Heath's opinion was that the severe and continuing pain from this injury would have been apparent to any observer, because the child would have had great difficulty in moving, would have adopted a bent posture and been holding her abdomen. That injury was probably caused within the last fortnight of life, possibly within the last 48 hours.

We find that physical abuse of Kimberley was inflicted almost incessantly, from about the late autumn of 1985, and continued throughout the New Year, increasing in intensity and severity.

When seen by Mr. Ruddock on 12 March 1986, Kimberley was already suffering severe physical and emotional abuse. Clear evidence of both conditions was obvious. They should have been recognised, and should have led to urgent action. How Mr. Ruddock failed to see the blindingly obvious is explicable only by the fact that he was blinded by his incompetence in assessing clear deception by abusing parents, something that all social workers must constantly be alive to. Unseen for the next ten weeks, Kimberley was a child so hideously abused that only swift official intervention could have spared her serious injury, permanent psychological harm, and death.

# CHAPTER 6

# KIMBERLEY'S TEMPESTUOUS EARLY LIFE

The Carlile family first came to the notice of Wirral Social Services in May 1982 when Kimberley, the youngest of three children, was 7 months old. Mrs. Carlile had requested urgent help to escape the violence of the children's father. She was instantly transferred, with the children - X was then $4\frac{1}{3}$ years old and Y, $2\frac{1}{2}$ - to the Women's Aid Unit in Birkenhead. Thereafter for the next two years, she and her children, who lived constantly in an environment unconducive to proper child development, were seen by social workers on a regular basis, and sporadically by health services.

We were told that it was a regular practice of the health authorities in Wirral to make an appointment for a child to attend for a hearing test at the same time as a nine-month assessment, at which the mother attends. The timing of this appointment is arranged so that it takes place two weeks either side of the child reaching the age of nine months. If the child fails to attend, the procedure is to make a second appointment within 4 weeks. If there is a further failure, a home visit is undertaken by the health visitor. Kimberley was nine months old on 3 August 1982. On 18 and 19 August 1982 the health visitor launched the procedure, but was unable to gain access. She gained access, however, on 23 August, which turned out to be a bereavement visit.

On 6 August 1982 the children's father had died suddenly of a cerebral haemorrhage, following a fall in the street. The social worker who visited shortly afterwards reported that Mrs. Carlile was coping well and managing to maintain a good home. She was apparently devoted to her children. The suggestion that the children should be received into voluntary care was thought unwise, since it "would exacerbate the situation" of a family adjusting to being a single-parent family.

Simultaneously with the health visitor's visit, a report was made by a senior social worker to the Director of Social Services seeking a grant for Mrs. Carlile to pay for the mounting debts in respect of rent, funeral expenses, laundry bills and the like. The report added: "Social work support will also be provided to help Mrs. [Carlile] overcome her emotional anxiety and any of the problems which might possibly arise in relation to her three young children". During the following months social workers continued to note the strong bond between Mrs. Carlile and her children "who receive an excellent standard of care, despite the difficulties of the last few years".

Repeated attempts were made by the health visitor on a monthly basis to gain access to the family. The test for hearing should have been a priority. Eventually in February 1983, Kimberley was seen by the health visitor who recorded that the child was vocalising well, an indication that the child was not deaf. Her hearing ability would, however, be tested at the two-year developmental assessment, in November 1983.

About this time Kimberley began attending the Under-Five Resource Centre Day Nursery. On 3 March 1983 a social worker reported that the Matron of the Day Nursery had rung to say that Kimberley had a bruise on her forehead, consistent with an accident. She also appeared to bear the scars of ulcers at the top of her legs. These were attributed to poor supervision and infrequent nappy changing. A fortnight later it was noticed that Kimberley had not been attending the Day Nursery, and worries were being expressed about X and Y who were attending Brentwood Nursery. A social worker reported that up until Christmas 1982 she had been satisfied with the childrens' welfare, but the picture had changed. Mrs. Carlile, who had been seeing the doctor for depression, had become "evasive and difficult to pin down".

In the report of 13 April 1983 the social worker noted four areas of concern: "possible low standards of care of children; irregular attendance of children at school; Mrs. [Carlile's] handling of finances and further debt; our lack of information about co-habitee". Although the Intensive Family Casework Team was actively involved with the family, by June 1983 contact with the nursery and the social worker was ended. The case was "dormanted" - an adjective used impermissibly to serve as a verb, no doubt connoting that the case was to be put to sleep - due to Mrs. Carlile's rejection of social workers in her house.

The new co-habitee in Mrs. Carlile's life, David Carlile, was well known to the police as a violent man. Shortly after co-habiting began, he received in May 1983 a 3 months prison sentence for assault. He then married Pauline in September, but it was not until later in the year that Social Services were aware of the marriage. A memorandum of 3 November 1983 from the Director of Social Services to the Director of Education commented that "from our knowledge of Mr. Carlile, the three children may be at risk". That fear of risk to the children persisted, so long as the children lived in the same household, which they did for another 6 months. The day after that memorandum, Mrs. Carlile appeared before the Wallasey Justices. She was granted a conditional discharge for 12 months plus an order for £25 compensation, for obtaining £46 by deception. She had forged entries, using wax impressions, in a Post Office Savings Bank.

On 17 November 1983 Kimberley was seen at the Water Street Clinic, Wallasey for her 24-month developmental assessment. We considered the results of that developmental assessment in the last chapter. We do not need to repeat them from a medical standpoint, save to say that it does not follow from the fact that Kimberley's weight showed her to be below the 3rd centile that this was due to abuse or neglect. What it does is to flash an amber light to the effect that if there is no physical disease the child is failing to thrive. Given the medical officer's adverse comments on Kimberley's speech and on her physical development, there was more than ample material to alert those responsible for Kimberley's welfare.

When follow-up examinations are required - as was the case with Kimberley Carlile - a recall appointment is sent. This appointment was fixed for 15 March 1984. Mrs. Carlile never kept that appointment. Before that there were signs of the impending troubles that led Social Services to receive the children into voluntary care.

On 1 February 1984 both Carlile parents were arrested on theft charges. All the children were taken to a place of safety for the day. Mr. & Mrs.

Carlile were released on bail and went home. A fortnight later a social worker made a home visit. The report said that the parents had "little insight into the reasons for [X's] rudeness in and out of the home, [Y's] dumb insolence and Kimberley's temper tantrums". Kimberley had been attending the Under-Five Resource Centre Day Nursery. By 28 February it was reported to Social Services that she had not been attending. Later that day a social worker made a home visit, only to find Mrs. Carlile in tears "and [Y] and Kimberley not in nursery again, due to worry about arrears and Kimberley's temper tantrum on the way home on Friday". Following a further home visit on 9 March the Matron of the nursery contacted the social worker to say that Kimberley and Y had arrived late and had not been picked up at the right time. When she chided Mr. Carlile, he retorted by saying that the girls would not be attending in future.

On 20 March 1984 a neighbour reported her worries at the level of violence in the Carlile household. On 28 March a social worker made a detailed report. She ended: "Although as a department we have done all we could to-day, I believe that in this case there is still cause for concern for the children involved". Yet, by the end of April, following a case discussion within Social Services, a decision was taken to terminate involvement. A week later Mrs. Carlile was arrested on suspicion of theft and obtaining property by deception at King Street Post Office, Wallasey. On 1 May the police made a Place of Safety Order on the three children. The sequence of events that followed were, in brief: 4 May, children received into voluntary care; 25 May, discharge from voluntary care; 3 July, children received back into voluntary care, when Mrs. Carlile went into hospital for treatment on a broken jaw; 13 July, children returned to mother at Chester Women's Aid Refuge; 13 August, children return into voluntary care, as mother being imprisoned; 4 October 1985, children discharged from voluntary care, and leave for Greenwich.

During the whole of the early months of 1984 Kimberley was not seen by the health visitor, as well as not being taken for the follow-up examination on her developmental assessment. The reason why there was no contact with health authorities was, we were told, the absence of the health visitor; this resulted in only priority visiting being undertaken on her caseload. Kimberley, we were told, did not come into the priority category, as 30% of caseloads in the particular area would have children from a similar background.

Mrs. Carlile appeared in court on 2 May. It was the prelude to a further unsettling period for the children, culminating in her imprisonment three months later. Social Services responded to the need to protect the children. As the chairman of the case conference, convened for 3 May, aptly commented: "If the children go home, they will go from crisis to crisis". For Kimberley at least, the turbulence of the last nine months and her stunted growth were soon to yield to a sustained period of happy contentment with her foster-parents and the restoration of her physical and emotional development.

CHAPTER 7

# KIMBERLEY AND HER SIBLINGS IN VOLUNTARY CARE

From the summer of 1984 until 4 October 1985, when the family was re-
united in Greenwich, Kimberley and her two siblings were in voluntary care
and fostered in the Wirral. Kimberley and her older sister lived with Mr. &
Mrs. Whiteley; X, the boy, was fostered separately.

The process of being received into the voluntary care of Wirral Social
Services began with the police Place of Safety Order of 1 May and was
continued with the parents' agreement until 25 May 1984. At the case
conference of 3 May, convened by the Social Services Department, Wallasey,
most of the agencies involved in child care and child health were represented.
The health visitor representative (supported by her Nursing Officer) was
asked about health services' involvement with the family. She referred
specifically to Kimberley's 24-month developmental assessment of the
previous November. She also mentioned the medical observation about the
"negativistic" attitude of the child and her limited language. She indicated
that a follow-up examination had been arranged, but that had not taken place.
The Nursing Officer present at the case conference said that normally a health
visitor would visit twice a year, and that more frequent visits could be
arranged. The meeting recommended that the health visitor should continue
to visit whenever possible. This recommendation was not repeated at the
second case conference, held on 15 August 1984. No visits from any health
visitor took place between that time and 4 October 1985, when the children
left the Wirral to be re-united with their mother. Nor did Kimberley have a
follow-up examination, or undergo her 36 month developmental assessment
in November 1984.

Paragraphs 1 (n), (o) and (p) of the 'Pattern of Health Visiting Normally
Undertaken' of Wirral Health Authority, dated 14 March 1983, provides
respectively for "one visit between 2-3 years: Three-year screening with
Health Visitor at clinic: One visit between 3-4 years". The occasions that
Kimberley was medically examined, before the day of departure from Wirral
on 4 October 1985, were on 24 May 1984 and by a general practitioner on
25 August 1984. On the former occasion the doctor noted that, apart from a
"chesty cough", she was well. She weighed 11½ kilograms and her height
was 2 feet 10 inches. Neither weight nor height was plotted on her percentile
chart. Had they been, a marked, even dramatic improvement in her physical
development, to a point just above 10th centile for weight, would have been
recorded.

At the second case conference on 15 August 1984 (at which the health
visitor and her Nursing Officer were again present), the chairman asked
pointedly whether the children were fit and well, and whether there was any
medical concern. The key social worker replied that Kimberley had taken to
soiling recently, "but this was understandable at the age of two, and given
the circumstances". When asked by the chairman whether the children had

been medically examined, the social worker said that this had been arranged for later that week. The health visitor had intervened on occasions, to say that the children would be registered with the foster-parents' doctor; that she had called, but failed to see the children at the beginning of June; and that the expected new baby in November would affect the family situation. But nothing emerged about the report on Kimberley's 24-month developmental assessment or the failure to undergo any follow-up examination.

The main recommendation of the case conference was to initiate the process for a Section 3 resolution and plans for long-term placement of the children. The chairman of the case conference had expressed his worries about the constant business of preventing incidents in the Carlile household. He did not favour the idea of voluntary care, and thought that the long-term future of the children had to be made secure by some action. He called for actual consideration to be given to care proceedings, wardship, or a Section 3 resolution. The preference was for the latter, with which the local authority's senior solicitor agreed. Whether the local authority finally decided to take a resolution or not, we would have expected that, in the processing of the case for submission to members of the local authority, much more detailed work would have had to be done to justify the assumption of parental powers by the local authority.

The second case conference of 15 August 1984 had been preceded by a period of some 6 weeks from 25 May until 3 July, during which the children were back home but not considered to be at risk. On 3 July Mr. Carlile was released from Risley Remand Centre, only to commit assault on his wife in which she suffered a serious fracture of her jaw. During the following days during which the children were moved for a week to foster-parents and then kept for a month in a safe place, social workers managed to persuade her to accept the voluntary care of the children for 3 months. She was reminded constantly that if she were to return, with the children, to her husband, the Department might apply for a court order. Mr. Carlile was back in custody on remand in respect of the assault charge, and his wife was remanded until 3 August on the theft charges. On that day Mrs. Carlile pleaded guilty to two offences of obtaining property by deception and received a sentence of three months' imprisonment. On each of the two charges, the sentences were to run consecutively. The judge said that her conduct had disclosed a long pattern of dishonest dealing with other people's money. Kimberley, X and Y stayed temporarily with their mother's aunt. On 13 August 1984 the two girls were placed with the foster-parents, Mr. & Mrs. Whiteley. The two children quickly settled down. There was nothing of substance relating to Kimberley that gave any cause for concern about her welfare. By all accounts she flourished.

The question that continued to exercise Wirral Social Services over the following months was, what action should be taken, as and when Mrs. Carlile was released from prison. (Her actual release was delayed until 3 December 1984, due to the birth of her fourth child, a daughter, Z). We proceed to describe the deliberations of Social Services both during that period, and during the period when Mrs. Carlile left prison, settled finally in London with Z and began seeking the return of her three children to live with her and her baby daughter, together with her new co-habitee, Mr. Hall.

The main social worker involved with the Carlile family produced a note for the case conference of 15 August setting out the positive and negative factors for taking action to protect the children. Three factors weighed against anything more drastic than voluntary care. They were: the children had not suffered any physical harm; the periods of voluntary care had been short; and "there is little hard evidence that the children are disturbed in their behaviour". What was being done to ascertain the condition of the children? More particularly, what steps were taken to find out the development of Kimberley, in the light of the unsatisfactory assessment made on 17 November 1983, and the absence of any follow-up?

The key to all future considerations about the placement of the Carlile children is to be found in the arrangements made for the statutory Case Review to be held on 1 April 1985. Wirral Social Services sent out invitations for attendance at the Case Review to the two sets of foster-parents, the head-teachers for the schools attended by X and Y, and to Mrs. Carlile. Her invitation was sent "c/o N. Hall", but no separate invitation was sent to him, although by this time it was known that he was co-habiting with Mrs. Carlile and Z. On 27 March Mrs. Carlile told Wirral Social Services that the two of them were "sharing accommodation", and the meeting of 1 April agreed that Kensington & Chelsea Social Services Department would be asked to investigate his background. No invitation was sent to the health visitor and/or Nursing Officers who had attended the case conferences of May and August 1984, or indeed anyone connected with the health services. Thus the earlier concern about Kimberley's development and lack of follow-up of her doubtful hearing and physical development had vanished from the social workers' minds. The sole focus of their considerations was the future of the 3 children collectively. The main, if not exclusive obstacle to discharging the voluntary care was the hovering presence of Mr. Carlile. Once he was firmly out of the picture and would not be involved in the children's lives, and once Mrs. Carlile was properly housed, no other consideration was alive to forestall the reunion of the three children to their mother. Those in attendance at the case review on 1 April were the Deputy Area Officer for Wallasey Area Office, (who took the chair), a team leader and a social worker from that office, plus Mrs. Whiteley, Kimberley's foster-mother, and a class teacher from X's school. After reading reports and hearing from those in contact with the children, it was felt that all three were progressing satisfactorily.

The meeting concluded that the plan would be to reunite the children with their mother ("plans should be made with the aim of eventual rehabilitation to their mother"). Mrs. Carlile had not been able to attend, but she was written to the day after, telling her what had taken place. She was told that "it would be necessary for us to work out a rehabilitation programme with dates fixed for visits etc ...". On the same day Kensington and Chelsea Social Services Department was informed by letter, asking whether one of the social workers in Kensington could liaise with a Wirral social worker "and check out her present situation, accommodation, circumstances etc." The change in tack had been adumbrated the previous autumn, shortly after Mrs. Carlile was imprisoned. Social workers went to Askham Grange Prison, near York, to explain to her that Social Services had set in motion the procedure for the local authority assuming parental powers by way of a Section 3 resolution. Wirral Borough Council's lawyers had doubted whether there were adequate grounds for assuming Mrs. Carlile's parental rights, since the primary concern of the social workers was the extremely violent home environment, exposure to which was having a marked effect on the three children. Even Mrs. Carlile's imprisonment for fraud was thought to be an insufficient ground for a parental rights resolution. On 5 November 1984 Mrs. Carlile was told that for the time being the children would be remaining in voluntary care, but if, on her release from prison, she made any move to get the children back, the local authority would instantly make the children wards of court. The aim was clear. Mrs. Carlile could eventually have the children returned to her, so long as Mr. Carlile was no longer part of her, and therefore the children's, life. It was his habits and mode of life that prevented the children being restored to their mother, and not hers.

# CHAPTER 8

# THE CARLILE FAMILY AND KENSINGTON & CHELSEA SOCIAL SERVICES

Kensington and Chelsea Social Services Department was briefly involved with Mrs. Carlile, Mr. Hall and Z, between April and September 1985. The initial referral from Wirral on 10 April went to the Kensal Neighbourhood Team but, when it was apparent that the family did not have a permanent home in the Borough, subsequent work was undertaken by the Homeless Persons Unit in the Housing Department and by a social worker specialising in work with the homeless. The referral letter from Wirral, dated 2 April 1985, advised that Mrs. Carlile had moved to London, provided some background information, and asked: "Would it be possible for one of your social workers to liaise ... and check out her present situation, accommodation, circumstances, etc?"

In May, Mrs Carlile and Z were nominated by Kensington and Chelsea for two bedroomed accommodation under the Greater London Mobility Scheme. The nomination was changed to one for three bedroomed accommodation in July, to allow for the possibility of the three children in Wirral's care returning to their mother. A senior officer from the Homeless Persons Unit visited the family on 16 August 1985 to give details concerning the nomination, and the tenancy in Greenwich was taken up on 2 September.

Mr Moorhouse, from Kensington and Chelsea Social Services, assumed responsibility formally for work with Mrs. Carlile , Mr. Hall and Z, on 7 May 1985. He had interviewed Mrs. Carlile at the end of April, following a referral from the North Kensington Law Centre. Mr Moorhouse contacted the Kensal Neighbourhood Team and then, near the middle of May, telephoned Wirral to let them know he would be carrying the case.

From his evidence, and from that given by his supervisor, Mrs Sharpe, it seemed to us that Mr Moorhouse's involvement had three objectives: first, to help with the accommodation problem; second, to assess the quality of care received by Z whose welfare was clearly seen by Kensington and Chelsea Social Services to be their responsibility; and third, to provide Wirral with information to help them with their decision about whether to reunite the three children, who were still in voluntary care, with their mother.

The accommodation problem was dealt with through the Greater London Mobility Scheme and Mr Moorhouse never felt concern for the standard of care received by Z. The information for Wirral was provided principally in a report, dated 4 July 1985, following discussions which Mr. Moorhouse had with his supervisor. The report contained details concerning the referral, the "current history", the relationship within the family, Mr. Hall's past history, and the housing position. The conclusion stated that : "Mr Hall and Mrs Carlile appear to have a stable relationship at the present time. However, I do have only very limited information on Mr Hall and the relationship is of short standing, therefore I am unable to comment on whether this is likely to last". Mr Moorhouse confirmed that this commendably cautious assessment was intended precisely to be "a very guarded comment", because he had insufficent information to justify a more emphatic prediction. He told us that in his telephone conversations with Wirral, he would have been "quite positive about Mr Hall", but did not expect his comments on Mr Hall to be the decisive factor in determining whether he would make a good father to the three older children. The conclusion of the report continued: "I have not seen either Mr. Hall or Mrs. Carlile with her older children and despite being pushed by both Mrs. Carlile and the North Kensington Law Centre to make comments on the rehabilitation of the children I feel unable to give any opinion".

Mr. Moorhouse knew that Wirral Social Services would have far more information concerning the children who were still in voluntary care, and would have had opportunities of observing Mrs. Carlile and Mr. Hall interacting with the children during visits. He recognised that any plan to return the children was going to be difficult. He was not convinced that Mr. Hall, a man without "a great deal of child care experience", appreciated what he would be taking on. Mr. Moorhouse was worried that there had not been much contact with the children, and that such a substantial increase in the size of the family would be a major challenge for anybody. As he put it: "Any family would have found it quite difficult to actually take on three new children, just like that, that they hadn't seen for at least a year".

The final paragraph of the report suggested that: "This does appear to be a situation which might benefit from personal contact between your social worker and this Social Services Department. We would be very happy to participate in some kind of contact and after discussion to offer what help we can that seems to be appropriate to you." Unfortunately this was an offer that was not taken up with Kensington and Chelsea by Wirral Social Services, and was never even suggested between Greenwich and Wirral. Mrs Sharpe, with unhesitating forthrightness, told us in her oral evidence the advantages of holding such a meeting: "I felt it was absolutely essential that we somehow had this personal meeting and that was why it was in the report, because I don't think over a telephone you do actually say all the things that you might say on a face-to-face meeting, and I equally don't believe what you put in letters either is the full story." Given Kensington and Chelsea's housing policy, it was known by this time that the family would not be staying in the Borough, but Mrs Sharpe made clear what her expectations would have been if there had been a possibility of the children in care being discharged to her area: "If they were coming from another authority to Kensington, I would have expected to have some kind of personal contact and in the personal contact I would have hoped that they would bring the file so we could have a look at that. I would have hoped that we could have made a planned return."

Mr. Moorhouse stayed in contact with Wirral Social Services and continued to visit the Carlile family. His last visit was made on 28 August, when he saw Mrs Carlile and Z. Mr. Hall was reported to be decorating the new property. Mrs. Carlile was said to be "very happy with offer and is already making plans to move in." She had not "been in contact with Wirral yet" but was "hoping to do so in the near future." Mr. Moorhouse explained that he would not be working with them any more as they "were moving completely out of my area". He asked Mrs. Carlile's permission to contact Greenwich, although this was an act of courtesy rather than an offer which Mrs. Carlile could refuse. In the middle of September Mr. Moorhouse spoke to his counterpart in Wirral, describing the action that had been taken and explaining the case was now closed to Kensington and Chelsea.

Mr. Moorhouse wrote a report to Greenwich on 28 August 1985, which was received in Area 4 on 5 September. By then he knew that Wirral were planning to return the children to their mother, but he told us that he expected - rightly, in our opinion - Wirral to provide Greenwich with all the relevant information concerning the children and the plans for them. The purpose of Mr. Moorhouse's report was to provide Greenwich with information he had gleaned and to describe his work with the family. The report contains similar details to those sent to Wirral but its conclusions are different.

Mr. Moorhouse described his involvement in these terms: "My work with this family has been quite limited, mainly in liaising with the various agencies and providing a short report to Wirral of the current situation. In a limited sense I have monitored the family while in temporary accommodation and helped them cope with the stress of transient living." We consider this a fair description of the part played by Mr. Moorhouse, although it is ironic that this limited role was characterised by greater actions, in terms of direct contact with the family, than anything that occurred subsequently. After commenting favourably on the family's resourcefulness and ability to manage its affairs, Mr. Moorhouse concluded: "I understand, with the resettlement of Mrs. Carlile in permanent accommodation, that plans will go ahead with the rehabilitation of the children from Wallasey, this being co-ordinated by Wirral Social Services. I, therefore, suggest that any future contact should be made to that authority". The key relationship had become that between Wirral and Greenwich Social Services Departments.

Despite some minor problems with communication, we consider Kensington and Chelsea discharged their responsibilities to the Carlile family conscientiously and efficiently, working hard to liaise with the relevant agencies. We found their cautious social work judgments sound, and accepted their descriptions of the limited role they played. We were particularly impressed by Mrs. Sharpe's evidence and saw in her relationship with Mr. Moorhouse the kind of supervision we would have hoped to have seen in Greenwich, and to which we advert in chapter 30.

# CHAPTER 9

# CARLILE FAMILY RE-UNITED

The three children's contact with their mother, even after she came out of prison at the beginning of December 1984, was extremely limited. This was due to the fact that she did not immediately settle down - moving from the Wirral just before Christmas, to York and then to Wigan, until mid-February, when she moved to London and began cohabiting with Mr. Hall. Even then she had inadequate accommodation for anybody more than herself and the baby, Z. Not until she was re-housed on the Ferrier Estate in September did she realistically expect to have her children returned to her. During that month, however, she took steps to arrange for the hand-over of the three children, pursuant to the commitment of Wirral Social Services on 1 April 1985 to discharge the children from voluntary care as and when the time for reunion with their mother was propitious.

On 1 October 1985 Mr. & Mrs. Whiteley, who since April had anticipated the ending of their foster-care of Kimberley and Y, were informed of the collection of the children by their mother on the following Friday, 4 October. Mrs. Whiteley said that she would arrange for the children to be medically examined before delivering the children to Edgehill Family Group Home at 3 pm, the time arranged for collection being between 3 and 4 pm. X's foster-parents were similarly alerted.

A social worker from Wirral Social Services went in the early afternoon to Edgehill Family Group Home to see the children collected by their mother. The Whiteleys had just arrived; and X had already been delivered by his foster-mother. At 4 pm Mr. Hall rang to say that the car had broken down on the motorway, at least two hours away from Liverpool. The staff at Edgehill Family Group Home arranged tea for the children and were proposing to look after them until Mrs. Carlile arrived. The staff were then given the names, addresses and telephone numbers of the foster-parents, in case the children had not been picked up that night. Apparently there was some problem about providing sleeping accommodation at the Home.

The social worker left at this point. On the Monday morning the social worker rang to find out if the Carliles had arrived on the Friday night, and was told that they had turned up just after 8 pm. The children seemed pleased to see their mother who told the staff that they would all be staying overnight at Mr. Hall's parents' home in Liverpool. They would travel to London the next day.

The Wirral Health Authority was notified on 8 October 1985 of the movement of the children out of the care of Wirral Social Services, into the care of their mother. The notice gave 49 Cambert Way, London SE3 as the address, but the name of the general practitioner was marked "N/K".

Thus, in this dismissive fashion, Kimberley and her siblings passed out of the care of Wirral Social Services into the care of their mother, who for three years had undergone an unsettling, if not disturbing life, punctuated by bouts of marital violence. In addition, the children were being pitchforked into a reconstituted family with an untried step-father. The protective element of voluntary care dropped away, without any comparable replacement, save for a mild desire for a transient watch over the three children. "Some sort of monitoring of the case could be carried out while the children settle back with their mother", were the signing-off words from Wirral Social Services to Greenwich Social Services.

# CHAPTER 10

# RESPONSIBILITY OF WIRRAL CHILD CARE AND CHILD HEALTH SERVICES

Kimberley Carlile lived in the Wirral for all of the first four years of her life. The Carlile family was known to many agencies there, but the principal responsibility for Kimberley's welfare fell to the Health Authority and the Social Services Department. Although both had reasons for being concerned about Kimberley, no pattern of consistent care can be detected in the services provided for her.

Kimberley was born prematurely on 3 November 1981 and the medical examination at six weeks noted "Follow up for prematurity". She was examined again in June 1982, but no weight was recorded. After Kimberley reached the age of nine months the health visitor experienced the same difficulty gaining access as others were to have in attempting to see Mrs. Carlile and her children. At her 24-month examination on 17 November 1983, Kimberley was described as a "small child. Very negativistic". It was noted that she was "below 3rd centile for weight". This was the last time Kimberley's weight was plotted on a percentile chart. At this examination it was intended that she should be seen again in two months time, but no effective follow-up was achieved. Not for the last time in her life, Kimberley was allowed to drift, free of care.

Mrs. Carlile was offered an appointment to follow-up the 24-month examination, but she failed to keep it. During the early part of 1984 the health visitor had periods of sick leave and only priority visiting was undertaken on her caseload. Kimberley was not considered a priority, despite the compelling facts that she was (a) a premature baby; (b) failed to grow; (c) of doubtful hearing; (d) exhibiting poor language development; (e) living in a disturbed and violent family environment; and (f) often not brought by her parents to appointments with health services.

At the case conference called by Social Services on 3 May 1984, the health visitor is recorded as having given an account of the 24-month examination of Kimberley: "She was small for her age, very negative in her attitude, which was normal for a two year old. Doctor reports that the mother said the child could talk but only to say "bye-bye". She was supposed to return, but did not". The chairman of the case conference, the Area Officer for Wallasey Social Services, asked how often the health visitor could visit the children. The nursing officer said "this would normally be twice a year", but the health visitor was more optimistic, predicting that "they could possibly go more". One of the conclusions of the case conference was that "all agencies will continue to monitor the situation very carefully". Regular health visiting was not achieved, nor could we find any evidence to suggest that the health authority did honour its commitment "to monitor the situation very carefully".

At the case conference held on 15 August 1984, the health visitor reported that "she had called to see the children once at the beginning of June but nobody was in". To his credit, the Area Officer, chairing the case conference again, did press for information concerning the children's health, asking if they were fit and well, if any medical concern was felt about them, and if they had been medically examined. There is no record of him having received any informed advice concerning the children's health.

The notes of the conference made it clear that the chairman found this "a worrying case". This worry, and the decisions of the May case conference did not, however, spur the health authority into action. Miss Rowlands, Director of Nursing in Wirral Health Authority, advised us in her written statement that Kimberley, after being placed with foster-parents, Mr. and Mrs. Whiteley, in August 1984, "was not seen by a health visitor at any stage thereafter". Miss Rowlands told us this was "not consistent with Wirral Health Authority policy" but she could "offer no positive explanation why the policy was not adhered to"; although Miss Rowlands did point out to us that the health visitors carried high caseloads and that at the time "colleagues were absent on maternity leave and sickness".

According to the documentation, Wirral Social Services notified the Community Administrator of Wirral Health Authority of the children's discharge from voluntary care and their transfer to 49 Cambert Way on the Ferrier Estate. The school medical records from Wirral, concerning X, Y and Kimberley (she had undergone a medical examination while attending the nursery), eventually arrived in Greenwich in February 1986. One page of each set of records had a red star stuck on them. The red star, in Wirral language, meant that the "child had been subject of a case conference". The significance of this was lost on Greenwich Health Authority which had its own records' language. The red stars had black 'R's in them. The 'R's were placed there, according to Miss Rowlands, because a "higher clerical officer" was told that the "child's name had been placed on Register". Miss Rowlands did not know who had provided this "incorrect information". In any case Greenwich Health Authority's curiosity was not aroused. Kimberley's health records did not arrive in Greenwich until after her death.

Wirral Social Services Department first came into contact with Mrs. Carlile in May 1982 when Kimberley was nearly seven months old. For much of the time from May 1982 until October 1985 the Social Services had some involvement with the Carliles. This involvement is recorded fully, if somewhat purposelessly, in the substantial file kept on the family and made available to the Commission.

On three occasions X, Y and Kimberley were received into voluntary care. The first two occasions were for short periods but their last spell in care lasted from 13 August 1984 until 4 October 1985. The recording on the file provides testimony of the conscientiousness with which many of the Social Services staff approached their responsibilities. As far as we know, the children, and certainly Kimberley, were well looked after while they were in care. The conclusions of the case conference leave no doubt, however, about how seriously the case was viewed by Social Services personnel. At the end of the case conference in May 1984, as we have seen, all agencies were "to monitor the situation very carefully". The chairman of the August case conference confirmed that "this was a worrying case"; and that he "did not

61

think that voluntary care was a good idea, and the best thing would be for some action to secure the future of the children." At the end of the conference he "asked everyone to consider care proceedings, wardship, to make [sic] application to the Social Services Committee for a Section 3 resolution whereby the children would remain [in care] until they were 18". Would that Kimberley had done so.

We do not discuss in detail why the chairman's views were not acted upon, and why the children remained in voluntary care. We do, however, consider that the Social Services Department's responsibility for the children, and the anxiety expressed concerning their future, required that any move to re-unite the children with their mother would have to be approached with considerable caution and would be planned very carefully indeed. After all, Wirral was now home to the children; Kimberley's foster parents had taken her through fourteen crucial months of her growth and development, and the children's social worker was their champion and their link to the past.

We saw no evidence of careful planning having taken place. It was as if the workers were so preoccupied with Mr. Carlile that, once he was out of the way, their concentration on the needs of the children waned; and as if the possibility of the children moving from the Wirral was seen as an immediate end to the Social Services Department's responsibilities. The children were despatched to an unknown and uncharted future.

Most disappointingly of all, the Social Services staff who had been most involved with Kimberley would not, after she died, assist us in trying to understand what had happened in order that we might try to make a contribution to the aim of doing better for future children at risk.

A CHILD IN MIND:
PROTECTION OF CHILDREN IN A
RESPONSIBLE SOCIETY

# PART III

## EVENTS UNDER INQUIRY
*4 October 1985 – 8 June 1986*

CHAPTER 11

# SOCIAL SERVICES' RESOURCES

## Overview

It is unreasonable to expect a precise relationship to exist between the macroscopic issue of resources and the microscopic, more intimate circumstances surrounding the death of a frail four-year-old. None of those most closely involved with Kimberley was blaming lack of resoures for all that went wrong; clearly not. Nevertheless, we became convinced during our Inquiry that the issue of resources should be dealt with, if a full and comprehensive account was to be given.

We cover a range of levels within the "child protection system", because each has its part to play. While in any particular case one aspect may be more important than another, we believe it is important to remember the collective responsibility we, as a community, share for protecting children. Resources framed and fuelled the services that were available to help Kimberley, and consequently helped to shape and define the system in which she and the staff in the welfare agencies should have come together. We had presented to us a picture in which the relevant branches of the Health Service, and the Social Services, felt they were under considerable pressure during the period of Kimberley's life spent in Greenwich.

Resources are directly related to services, in the sense that you get only what you provide for. Resources were available in this case: Kimberley had a health visitor and a social worker; the Carlile family had a health clinic and a general practitioner; the older children had a school to go to, and Kimberley was offered a nursery school place; the Court Welfare Service was willing to extend its role with the family, and the police would, no doubt, have helped, if asked.

Resources are indirectly related to services in their effect on the background within which the services are provided. This background is made up of such components as training, supervision, working conditions, working systems, staff morale and public confidence. The relationship between what happens in a particular case and its general background is bound to be difficult to define and even then, tenuous. The conclusion that a child's avoidable death cannot be attributed directly to the lack of one identifiable resource should not, however, preclude consideration of the broader relationship between a case and its setting. It is this less tangible relationship that will involve the competence and skill of the human resources that form the most central, vulnerable and valuable resource of all.

As we heard of letters and memoranda, concerned with staffing issues and unallocated cases, trundling up from the Area Office and whizzing back again, we wondered if we were witnessing, un-Trumanesque-like, a revolving buck which stopped at no-one's desk. Another description of the same process suggested that it was a circle line, with a train full of memos, discussions and concerns going round in loops. To change the metaphor, the boomerang of accountability left the impression of returning to hit the originator who had turned his back on it.

As we heard more evidence, we became dissatified with any of these descriptions for two reasons: first, it suggested a cynical ducking of responsibility; and, second, it suggested a complete lack of concern and action. None of these conclusions is justified. The circular motion was more accurately perceived as the blurred image of various compartments speeding past each other in the complex network of resource provision. Every one of the many levels in the complex organisations involved could make decisions about resources, with the decisions made at one level impinging on the others, and with levels between organisations interacting. At the head of this structure is central government; Kimberley was at the other remote, receiving end.

Any democratic government exists to serve the nation it has been elected by and, in any civilised country, will be particularly concerned for its most vulnerable people, with none so vulnerable as children at risk of physical, sexual or emotional abuse, or severe neglect. Acceptance of the fundamental duty to protect our children is one of the reasons why such a powerful reaction often occurs when, as a society, we fail to prevent children being killed in circumstances when they could, and should have been saved. Central government serves children in many ways and makes various financial arrangements for their benefit. As local authorities have a major role to play in protecting children, one of the more important economic decisions made by the central government on behalf of children will be the level of help it provides to local authorities, especially if it accepts the onerous responsibility of setting spending targets.

These decisions operate at a general, and a specific level. Given that a nation's economy is there to serve its people, as well as vice versa, central government has the difficult task of determining how much is to be provided from central coffers, and for what. Social Services share of GRE (Grant Related Expenditure) has grown in England as a whole from 9.7% in 1981/2 to 11.1% in 1984/5, with the total increase rising from £1,642.6 million to £2,204.8 million for the same period. Central government will be wanting to ensure that GRE calculations are effective, fair and accurate. A universally acceptable, and precise method of measuring spending need has been sought by successive governments without the magic formula yet being found.

Central government will also want to take into account the large increases of reported child abuse cases that have occurred in the last few years. ADSS[1] figures, released in the summer of 1987, gave the results of a survey covering 100 local authorities, which showed in 1986 an increase, compared with the previous year, of 22% in the number of children on child abuse registers and "a huge increase in the referral rates and the work associated with investigating child protection cases and providing follow up services." (ADSS press release, 21 July 1987.) The NSPCC's register research, covering geographical areas that include over 9% of the children in England and Wales, showed that in 1985 "some 1,586 children were placed on child abuse registers maintained by the NSPCC. This represents a 42% increase in reported cases compared

---

[1] Association of Directors of Social Services.

66

to 1984". Another increase was reported in 1986 with 2,137 children placed on these registers, "a 34% increase in registered cases compared to 1985." (NSPCC research briefings numbers 7 and 8).

The DHSS, in considering responses to its circular "Working Together" and in preparing to publish the final version of the circular, will want to review carefully whether the final recommendations have resource implications.

We also want to commend to all those involved in protecting children from abuse, consideration of how we can give appropriate assistance and remuneration to those who act as agents on our behalf. If we do not believe our agents are up to the task, we must change them or improve them. If we are willing to place our trust in them, we must back them. Unsupported frontline troops, lacking confidence, do not win battles, let alone wars.

At a specific level, individual authorities must not be treated unfairly. Greenwich's Social Services GRE grew from £9.9 million in 1981/2 to £14.6 million in 1984/5, but we received evidence to suggest that Greenwich does not fare well in the way its present Social Services GRE is calculated, partly because, unlike most other inner-city authorities, it has a rising population. (While Greenwich is strictly an outer-London Borough, it is now generally regarded as having the main characteristics of an inner-London Borough).

It is beyond our terms of reference, and beyond what can reasonably be considered relevant to what happened to Kimberley, to go into these complex calculations in detail. We know that this issue has been part of discussions and correspondence between the Borough and central government, with particular concern being expressed for child care and child abuse. This culminated in a letter sent to the present Under Secretary of State for Health in November 1986. We hope that these discussions will reach a satisfactory resolution as soon as possible.

It is likely that a poor relationship at the top, between local and central government, will have repercussions throughout the various layers of resource distribution. It sets a bad example; and it is hypocritical to urge good relationship on others if we do not work as hard as we can on our own.

Central government does not make available resources which are earmarked specifically for Social Services. Every council has to establish priorities to determine allocation of its resources in the light of local circumstances and statutory obligations. A council has not only to set priorities between the various services it provides but also, even within Social Services, it has hard decisions to make about the distribution of resources between different client groups. Even within one client group a council has to distribute resources between different areas and it was impressed upon us, more than once, that the Ferrier Estate is not the only needy part of Greenwich.

One of the apparent strengths of Greenwich Borough Council has been the good relationship, reported on both sides, between the Directorate and members of the Social Services Committee, with both refreshingly willing to accept responsibility for the consequences of their decisions concerning resources.

# Social Services Resources in Greenwich 1982 - 1987

The present Director of Social Services, Mr. Martin Manby, took up his post with Greenwich in July 1982. When he arrived he found a report from the Assistant Director, Mr Devaux, arguing that the Social Services Department simply could not manage on the level of resources at its disposal. The appointment of the new Director coincided, more or less, with a change in the policy of the Council. After the municipal elections in May 1982, the administration of the Council changed, although remaining Labour. The previous Labour administration had a policy of cutting, or controlling, expenditure in order to keep within government guidelines. The new administration rejected such stringent financial control.

One of the major problems facing the Social Services Department, and other departments of the Council, at that time was the introduction of shortfall levels. This was a financial device for restricting staffing costs. Thus, while the Social Services Department had an establishment of 100%, it had money in its budget to fill only 84% of its posts. The required saving was first reduced to 10% and then removed altogether by the new Council.

The new administration, in round terms, provided £1 million to restore what was seen as cuts imposed by the previous administration, and then, a further £1 million was provided for growth. Both the £1m "re-instatement" and the £1m growth occurred in the 1983/84 budget. One of the consequences of the increased expenditure was a significant reduction in the number of unallocated cases, although there still remained some unallocated cases by the middle of 1985.

This fresh approach of the new administration was curtailed by ratecapping and in recent years it has been accepted that most areas of growth are going to have to be financed through a re-distribution of existing resources. Nevertheless, two significant packages have been introduced recently. Following a DHSS inspection in Greenwich, a further £150,000 package was provided in the winter of 1985/86, for child care and child abuse services. A further £450,000 package was considered for the 1987/88 budget. This package, among other things, proposed an additional Assistant Director post, and increase in the social work establishment including increases for the Ferrier Team, two team manager posts and some extra clerical assistance, establishing "a shortage grade" taking social work salaries beyond the top of level III, and a "vacancy pool" of 5 social workers and a team manager.

Overall, between 1982/83 and 1987/88 the Social Services Department's budget, after accounting for inflation, grew by £7 million, an adjusted increase of some 40%. We accept that Greenwich Council has not been complacent about the problems it faced and has not been standing still. The Director confirmed that "over the course of the past five years there has been a significant increase in the Directorate budget overall, in the staff establishment and the amount of money spent in real terms over that period".

# Resources for Child Care in Greenwich 1982 - 1987

Of the 40% adjusted growth in the Social Services' budget between 1982/83 and 1987/88, we were offered the estimate that approximately 43% of this increase was for specific child care policy. This increase in expenditure in real terms included a 59% growth on day nurseries, a growth of 100% on childminding and 31% on fieldwork staffing. A Children's Services Section has been built up, while increasing use of "Section One"[1] money and the development of fieldwork projects have been aimed at helping families with children.

The package of £150,000, agreed in 1985/86, included such items as a "staff member to plan and co-ordinate child abuse training", "five administrative assistants for child abuse/child care support activities" and "an extension of IT (Intermediate Treatment) and project work". The more recent £450,000 package also included many increases that would directly and indirectly augment resources for child care, including the staffing increases already mentioned, applying the "shortage grade" to social work posts in the Family Finding Unit from 1 July 1987, and establishing one additional social worker in the Children's Services Section.

We have no doubt that Greenwich Council was concerned about the resources available to Social Services in general, and for child care in particular. As for all Social Services Departments, the issue for Greenwich is, first, to judge whether the total expenditure available is adequate to meet the Council's policies; and second, with the rapid changes in the demands being made on the Department, to judge whether resources are distributed in the most effective manner and whether priorities and working practices have adapted quickly enough to these changes. Concerning the overall provision, we heard often the view that Greenwich was starting from a low baseline in 1982. The "Caring Under Threat" document showed, using comparisons up to 1983/84, that despite the fact that Social Services was the main committee spender in Greenwich, nevertheless Social Services' expenditure per capita was significantly less than in any other Inner London Borough. By the same comparison, it also showed that the fieldwork staff per thousand population in Greenwich was significantly lower.

In terms of these changes in demand, our particular interest is, of course, in the work concerned with child abuse. We were presented with the quarterly statistics showing the number of children on the Child Abuse Register from 31/3/82 until the quarter ending 30/6/87. The numbers on the Register can be used as one measure of workload. Any rise will be translated into the extra time required for applying the child abuse procedures, including dealing with the increasing number of "initial" and "review" case conferences. In addition to the basic numbers more work will have been needed to meet the rising standards of practice and levels of expectation that occurred during this period.

---

[1] This refers to the provision in the Child Care Act 1980 (previously, Section 1, Children and Young Persons Act 1963) which authorises measures designed to prevent children coming into care.

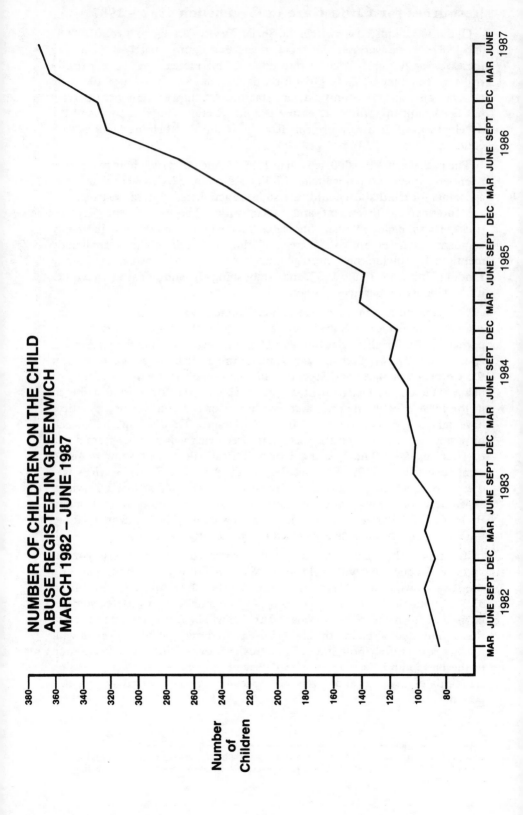

NUMBER OF CHILDREN ON THE CHILD
ABUSE REGISTER IN GREENWICH
MARCH 1982 – JUNE 1987

Number
of
Children

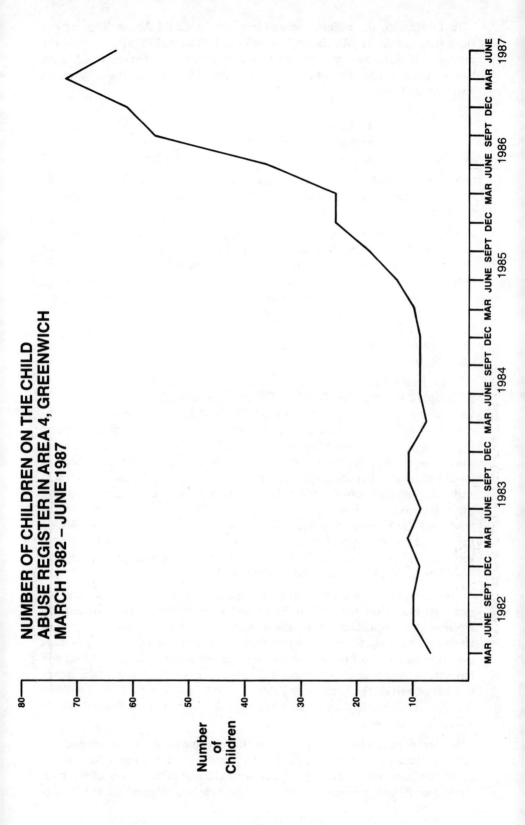

NUMBER OF CHILDREN ON THE CHILD
ABUSE REGISTER IN AREA 4, GREENWICH
MARCH 1982 – JUNE 1987

Number
of
Children

In Greenwich the number of children on the Child Abuse Register has risen from 82 on 31 March 1982 to 363 on 31 March 1987. For Area 4 the numbers of children registered for the same period rose from 7 to 72. This has not been an even rate of growth. The figures for three of the intervening years are as follows :

|         | Total | Area 4 |
|---------|-------|--------|
| 31/3/85 | 141   | 10     |
| 31/3/86 | 235   | 24     |
| 31/3/87 | 363   | 72     |

The most rapid increase has been seen in the more recent years, with the sharpest ascent starting roughly at the time that the Carliles came to Greenwich.

The increase in Greenwich has been part of a national trend which we described earlier. A sufficiently detailed breakdown of this trend does not exist for us to compare Greenwich with other local authorities, but we suspect that the Director is right in assessing that his Department faces one of the steeper rises. In his report to the Social Services Committee in July 1987, the Director suggested that: "Although there has been a marked increase in the reporting of child abuse across London and nationally, the increase in child abuse" - by which is meant, presumably, reported child abuse - "appears exceptional ...".

Concerning the two issues which we identified earlier, Greenwich will have to compare its total provision to the consequences of this increase. In the same committee report, introducing the £450,000 package, the Director continued to have serious doubts about the level of provision. "The Department's approach to this work is committed and responsible but there are simply not enough staff to deal with the work and this causes severe difficulties in allocating child abuse cases, children in care and on Supervision Orders and other statutory cases". We insist that within Social Services expenditure the protection of children must be a priority, because of the nature of the work and the consequence it has for the kind of society we live in. We do this in full awareness that reports on various other client groups, and other services, will be pressing their claims. However, for us to urge anything less would be to fail Kimberley, and children at future risk.

**Given the national explosion in reported cases of child abuse, we recommend that all Social Services' Departments fundamentally review the organisation of their services, and the distribution of their resources, to make sure that they are as well equipped as possible to respond to this trend.** We suggest that radical adaptations will have to be made, and that either to carry on as before hoping that minor tinkerings will do the trick, or to proceed with major reorganisations without specifically addressing this issue, risks leaving children in danger and staff in a hopeless position.

In Greenwich, when the issue of resources came closer to the ground, we saw a picture of Area 4, and the Ferrier team within it, as an office caught up in the pressures of change. We heard evidence of pressures of work on clerical staff, new developments, such as the decentralisation of the Ferrier team, a complete turnover of team managers, staff mobility and difficulty in allocating cases. We also visited the Area 4 office, and the sub-office on the Ferrier Estate, to see for ourselves the conditions under which staff were working.

To deal with the conditions in the Area 4 Office first, we would like to ask those responsible for providing office accommodation in Greenwich to consider whether the Area 4 Office provides suitable working conditions, and whether it provides the kind of place where clients can be satisfactorily welcomed and seen. When we visited Area 4's premises, the reception area was unwelcoming and bleak. We could see no signs of toys, or children's books, and few other features existed to redeem the beleaguered appearance of the building.

The interviewing rooms were like monastic cells and simply not large enough in which to interview a family. (We describe in more detail the precise conditions of the interview room in Chapter 19). Yet this was the environment in which Mr. Ruddock had the crucial meeting with the Carlile family on Wednesday, 12 March 1986. When individuals come under pressure, reliance cannot be placed on their strength (which comes from personal qualities, knowledge, training and experience) to transcend their confining environment. In such a setting, muddled, troubled and cramped working environments will threaten to produce muddled, troubled and cramped thinking and work.

The Ferrier team was by no means alone in its difficulty to manage on existing clerical resources. Money for clerical services and administration is not a popular cause today. To diminish the need for these services, it would be necessary to get rid of as much red tape, and as many regulations, as possible. Social Services, especially those concerned with child abuse, are heading the other way and becoming the subject of increasingly complex procedures. If that is the way to get the job done well, the clerical and administrative consequences will have to be taken on the chin. Failures in this area of work have been found by many previous inquiries to have played a crucial part in things going wrong. As the Paul Brown report[1] commented: "Adequate administrative back-up is not a luxury for social workers, it is a necessity." We echo that sentiment.

On the decentralisation issue, we would simply urge that if individual teams are to be established within the communities they serve, it is essential that specialist knowledge and expertise is readily available to them. Local knowledge will need to be supplemented by knowledge of departmental procedures and legal frameworks. It must also be acknowledged how fragile isolated teams can be, so that, if they are to provide emergency and statutory services, failsafe mechanisms must be established to safeguard the service, for example, at times of staff shortage. The workload of the decentralised teams should be carefully reviewed to judge how far their very availability effects referrals, both in terms of number and in terms of how consistent their pattern is with the Department's priorities.

So far we have been looking at the general resource issues that will have formed part of the Social Services background. We now come to two subjects

---

[1] Report of the Committee of the Inquiry into the case of Paul Steven Brown, 1980, HMSO, Cmnd 8107, p.19, paragraph 36.

which we believe had a direct bearing on the way the Carlile case was handled. Area 4 has three teams in it, each led by a team manager. During the course of 1985 and the start of 1986, three new team managers were appointed in the Area for each of the teams. This complete turn-over meant that the Area had no experienced, first line managers. This position must have made considerable demands on Mr. Neill as he helped his three new managers begin to tackle their jobs. They would have needed to be especially dependent on him in the early stages, since the quality of the advice, information and knowledge available to them from their own peer group would have been very limited. Ideally, at a time of such radical change in an area, we would hope to see the active involvement of more senior management in Social Services and we would like to see consideration of temporary, extraordinary arrangments to cover the running-in period of new staff, if there has been a turn-over such as this. The move from being a full-time practitioner to first line manager is one of the most significant that will be made within the social work career structure.

Good practitioners do not necessarily make good managers (or vice versa for that matter). Practice skills and managerial skills are related, but are not the same. Consequently, we would like to see properly structured induction programmes for new team managers and we would want to see them provided with the kind of management training that will help them master the team manager's role. This training will include preparing them for the tasks of a supervisor. Also, if team managers are to concentrate on their managerial and supervisory responsibilities effectively, and if the needs of their team are to come first, we doubt if it is reasonable to expect them to carry cases as well, and certainly not child abuse cases. Employers must be satisfied that they are not being unreasonable in what they ask of their staff. The DHSS Inspection in Greenwich in 1985 found that certain aspects of the case conference system placed "an unfair burden on the individual team managers".

Perhaps the most significant resource issue of all for Kimberley was the staffing position within the Ferrier team. Determining the appropriate establishment for a team requires a sophisticated matching of what staff can achieve in their time, with the anticipated requirements of the expected workload. We cannot comment on the distribution of resources between Areas, but we would ask for consideration to be given to the referral rates within Area 4 to assess the appropriate level of establishment for the Area as a whole, and to assess the distribution of resources among the three teams in Area 4, A and B teams and the Ferrier team. The fact that the Ferrier team became depleted in 1986 we believe to be perhaps the most important reason why the Carlile case was never allocated to a social worker by Mr. Ruddock. Many team managers would have found allocation of difficult cases in a busy team a hard enough process at the best of times, but with two experienced social workers leaving the Ferrier team, it must have been especially troublesome. We cannot comment on the quality of support Mr. Ruddock, as a new team manager, received from other members of his team, but we heard evidence which suggested that the team was unhappy about certain proposed changes in the Area and this might have created an even more unhelpful atmosphere in which to allocate cases.

At a crucial period in the Carlile case, early in 1986, Mr. Ruddock would probably have been principally concerned with trying to allocate the caseload of Mrs. Olive Swinburne, one of the experienced social workers on the point of leaving the Ferrier team. Anyway, for what ever reason, Mr. Ruddock decided to shoulder responsibility for the Carlile family, having in mind the possibility that the case might be referred to another agency. We agree with him that whether, and when, he formally allocated the case to himself is not important, given that he has never denied that he carried personal responsibility for the case during the crucial period in 1986. We do not think he should have accepted, or been allowed to accept this responsibility. He had enough to cope with in his new job without taking on such a case. However, we accept that he did it for the best of motives, at great cost to Kimberley, and to himself.

Greenwich is not alone in suffering from the loss of experienced social workers followed by difficulties in finding suitable replacements. Nevertheless, this issue was of such relevance to this particular case that **we recommend that consideration be given to seeing if action can be taken to manage the turn-round of staff more efficiently. We recommend specific consideration be given whether the departure of a member of staff can become a longer process, so that proper planning can take place.** This might involve social workers being required to give longer periods of notice. We know that this will have a knock-on effect if all employers make the same requirement. The second area that could be explored is the possibility of providing emergency cover for an Area in particular difficulty. This might involve having some form of bank upon which the Social Services could call when needed, maybe similar to the education system's use of supply teachers or the health service's use of a bank of nurses. In the case of Greenwich, by the time the Inquiry started sitting, action had already been taken to establish a back-up team of social workers. Finally, attention should be given to the attempt to create attractive recruitment packages. Greenwich will need to consider such matters, if it is to compete successfully with other Social Services Departments which are trying to recruit similar staff. If serious recruitment difficulties are being experienced, liaison with other local authorities might indicate whether this is a local problem or part of a problem that needs to be tackled nationally. If it is local, then local authorities might benefit from combining to identify, and to remedy the local causes of the problem.

## Unallocated Cases

We heard a variety of submissions concerning unallocated cases. We identified three categories of unallocated cases:

1. A case where it is clear that it should be allocated but, for whatever reason, no one will accept responsibility for it;

2. A case where it is not clear if it is going to require further work, and so the decision is left until further inquiries have been made; and

3. A case where the nature of the work is clear, but it possesses insufficient priority to be allocated immediately; at the same time, it does not lack enough priority to prevent it being rejected immediately. So it is left in suspended animation.

Concerning the first kind of case, we say, unequivocally, this is not acceptable with a child abuse case. This is not a comment directed specifically to Greenwich, but to all local authorities, especially as during the course of the Inquiry we heard of a number of authorities that were unable to allocate child abuse cases. If cases of children on the child abuse register, or cases of children at risk of abuse, are not being allocated, then they are not being provided with a child protection service. Some kind of temporary covering mechanism is unlikely to offer them the safeguard they need. If this is the position, the system has simply broken down; the system must either be repaired immediately, or emergency arrangements will have to be made to provide another system. (Unless as a society we are prepared to tolerate such an unreliable system existing for children).

Concerning the second category, we believe that it has two potential dangers: first, ambiguity might exist concerning accountability for the case while it is unallocated, with the likelihood that the team manager will be left literally holding the baby; and second, there is a risk that an unallocated case will drift into oblivion. If this category is to remain as part of the way a Social Services' Department operates (and we are not convinced it is a better process than immediate allocation, followed, where appropriate, by prompt closure) then a definite plan of action must be made, to be completed within a specified time-scale and with clear accountability. The last category might be appropriate if there is a reasonable assumption that better times lie ahead. We would be worried, however, if it is used as a way of avoiding hard decisions and of disguising lack of resources, or if it is used as a method of pretending that an office can do more than its resources actually permit. We are worried that the generic nature of the services provided by Social Services Departments may conceal in its breadth the particular needs of specialised parts of that service.

A good example of the kind of hard decision that may have to be faced was provided by Mr. Ruddock in his final submission, when he suggested that it might be necessary "to define much more narrowly the boundaries within which Social Services will be provided and without which they will not." Mr. Ruddock closed his final submission with a summary of what he saw as the adverse and the beneficial consequences which might arise from such a strategy: ".... a substantial increase in the unmet need for Social Services, a decrease in job satisfaction for Social Services staff, with the reduction of opportunities to carry out preventive and developmental work and, coming full circle, possible political unpopularity for elected members among those whose need for Social Services is left unmet. The beneficial consequences, however, include greater uniformity in the standard of provision in cases where services are provided, the achievement of manageable caseloads for social workers and of manageable workloads for managers and thus the removal of the spectre of disasters resulting from overload, and (most importantly) a realistic expectation that dangerous cases *can* be competently handled...".

Issue might be taken with this analysis, but it points to the kind of a balance of advantage that will have to be sought where there is any serious gap between demand and supply, between needs and the resources to meet them. The bottomless pit, which we often had opened for our inspection, cannot be filled: better to be strict about what we do, and do it well. Then we can take pride in our work and demonstrate its worth.

There are no doubts that holding unallocated cases was a source of anxiety for social workers and middle managers. Mr. Neill described it as like "holding a time bomb". These decisions have to be taken at Area level, but the reason for a decision not to allocate a case must be defined, so that the issue of responsibility can be dealt with.

We ask Greenwich Borough Council to satisfy itself that the politics concerning unallocated cases is clear. In a recent Social Services Committee report (July 1987), under the heading "Child Abuse", we read that: "The pressure of work falls directly on social workers dealing with families, and on their Team Managers, who supervise the work, and have to take responsibility when statutory work cannot be allocated". Councillor Draper, in his written statement to us, showed that the Social Services Committee had always taken the existence of unallocated cases seriously, but confirmed that no formal policy on the subject existed. We accept Councillor Draper's, and Mr. Manby's evidence that among councillors, and within the Directorate, there was, and is a readiness to take responsibility for what flowed, and flows from their decisions concerning policy and allocation of resources. We heard of steps taken to relieve Team Managers of responsibility, and for this to be transferred to the Directorate when the Team Managers had notified their Area Managers that statutory cases could not be allocated. Also we welcomed Councillor Draper's insistence that the Social Services Committee "fully recognises that it has a responsibility to provide an efficient child protection service in Greenwich. It would not wish to off-load that responsibility on to any member of staff if it was not possible for it to be discharged by him, having regard to the resources available". Problems arise when it is hard to establish directly the effects of particular decisions and the causes of individual cases being handled badly.

**We recommend that any Social Services Department accommodating unallocated cases must establish the appropriate criteria whenever a case remains unallocated, and policies to determine what happens next, including a clear definition of accountability for each case.**

## Conclusion

Any service can be delivered only in proportion to the resources made available. It is the responsibility of staff providing direct services to clients to make sure that the best possible use is made of their available time. Decisions should always be based on the needs of clients, and working methods and priorities must be constantly evaluated. The contributions that can be made by other agencies, organisations and people in the community should always be borne in mind. It is the responsibility of senior management, local and central government, to provide the overall resources and to determine the broad pattern of priorities for these resources, taking responsibility for decisions leading to no, or limited, services being provided.

Given the imprecise art with which these calculations are made, goodwill and trustworthiness must exist at all levels. There is ample scope for anyone to behave as manipulatively within the organisation as Mrs. Carlile and Mr. Hall did outside it. Blame can always be put on others. Before making a criticism, it is good practice to make sure we have our own house in order and to test any of our impending criticisms by the standard: "Will this do anything to help clients?" Indeed, this would be an effective criterion for most judgments in the world of welfare services.

Those nearest to the clients must make sure that as many clients are reached as effectively as possible with the means at their disposal. Those with control of the large scale resources must ensure their expectations match the consequences of their decisions.

# CHAPTER 12

# CHILD CARE POLICY IN GREENWICH

Greenwich, like many local authorities, has seen a recent drop in the number of children in its care. In 1982, 550 children were in the care of the Borough and by the start of 1987 this number had fallen below 400. This trend is in line with the Department's emphasis on preventive work and on services to children under five; and with its child care policy to keep children in their own families or, when children do need to come into care, to keep the period in care to the minimum consistent with the child's welfare. The child care policy provides a clear statement that children have a right to family care, either in their own families or through adoption and fostering, although the policy statement claims to be unusual in also recognising the value of residential care as a resource for children with special difficulties or needing a period of special help.

While fewer children were in care, many were being helped in the community; the falling number might have been partly attributable to increasingly effective preventive work. By January 1987 Greenwich Social Services Department was supporting over 500 children in the Borough who were not in care, but were either on the Child Abuse Register or who were subject to Supervision Orders. If the Director had extended his comments to refer specifically to assessing allegations of child abuse, he could have been anticipating this Inquiry, when he reported to the Social Services Committee (January 1987) :

"The Department can be held to account for its work with these groups of children almost to the same extent as for its work with children in care".

Kimberley was not in care, but there can be no doubt of the extent to which the Social Services Department and its staff are to be held accountable for the work with her and her family. We have often heard a distinction made between statutory and non-statutory work, with highest priority going to the first category and preventive work with children being allocated to the second. This distinction in child care is both inaccurate (given a local authority's duties) and risky. If it is still needed, then Kimberley provides proof that in child protection investigations, assessments and prevention must have the highest priority, and are every bit as important as working with children in care. **We recommend that no such distinction be made in child protection**.

The Greenwich Child Care Policy, agreed by the Social Services Committee on 20 April 1984, opens with the statement: "The main strategy of the Department is to help families with children at risk at home and to avoid the need for public care ... All possible ways of maintaining families in the community should be explored before looking at separation as the way to safeguarding children". This strategy is enshrined in the first aim of the policy statement which confirms: "The primary aim of all of our intervention with children and families is to ensure that children are positively sustained within, or returned to their natural family, and to prevent inappropriate separation of children from these families". The aim is similar, we suspect, to aims that will be found in other Departments' child care policies, where they exist. We have misgivings about the balance of this policy.

We recognise that we are taking one statement in a long document out of its context, but we would like to see greater importance given, at the outset, to the need to protect children. In the policy statement an imaginative and vivid list of the fundamental needs of children does not explicitly refer to the basic need a child has to be safe and to be protected from neglect and from physical, emotional and sexual abuse. (Similarly we would have welcomed greater emphasis for child protection in the "Caring Under Threat" document). We cannot say that the balance of aims in the Child Care Policy affected directly the work done with the Carlile family, and there was no evidence to suggest that the staff involved were motivated to keep the family together at all costs. Social workers are bound, however, to be influenced by the perceived philosophy of their Departments, and anything that detracts from an impartial assessment of a child's needs will be unhelpful.

In the child care policy, only one page is devoted to the topic of child abuse. Other documents, of course, will provide separate guidelines and procedures. The section on Child Abuse states: "The primary consideration in cases of child abuse is the protection of the child. The abused child has the right to expect swift, effective intervention to prevent further suffering when his/her situation is brought to the attention of the Social Services Department". This clear statement needs to be incorporated in the Department's "main strategy" and "primary aim", and the sentiment it expresses needs to be integrated in the whole document, and not compartmentalised in a section that might be seen to apply only in the direst circumstances.

We have noted the Director's statement to the Social Services Committee (January 1987) which we have echoed: "The policy now needs to be directed ..... towards the Department's responsibilities for children at risk in the community. New strategies are required to address new problems, such as child sexual abuse ...". **We recommend that all authorities with, or in the process of producing formal child care policies, make sure that child protection has the prominence it deserves.**

# AREA 4 AND THE FERRIER ESTATE

## Area 4

The Fieldwork Division of Greenwich Social Services Department is composed of: the hospital social work service; childrens services section; community services section; specialist services section and 5 Area offices. Each Area office is staffed by social workers, family aides and administrators, and is the base for the Home Help Service. Area 4 is situated in Kidbrooke Mini-Town Hall and serves six wards: Blackheath, Ferrier, Kidbrooke, Sherard, Well Hall, Deansfield and small parts of other wards. The total population served by Area 4 is approximately 40,000.

Three teams of social workers are found within Area 4 - "A" and "B" teams and the Ferrier team. In October 1983 Blackheath was added to the Ferrier team's responsibilities and the team's establishment was raised from four to six social workers, by the transfer of two social work posts from the "A" and "B" teams. As a result of these changes the Ferrier team serves a population of roughly 11,500 (with one social worker to nearly 2,000 people) and the "A" and "B" teams, not split into "patches", serve between them a population of about 24,000. The average caseload for Area 4, as reported to the Social Services Committee in February 1984, was 32.

In addition to being based at the Mini-Town Hall, the Ferrier team operates a duty system every morning on the Ferrier Estate at a Neighbourhood Centre in Ebdon Way. At the time of the Inquiry, plans were going ahead to move the Ferrier team into a joint Social Services and Housing Estate Office on the Estate.

## The Ferrier Estate

The Carlile family moved onto the Ferrier Estate in September 1985. It was the end of a long journey for Mrs. Carlile which had taken her through Merseyside, York, Wigan and North Kensington. Although both Mrs. Carlile and Mr. Hall originated from the Liverpool area, this estate was to be the new home for them and also for all four children (the three in voluntary care of Wirral being discharged to their mother on 4 October 1985).

The Ferrier Estate is situated on either side of the Kidbrooke Park Road, next to Kidbrooke Station and close to Rochester Way, part of the busy A2. It was originally a GLC show-piece, built on the site of an old RAF base. If it was hoped the Estate would be a suitable site for relatively affluent people commuting to the city, this aspiration must have been short-lived. Although you would not think so to look at it, the Ferrier Estate is nearly new. But, as with some people, there are the marks of some premature ageing from having had a hard life, struggling to make ends meet. The first part of the Estate (the side of the Estate containing the Social Services Neighbourhood Office in Ebdon Way) was built by the beginning of the 1970s, and the other

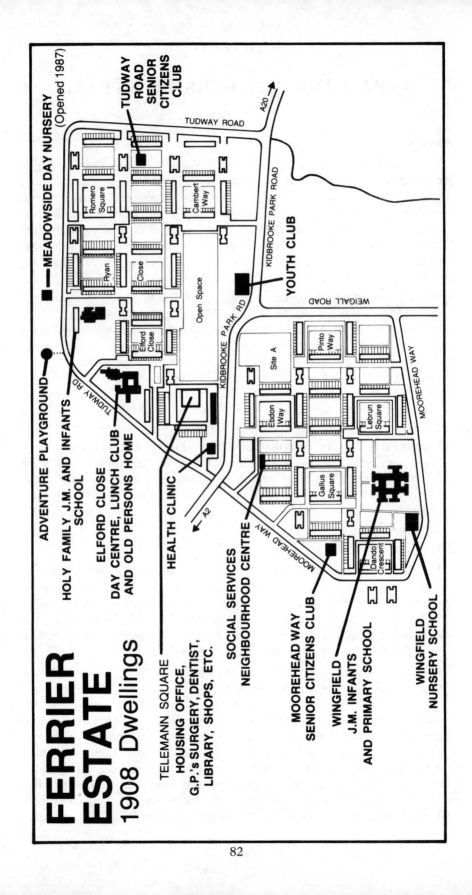

# FERRIER ESTATE
## 1908 Dwellings

MEADOWSIDE DAY NURSERY (Opened 1987)

TUDWAY ROAD SENIOR CITIZENS CLUB

TUDWAY ROAD

A20

KIDBROOKE PARK ROAD

YOUTH CLUB

WEIGALL ROAD

Romero Square

Cambert Way

Ryan

Close

Open Space

Elford Close

KIDBROOKE PARK RD

TUDWAY RD

Site A

Pinto Way

Ebdon Way

Lebrun Square

Gallus Square

Dandol Crescent

MOOREHEAD WAY

A2

ADVENTURE PLAYGROUND

HOLY FAMILY J.M. AND INFANTS SCHOOL

ELFORD CLOSE
DAY CENTRE, LUNCH CLUB AND OLD PERSONS HOME

HEALTH CLINIC

SOCIAL SERVICES NEIGHBOURHOOD CENTRE

TELEMANN SQUARE
HOUSING OFFICE,
G.P.'s SURGERY, DENTIST,
LIBRARY, SHOPS, ETC.

MOOREHEAD WAY SENIOR CITIZENS CLUB

WINGFIELD J.M. INFANTS AND PRIMARY SCHOOL

WINGFIELD NURSERY SCHOOL

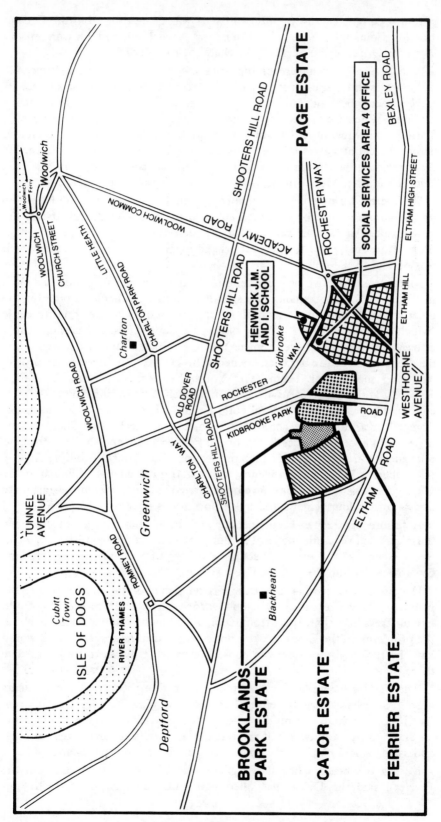

part was completed shortly afterwards. It was taken-over from the Greater London Council by Greenwich Council in April 1980, under a Compulsory Transfer Order of the Secretary of State for the Environment.

The Estate is a mixture of high-rise concrete tower blocks, "stacked" maisonettes and houses. It contains approximately 1,900 homes, accommodating between 6,000 and 7,000 people, with most of these coming from outside the area. When we visited the Estate we found one of its more remarkable features to be how unremarkable it was. Many worse estates are to be found across the country, so that the "survivors" in Ferrier are not even awarded the kudos that goes with bringing up a family successfully in, say, the East End of London, Moss Side in Manchester, or Toxteth in Liverpool.

We visited during a week-day morning - mainly in the rain - and saw few people about except for workmen engaged in repairs. Although it was the school holidays, no children were to be seen. The one place teeming with life was the surgery of the general practitioners in Telemann Square, which was packed to the gills.

Many attempts have been made to make the Ferrier Estate a decent place in which to live. It contains two schools, a nursery school, a home for the elderly (which we visited), a youth club, a community centre, a health clinic (which we also visited), a housing office and play groups. It has shops and a pub. Many initiatives have been started on the Estate since it was built. The neighbourhood centre has been opened. This centre is an inter-agency project involving the Ferrier Team, The Youth Service, The Adult Education Service and the Citizens Advice Bureau, as well as providing a base for other community groups such as local childminders. The Ferrier Team itself has engaged in a number of community projects on the Estate. There can be little doubt about the accessibility of the Ferrier Team and the need for, and relevance of its service, with a high proportion of the referrals coming directly from clients, 71%, and with 60% coming from residents calling into the office in person. Renovations have been carried out on the Estate: each square has its own colour scheme and lights and drains have been improved.

A leisure centre has been opened, and ILEA has moved into a "new horizons" centre, while the local authority plan to set up a joint Housing and Social Services office on the Estate. (This venture was the subject of some controversy within the Area 4 Team.)

Despite these attempts to put the Ferrier Estate on the map of reasonable places to live, we heard hardly a good word for the place. However, we would like to stress here that, apart from Councillor Fay who spoke feelingly about the problems on the Estate, we did not consult with the residents who would have been the only people who could tell us what it was really like to live there.

The Ferrier Estate lacks a post office, even though most of the residents are on Supplementary Benefit. There are few play facilities for children. Until recently there was no day nursery within walking distance. The rents are high (apparently over half the tenants on the Estate are in rent arrears) and asbestos and pharaoh ants have been discovered on the Estate.

Mr Hayter, headteacher of Wingfield school, (the primary school for the Ferrier), said the Estate was filled with vulnerable families which "put intolerable pressures on the school and the Social Services team." At the time of his giving evidence, Mr Hayter told us that 72% of the children have free school dinners, 38% are from single parent families and 63% come from families with unemployed parents. Children from 23 different nationalities go to the school. We heard from P.C. Williams, who had been a "home beat officer" on the Estate, that Cambert Way, where the Carliles lived, was one of the parts of the Estate that had a high crime rate. P.C. Williams also said that it was the kind of Estate where people kept themselves to themselves.

We were told that "those who can, move off the Estate" and that "the overwhelming majority of people who live on the Estate would rather live somewhere else." The Estate in its layout was described as "self-contained" and this added to the impression that once in, it was a hard place to get out of. Attempts to improve the Ferrier Estate have foundered on a hostile environment: they have been like trying to cultivate a garden flower on a mountainous crag.

Many of the people on the Estate came there via the Greater London Mobility Scheme. Many of these, like Mrs. Carlile and Mr. Hall, came from being homeless in another part of London where they had lived in bed and breakfast accommodation. These relocated people will have no roots, no friends and no extended families within Greenwich. The problems arising from such a scheme seem to us very predictable.

No one should be surprised when the dumping ground at the end of the process ends up being described as "a concrete ghetto". It is irresponsible to set up such a scheme without having the means of tackling the predictable consequences. Under these circumstances it is bound to be hard to establish any sense of community on an Estate like the Ferrier. We heard of families being isolated and, as we have already mentioned, of people keeping themselves to themselves, although we remembered that at least one neighbour took the trouble to make the telephone call (to which we refer later) expressing worry about the care of Kimberley.

This then was the place where the Carlile family was going to set up home: where Mr. Hall was to become father of four children and a fifth soon afterwards; Mrs. Carlile was to be reunited with three children she had seen little of in the previous fourteen months, and where three children were coming to, from established foster homes, in order to start a new life. For Kimberley it was to be a short one.

# CHAPTER 14

# GREENWICH SOCIAL SERVICES: OFFER AND REJECTION OF HELP, OCTOBER 1985

Even before the request arrived from Wirral on 7 October 1985 for Greenwich to carry out "some sort of monitoring while the children settle back with their mother", Area 4 had become marginally involved in the projected reunion of the Carlile family, and was offering the assistance of Social Services.

In early September Kensington & Chelsea Social Services had informed Area 4 that a transfer summary was on its way, and asked for Area 4's address for forwarding the summary. Mr. Ruddock's predecessor as Ferrier Team Manager held a team meeting, which decided to await the report. The report arrived shortly afterwards. We have commented on it in Chapter 8. It assumed that, with the Carliles moving out of the Kensington & Chelsea area "with the resettlement of Mrs. Carlile in permanent accommodation ... plans will go ahead with the rehabilitation of the children from Wallasey, this being co-ordinated by Wirral Social Services" with Greenwich Social Services.

The co-ordination was reflected in a call from Wirral seeking Greenwich's assistance in establishing contact with Mrs. Carlile only for the purpose of making arrangements for the hand-over of the three children. Area 4 wrote on 18 September to Mrs. Carlile to the address on the Ferrier Estate, requesting that she should call at the neighbourhood office to discuss the return of her three children. The Carliles did not move into their new home on the Ferrier Estate until 27 September. Three days later Greenwich Social Services were told by Wirral Social Services via a telephone call that Mrs. Carlile was going up to Wirral, 4 days later, on Friday, 4 October, to pick up the children and to bring them to live with her and Mr. Hall. It was much too late in the day for Area 4 to become directly involved in the arrangements for, and even the actual physical hand-over of the three children to their mother.

Greenwich Social Services were told that Wirral did not expect any problems - "the problem before was Mr. Carlile's violence towards his wife". The request, which was to be echoed in the subsequent letter, dated 4 October 1985 and received on 7 October, was to "monitor the situation whilst the children are settling in". Area 4 responded by indicating that, since their letter had been sent in advance of the family moving into their new home, and had probably not been received, a fresh letter would be sent.

On the day before the hand-over of 4 October, Mr. Ruddock, then only just in post, wrote to Mrs. Carlile. He noted the imminent hand-over of "the three children from care" and expressed the hope that their return home would be "easy and without too many issues". Mr. Ruddock could be excused for not knowing that this was anything but a self-fulfilling prophesy. He ended his short letter: "However, should you feel we can help in any way, please call in to the Neighbourhood Office at 1 Ebdon Way on the Ferrier

Estate, and talk to a social worker. The office is open each morning between 9.30-12.30 on Monday to Friday".

Having regard to Wirral Social Services' minimal concern about the future of the Carlile children - the one disturbing factor of Mr. Carlile's violence towards his wife, having been removed from the familial scene - Mr. Ruddock's action was entirely reasonable. His duty was to offer his team's services. The offer was responded to, but not in the manner expected.

At about 10 a.m. on 10 October 1985 a reasonably well dressed young man with a child in a buggy - it must have been Z - appeared in the doorway of the Neighbourhood Centre at Ebdon Way. He was quickly identified as Mrs. Carlile's co-habitee, since he was waving the letter sent by Mr. Ruddock to Mrs. Carlile in the face of Mrs. Fitzgerald, the Ferrier team clerk who was acting as receptionist. Mr. Hall stood on the threshold of the office, obdurately refusing to go inside. He appeared "angry and edgy", even aggressive. His speech was loud - "almost shouting" - and he was abusive of social workers. The message was unmistakably clear. He and Mrs. Carlile wanted nothing to do with social workers whom he regarded as "the worst people who ever walked the earth". The encounter was mercifully short - long enough, however, for Mr. Hall to reject Mrs. Fitzgerald's offer for him to be seen by the duty social worker, but insufficient time to elapse for Mrs. Fitzgerald to feel intimidated by him. Mrs. Fitzgerald considered, sensibly, that the incident deserved something more than a message on the file. She wrote a succinct report of it. Later that day, Mrs. Fitzgerald's report was seen by Mr. Ruddock. Laconically, he wrote on the file: "Add to papers".

A month later - on 18 November 1985 - Mr. Ruddock saw a note on a referral record form that Mrs. Carlile had presented herself at the Kidbrooke clinic and had been interviewed by the health visitor, Miss Reader. Ms Roper of Area 4, when contacted by the clinic, informed Miss Reader that "the family does not want social work involvement and currently we [Area 4] have no concerns". Ms Roper recommended no further action. That recommendation was endorsed by Mr. Ruddock on that day, indicating further that the case was not to be allocated. For the remainder of 1985 there was otherwise silence on the Carlile family front. Greenwich Social Services predictably felt unconcerned about the reconstituted Carlile family "settling down" on the Ferrier Estate. Area 4 had been lulled into a false sense of sangfroid about the Carlile children, in part because of the unconcern communicated by Wirral Social Services, in part by Area 4's disinclination to ask for additional information about the family, and in part by the assertiveness of Mr. Hall that there was no wish, nor need for the attention of Social Services. There was, in our view, absolutely nothing for Area 4 staff to latch on to, calling for an investigation of suspected child abuse. And the discharge of the children from voluntary care possessed the hallmark of the end of a chapter in the childrens' lives. A new chapter was opening up.

# CHAPTER 15

# AN EARLY EVASION, 18 NOVEMBER 1985

A week after Mrs. Carlile had gone to Dr. Mahesh's surgery and obtained from him a referral note to the Brook Hospital "for speech therapy" for Kimberley, Mrs. Carlile went, unaccompanied by any children, to the Kidbrooke Health Clinic which is only walking-distance from the doctor's surgery on the Ferrier Estate. On November 18 she went ostensibly to obtain details of the service at the clinic that she would be wanting.

Miss Reader, the health visitor, was on the clinic premises, and conducted an interview. Mrs. Carlile volunteered the names and ages of the four children and willingly answered all the questions put to her. Miss Reader was told that the family had recently moved onto the Ferrier Estate, and that the three children - X, Y and Kimberley, who had been there only for six weeks - had "in the past" been in voluntary care, due to their mother's homelessness. She did not indicate that the voluntary care had been in the Wirral, or that the real reason for the children being received into care was the upheaval in the Carlile household, her own imprisonment, and her subsequent homelessness. Her partial concealment of the true facts was compounded by her not divulging any connection with Wirral. She gave the four children's dates of birth, omitted their place of birth and gave two addresses, prior to that of the Ferrier Estate, which were in Kensington. The three children in care had, of course, never resided in North Kensington where Mrs. Carlile and Z had been in the earlier part of 1985. Social Services at least knew that the voluntary care had been in Wirral, because they had had contact with Social Services there.

Miss Reader was clearly impressed by the fact of Mrs. Carlile turning up at the clinic unannounced and unprompted. Residents of the Ferrier Estate as a rule did not take advantage of the health facilities available. Miss Reader assumed, therefore, that Mrs. Carlile was a caring mother, concerned about her children's welfare. Miss Reader went on to ask about Kimberley and Z who, because they were under 5, constituted a special concern for a health visitor. She asked if they were up-to-date with their immunizations and developmental assessments. She was assured that they were. This was the second piece of evasion: Mrs. Carlile omitted to mention the fact of Kimberley's poor showing on the 24-month developmental assessment, and her non-attendance for the follow-up in March 1984. If Mrs. Carlile could be forgiven for not having recalled all, or any of those matters, she could hardly have forgotten the reason for the visit to Dr. Mahesh the week before, or that she had obtained from the doctor a referral note to the Brook Hospital, a referral which she never took up.

Miss Reader supplied Mrs. Carlile with the details of the service at the clinic, and she gave the telephone number of the health visitors' office. The meeting ended with Miss Reader saying that she would make a home visit to the family as soon as she received the children's previous health records. She invited Mrs. Carlile to contact her, should she have reason to need advice or help on the children's health.

Miss Reader's favourable view of Mrs. Carlile was reflected in the conversation which Miss Reader had with Area 4 later that day. She told Ms Roper, who was the Duty Officer, that Mrs. Carlile had presented herself at the clinic, and that she (Miss Reader) just wanted to check whether there were, according to Ms Roper's note on file, any "concerns about the family" because of the RIC (reception into care) in Wirral. (It was Ms Roper who had, on 30 September, taken the call from Wirral about the arrangements for the hand-over and discharge from voluntary care of the three children).

Ms Roper confirmed the good impression, by saying that "the family does not want social work involvement and currently we have no concerns". That Mrs. Carlile had in the past shown a marked attraction to violent men in her life, that she had recently served a prison sentence for fraud, and that her links with the three children over the previous 15 months had been tenuous - all these facts were not communicated to Miss Reader. Miss Reader, moreover, cannot have known that the three children's previous, and only homes had been in the Wirral because, if she had, she would have been able to indicate that fact when making her request that day to Greenwich Health Authority headquarters for the children's health records. School medical records arrived, fortuitously via the school health records office, only on 16 February 1986.

We make three observations about this encounter with Mrs. Carlile at the clinic on 18 November. First, Mrs Carlile was covering up about the earlier problems of the family and her own recent troubles. And she was not revealing the recurrence of Kimberley's speech problems, detected two years' earlier. Knowing that all three children had been in voluntary care - no matter in what part of the country - Miss Reader might have been more inquisitive about the socio-medical background. No doubt she was deferring probing questions until she made her home visit. Had she made that visit timeously, the absence of such questioning would not call for comment. We have no doubt that Miss Reader fully intended to make an early visit, but the volume of work deflected her from accomplishing it until 15 January 1986, following the incident over X at Wingfield School. Good professional practice demands that a "removal-in" home visit should be undertaken as soon as possible after the family's presence in the area becomes known, and not later than one month after.

Second, there was a lack of information a) elicited by Miss Reader from Mrs. Carlile; and b) emanating from Social Services. It is vital, if full collaborative effort is to be maintained in child protection, that the main agencies fully exchange all the relevant knowledge they have. To maintain bits of information in disparate documentary sources that are not collated is to handicap those who need to rely on optimum information. (We deal in Chapter 26 with the urgent need to establish an information system).

Third, we think that the visit to the clinic by Mrs. Carlile should have been made known to the family's general practitioner. Had contact been made with Dr. Mahesh, the fact of the visit of 11 November 1985, and its purport might have been discovered - again, to the benefit of protection for Kimberley. That this did not happen is another example of the failure of the multi-disciplinary approach in action.

# CHAPTER 16

# WINGFIELD PRIMARY SCHOOL AND KIMBERLEY'S OLDER BROTHER

During the morning of 9 January 1986, X, then aged nearly 8 went up to Miss Rouse, his class teacher, told her he had torn the zipper on his jacket, and that he did not want to go home because his father had already thrown him across the room that morning. X had joined Wingfield Junior School on the Ferrier Estate on 28 October 1985 simultaneously with his sister, Y (then aged 6) being admitted to the infants school. This was three weeks after their discharge from care and reunion with their mother.

Teaching staff at Wingfield quickly formed an opinion of X's character and behaviour, which indicated slight immaturity and attention-seeking behaviour. He was put into the nurture group - generally an hour long session with a teacher giving a high level of attention to only 4 children at a time. Miss Rouse told us that she found X "quite endearing and a bit of a clown". At times in a class situation he could be a nuisance because of his attention-seeking ways. She described one of these episodes:"He would pretend to faint. We have a mat where we do reading and sit down to have talks. He would stand up and say to me "I'm going to faint now", turn around 3 times and lie down flat on his back, sort of open one eye and then crawl to his feet once he got a little cluster of children around him or my attention".

Mr. Hall usually collected X from school; occasionally he was seen to be accompanied by Mrs. Carlile, with Z in a pushchair, and a large dog. X never showed any reluctance to approach the man whom he called 'Dad'.

In this way, Miss Rouse met Mr. Hall about a dozen times when he would take the opportunity to voice concern about X's reading. She found him to be somewhat intimidating and felt that she was unsuccessful in persuading him that it was unreasonable to expect X to read a book every night. He explained his anxiety by saying that he had had difficulties in reading himself and did not want X to grow up not being able to read. Miss Rouse and Mr. Cox, deputy head, whose assistance she sought, interpreted this as a parent taking an interest - albeit, somewhat inappropriately. Eventually they reached agreement to communicate with the home by sending messages back and forward through X's reading record. This achieved a slight reduction of pressure on X, and the amount that he was expected to read.

In making the allegation that he had been thrown across the room by his step-father, Miss Rouse told us that X showed no distress. His statement was made in his usual style "with sort of raised eyebrows and a smile on his face". Having been assured that he was not hurt, she waited until the next session which was P.E. and then placed herself near him while he got changed into vest and pants. She looked for any sign of marks on his body which might have substantiated his claim, but saw none.

There were three possible indicators of child abuse while X was at Wingfield School. At first there was the unrealistic expectation by his step-father about X's reading. This was taken to be parental interest in helping a son but not knowing how best to do so. There then followed the allegation by X that he had been thrown across the room. While staff kept an "open mind" about this incident, they believed that it could be explained by what Mr. Hayter, headteacher, described to Mr. Ruddock and to us, as X's fantasizing. It is possible that the attention-seeking behaviour of "fainting" could have been a third indicator.

With hindsight, the question must be asked whether X was fantasizing or acting out something which had happened to him or that he had seen at home. We have no answer to this, but are conscious that children seldom make false allegations of this nature.

## School's reaction to the incident

The incident of X alleging to Miss Rouse on 9 January that he had been thrown across the room by his step-father, was discussed with Mr. Cox. They decided to start monitoring X immediately.

Monitoring involved paying extra attention to the child - his physical state, behaviour and conversation, and recording this daily. His participation in the nurture group gave additional opportunity for detailed observation. This was an internal procedure and did not include informing the school doctor or nurse. At no time thereafter did X display any change in demeanour or attitude which could have been indicative of abuse to himself, or of the trauma occurring at home. There were no incidents involving Y. The following morning Miss Rouse asked X if anything had happened when he returned home the previous day, and was told that nothing had happened. When Mr. Hayter, the headteacher, returned to the school during that week after a long absence, there was a discussion between him, Mr. Cox, Miss Rouse and the two nurture group teachers. X's school attendance was good so they agreed to continue the monitoring.

It was only on 15 January that X's previous education records arrived from Wirral. When Mrs. Carlile had registered the children at the school she gave details of one previous school. It was only when Y's records arrived in November that it was realised that X must have been at a different school, thus necessitating a second request for the records. There was included in the records, when they arrived, a report of X's academic progress and a copy of Wirral Social Services child care review report, dated 1 April 1985. This review report indicated that the children had been in voluntary care. Wingfield staff nevertheless remained unaware of the childrens' turbulent past.

Later that day, there was a routine liaison meeting between Mr. Cox who acts as pastoral head of the school, Ms Gregory, educational welfare officer and Ms Roper, social worker. It was their considered opinion that there were insufficient grounds to invoke the formal child abuse procedure, and they confirmed that X would be monitored carefully at school.

Ms Roper told us that her monthly attendance at Wingfield School liaison meeting was an informal arrangement whereby she was given information which she passed back to the Social Services office for action, if appropriate. Unless another social worker had asked her to enquire about a particular child, she would be unaware of which children were going to be discussed each month.

News of the allegation by X and a copy of Wirral's Child Care Review form were conveyed back to the Area 4 office by Ms Roper. She then telephoned Miss Reader, health visitor, and, having told her of the incident, asked her to make a home visit. Miss Reader, who had still not received the health records, made her initial visit the next day and advised Ms Roper of the outcome.

It was during the meeting of 15 January that Ms Gregory first heard of the Carlile family. She learnt, and this could only have been from Ms Roper, that they were a family with past difficulties who were opposed to any social work contact. She subsequently reported to Ms Nuaimi, her senior. Thereafter, during her weekly visit to the school, Ms Gregory checked on X's situation and received reports regarding his attendance and attainment more favourable than for many other children who caused greater concern.

Mr. Ruddock, on hearing of the allegation, telephoned Mr. Hayter and Ms Nuaimi, senior education welfare officer, seeking clarification of what "pushed around" meant. Mr. Hayter told him of X's tendency to fantasize. These conversations were confirmed in writing with a request that education staff continue their monitoring and communicate any information which would substantiate or reduce the concern.

X had a school medical examination on 3 February to which his mother was invited but did not attend. Neither Dr. Kamalanathan nor Mrs. Coker, school nurse, knew of the allegation. Nothing abnormal was discovered and X was pronounced healthy.

A month later, in response to Dr. Hooper's request for a report on X, Y and Kimberley, Dr. Kamalanathan was told by Mr. Hayter that X and Y were making satisfactory progress in school. No note was made of this conversation, which Mr. Hayter could not remember but did not dispute. It seems unlikely that he shared the knowledge of X's allegation, or that Dr. Kamalanathan told him of the full content of Dr. Hooper's letter which stated that she had confidential information from Wirral in connection with child abuse procedures. Dr. Kamalanathan replied to Dr. Hooper with the information about X and Y which he had, and added that he had no knowledge of their social circumstances. There was no reference to Kimberley, no doubt because she was not attending the school.

The school monitoring continued uneventfully until 28 April when Mr. Hall suddenly requested a transfer of X and Y from Wingfield to Henwick School. Ms Gregory heard of the transfer at her next meeting at Wingfield and liaised with, and passed over the file to Mrs. Gibbs, education welfare officer for Henwick school, where internal school monitoring was continued.

The only observation of note, while at Henwick, was raised at the school meeting of 22 May when X was described as a scruffy child who was often late for school. This was not reported to Social Services, although it contrasted with Wingfield's reports on the children - that X and Y looked as if they came from an adequate and caring home and that they were good school attenders.

On the facts known and the perception of the events at the time, education staff acted reasonably, with the sole exception of their failure to inform school health personnel of their concern. At no time was any concern expressed at school for the welfare of Y.

# CHAPTER 17

# AN UNFULFILLED MISSION, 7 MARCH 1986

The first alert that Kimberley Carlile was suffering physical abuse in the Carlile household came in an anonymous telephone call to Greenwich Social Services early in the afternoon of 7 March 1986. The caller gave the address of the Carliles, but did not mention the family's name, giving only the initial "C". The call was taken by Mrs. Beryl Fitzgerald, a receptionist and clerk to the Ferrier Estate team in Area 4. With perspicacity, she identified the Carlile family, recalling that back in October 1985 she had encountered Mr. Hall when he visited the team office on the Ferrier Estate, in response to a letter offering the services of Area 4. Mr. Hall gave a dusty answer to the effect that he and Mrs. Carlile wanted no further contact with Social Services, and in particular social workers (see Chapter 14). On the Referral Record form Mrs. Fitzgerald entered the name of Mrs. Carlile, "4 children: Mr. Hall, co-hab." Mrs. Fitzgerald recorded the call : "Several neighbours very concerned about the children of this family, in particular a little girl about 4. Thinks she's being beaten, cries pitifully. Sure mother drinks. DO [Duty Officer] not available at time of call, informant will ring back". Under the heading "Further action recommended", she noted : "Phoned NSPCC - not known - home visit done", which was action taken later by the Duty Officer.

## The anonymous call

This call on 7 March 1986 was the only one received by Greenwich Social Services relating to the Carlile family. When the police were investigating the homicide of Kimberley Carlile three months later there came to light two witnesses who said they had telephoned Social Services about the Carlile family, but there was no record of any call other than the one received on 7 March. Miss Camilla Bacon and Mrs. Edna Barbanti, both of them neighbours of the Carlile family, gave evidence at the Central Criminal Court in May 1987. Miss. Bacon gave evidence to us of having made two anonymous calls. Mrs. Barbanti, an older woman, was not called before us; her evidence in the criminal proceedings was that she made her call at the end of February. We do not think that the call of 7 March came from Miss Bacon. Mrs. Fitzgerald who told us that the caller sounded like an older woman, was plainly aware of the importance of recording and acting on such a call; that she did on 7 March, with commendable speed and efficiency. It is inconceivable that she would not have treated Miss Bacon's calls in like manner, and there is no basis for suggesting that anyone else in Area 4 might have taken the calls and not acted upon them. The Social Services Department made a thorough investigation in mid-June 1986, at the request of the police, and discovered no trace of any other call. It is probable that the caller on 7 March 1986 was Mrs. Barbanti, although some adjustment in the date she mentioned in her evidence at the criminal trial would be necessary. It matters not whence the call came. It matters only that it was made. It proved to be genuine and was, all too unhappily, accurate.

## The response to the anonymous call

Mrs. Olive Swinburne, the Duty Officer of the day, and an experienced social worker, who had no prior knowledge of the Carlile family beyond the paucity of information on file, proceeded to act on the anonymous call. She rang the NSPCC, and was told that nothing was known of the family. She also tried to contact Ms Marilyn Gregory, the Education Welfare Officer at Wingfield Primary School - a note on file indicated an earlier contact by Ms Gregory with the Carlile family (see Chapter 16). After consulting with the Duty Team Manager, Ms Marilyn Streeter, it was decided, "in view of violence in the past, to visit the home", and to ask the health visitor Miss Reader, to go on a joint visit. Mrs. Swinburne rang Miss Reader.

Miss Reader was told of the anonymous telephone call of that day. Her note of the conversation with Mrs. Swinburne stated that Social Services had received phone *calls* (our italics) from neighbours "alleging that Kimberley was being beaten and cries pitifully". A great deal of evidence before us was directed to the disparity between a single anonymous call and multiple calls. In the end we are confident that the reference was only to the one call of 7 March, and that Miss Reader probably interpreted *calls* to mean several neighbours' accumulated worries about the Carlile family.

Miss Reader's note went on to record : "Requested that I visited as I had gained entry on my last visit and Mr. Hall, co-habitee, had refused Social Services intervention. I did not feel it was my role to follow through such allegations; therefore stated that Social Services should visit and act accordingly". It is likely that Miss Reader understood at the time that she was initially being asked to visit the Carlile home unaccompanied. Mrs. Swinburne is adamant that she intended to convey only a joint visit. We do not think that Mrs. Swinburne, who was alive to the statutory duty exclusively on Social Services to investigate, would have made a request for a lone visit by Miss Reader.

A refusal by Miss Reader to do the visit alone would certainly have been a reasonable decision. We think that Miss Reader's understanding of the suggested visit was a genuine mistake. She told us that, on the basis that the request had been for a joint visit, she would still have declined to go on such a visit. Indeed, on the occasion of the second call from Mrs. Swinburne, Miss Reader was positively asked to go on a joint visit, and did still refuse. She now accepts that there may be a valid health-visiting reason for a joint visit within the existing role of health visitors. We do not criticise Miss Reader for not having adopted a stance that she now accepts. All her training and practical work had taught her that the role of health visitors is preventive and educational, and that a health visitor is not to be engaged in crisis intervention. As Mrs. Pamela O'Connor, recently appointed Director of Nursing Services (Community) Greenwich Health Authority, told us, the way in which health visitors traditionally go about their work is to adopt a methodical, planned approach to child developmental surveillance. She fully accepted that health visitors may need to become involved in a crisis situation.

## The purpose of the visit

At about 5 p.m. Mrs. Swinburne and Ms Streeter, without the assistance of Miss Reader, went to the Carlile home on the Ferrier Estate. There is no doubt that the two of them were carrying out their duty to investigate the welfare of the Carlile children, and in particular to satisfy themselves whether the message contained in the anonymous telephone call, of physical abuse to Kimberley, was genuine or not. Mr. Hall told us that, on answering the knock on the door, he was informed that the two social workers had called "to see your children". They were not denied entry to the home, and began conversing in the sitting room where one child, Y, already was. The eldest child, X, came in soon afterwards. The two children appeared clean and tidy. They listened quietly and very attentively to the adults' discussion lasting about half-an-hour. When Mrs. Swinburne reflected on the visit over the weekend she concluded that the behaviour of X and Y had been disconcerting. It made her ponder further on her suspicions of child abuse.

The purpose of the visit was clearly focused on the primary need to see Kimberley and Z, the youngest child, but particularly Kimberley. In the event, which we proceed to describe, the purpose was frustrated. We have asked ourselves two questions: a) Did the two social workers have good reasons for failing to accomplish their mission of seeing the two younger children; and b) if so, was it reasonable on their part to postpone the fulfilment of that mission until the Monday morning?

Before we proceed to answer those two questions, we wish to indicate how we have approached our task of judging the quality of social work performed by Mrs. Swinburne and Ms Streeter. We have paid close attention to the Area Review Committee's and Greenwich Social Services child abuse procedure guides, which were operative at the time. Without dilating upon the precise provisions and the absence of important rules of practice in them, one thing is clear to us. It is never enough simply to comply with the letter of stated procedures. The procedures on the follow-up of anonymous telephone calls, for example, clearly needed supplementing. The standards which a generic social worker in Greenwich should apply in following up an anonymous telephone call cannot be gleaned solely from these procedures. There is always an overriding professional duty to exercise skill, judgment and care in following up an anonymous telephone call.

Where there is a refusal by parents to allow access to the child, a social worker is presented with a real difficulty. We are of the opinion that Greenwich's Child Abuse Procedures Guide was insufficiently clear or emphatic to point a way out of the difficulty. For example, the guide (para 4) states that "the child ... should be seen", whereas the guide should state that the child *must* be seen. **We recommend that the procedure for following up any referral of suspected child abuse should insist that all the children in the family be seen.** There are difficulties which existing procedures cannot help, because the law is defective. We have in mind the absence of any right of access to a child, the largely unknown power to obtain a warrant to search and inspect premises, and the excess of power in certain circumstances to remove and detain a child at risk where something less fearsome is called for. We have considered elsewhere (Chapter 25) how the law should be amended, and how it should work in practice. In arriving at our findings on the quality of the social work performed on the visit of

7 March, we have, therefore, made allowance for the problems that faced the two social workers.

Another example of a professional standard being applied to supplement the procedures laid down relates to the need for a speedy response to the anonymous call. The two social workers were down at the Carlile household within 3 hours of receipt of the call. No time limit is contained in the Greenwich procedure. Neither does one appear in the BASW procedure; nor in the DHSS draft guidance. The NSPCC's response to the DHSS draft guidance suggests (p.12) that "any alleged incident of child abuse should be regarded as serious and investigated urgently - within a maximum of 12 hours - whether or not the family is already receiving help. No distinction should be made between new, current or closed cases".

**We recommend that any child abuse procedure should state that a response must be made immediately to any referral suggestive of child abuse, and that in any event the action must be taken within 24 hours**.

We accept the submission made by Mr. Richardson, on behalf of Mrs. Swinburne, that when a social worker is forced by circumstances to do too many things at once, the fact that he or she does one of those things incorrectly - or, more so, fails to do something that in normal circumstances would have been done - should not lightly be the subject of criticism. It is clear to us that on that Friday afternoon Mrs. Swinburne was within a week of leaving her job to live and work on the South Coast, and was busily winding up and handing over her cases, and had quite enough on her plate without engaging in what might have turned out to be a fruitless exercise. If she and her colleagues in Area 4 were not exactly embattled, they were engaged in a struggle to combat the burdens of over-work and an increasing number of cases.

## Non-fulfilment of the mission

What perplexed us throughout the Inquiry was whether there had been a lack of persistence on the part of Mrs. Swinburne and Ms Streeter to see Kimberley on the visit of 7 March. When we first perused the documentation we thought that there had been such hostility emanating from Mr. Hall that the two women were almost being driven out of the Carlile home, and that they had done all that could reasonably be expected of them to gain access to the two younger children.

But when we had heard the oral evidence it was clear that, while Mr. Hall was highly indignant at the intrusion of his home by social workers, for whom he had, to put it mildly, no regard, there was no threat of violence, or even physical removal of the social workers from the home.

We have not found our task of deciding the question at all easy. But having read and re-read all the evidence, and having reflected on the issue at length, we are not disposed to criticise the two social workers, because of the circumstances under which they were working. We do feel, however, that other social workers might have said, in so many words: "We are not leaving until we have seen the two younger children", and leaving the home only when they had seen the children, or were shown the door in a manner that indicated termination of the visit. In which case, the evidence might have been enough to go straight away for a Place of Safety Order. We think that Mrs. Swinburne and Ms Streeter, without having received such a blunt demand, felt, not unreasonably in the circumstances, that they had come to the end of any useful discussion with the Carliles. The circumstances that have led us to conclude, on balance, that they should not be criticised for an unfulfilled mission are these :

1. There were inadequate procedural guidelines for following up anonymous calls.

2. There was widespread ignorance among social workers of the power to apply to a magistrate authorising the police to search the premises, under Section 40, Children and Young Persons Act 1933. And we think that it was not unreasonable to rule out an application for a Place of Safety Order.

3. There were immediately unverifiable stories told by the parents, which might or might not turn out to be true.

4. There was the determined resistance by the Carliles to allow access to Kimberley.

## Postponing fulfilment of the mission

While the initial response to the anonymous telephone call on 7 March was commendably swift, access to Kimberley was too long delayed. If it was reasonable to terminate the visit on the Friday evening after 30 minutes, there should at least have been a return visit within the next 24 hours. We think that, in fact, it should have been carried out later that evening. One of the parents' excuses, barely plausible, for denying access to the younger children was that they were in bed upstairs, although Kimberley may not have been asleep. Mrs. Swinburne's note, recorded that evening, was cryptic. It noted: "I asked if the children were asleep, she said they had been shopping *and the baby was sleeping so they both were in bed* (emphasis supplied). It was now 5 p.m. and I asked if they were in bed for the night. She said they would be getting up again later on". *If* Kimberley was not sleeping, there was no reason for not asking to see her at least, then and there. The explanation for their being in bed in the middle of the day was that the children had been out shopping that afternoon in Lewisham, and had come home very tired. But, according to Mrs. Swinburne's evidence to us, the two social workers were told that Kimberley (and Z) had not gone to bed for the night, but would be getting up later on. That remark should have been eagerly seized upon as a reason for coming back later that evening, either announced or unannounced, and either accompanied by the police, or unaccompanied. If the two social workers had decided that the re-visit could not wait 60 hours, until the Monday morning, they would have either had to return on that Friday evening, or would have had to make arrangements for the Standby Duty Officer to visit on the Friday evening or the Saturday morning. We do not regard this approach as a counsel of perfection. We think other social workers, working under normal conditions would have acted in this way.

98

The tale of the toddlers' tiredness, following a shopping expedition, may not have been a lie. It was verifiable neither then, nor later. There were, however, two matters that were capable of verification. The social workers were told that the health visitor had seen Mrs. Carlile and the children two weeks earlier. That was in fact untrue; it could be checked only as and when Miss Reader had been contacted. It was also said that the Court Welfare Officer, Mrs. Carrigan, had called earlier to see Mrs. Carlile. A visiting card was produced. (It has not been discovered in the Inquiry). It was true that Mrs. Carrigan had called by appointment on 5 March. Finding the family out, she had left her card. That too was verifiable only after the week-end. While social workers must always be sceptical of the manipulative acts of abusing parents, we do not think that these two lies could have been discovered for what they were at the time. They happened to be matters that could easily have been true. But these facts, verifiable only after the weekend, should not have deterred the two workers from pressing ahead with the urgency of seeing Kimberley.

## Place of Safety Order

Section 28 of the Children and Young Persons Act 1969 authorises the detention of a child or young person and his removal to a place of safety, if a magistrate is satisfied that the applicant has reasonable cause to believe that the child or young person is, roughly speaking, at risk of ill-treatment or neglect. Parliament obviously intended the power to seek a Place of Safety Order as an emergency procedure to ensure that a child in danger of abuse can immediately be taken out of danger and into safe hands. It is a rigorous measure, involving potential trauma to the child of removal from parents whose rights are being decisively interfered with. Recent research findings have indicated that in the past, Orders have been made in circumstances that were inappropriate. Critical comment had been widely publicised, and in December 1985 the Beckford Report had alluded to these comments and endorsed the view for cautious reliance on the Place of Safety Order.

The question which the two social workers had to ask themselves was : did they have enough evidence for them reasonably to believe that the two younger children - Kimberley, in particular - were in a situation of danger calling for instant action? The positive factors indicating intervention were : an allegation of serious physical abuse from an anonymous neighbour that had not been substantiated; the hint of an abusing parent by virtue of the incident with X in January; the refusal by both parents to permit access to Kimberley and Z; the unreasonable hostility of Mr. Hall generally to social workers, although not exhibited on this occasion. On the other hand, the anonymous caller did not say that she had seen any beating of the child or any injuries on her. But the caller did assert that she was "sure mother drinks". Any suggestion of alcoholism in Mrs. Carlile was sufficiently disproved by what the two social workers saw. X and Y were seen over the period, and appeared to be perfectly healthy. The home was clean and tidy. We think, nevertheless, that some social workers might reasonably have backed their justified suspicions and applied for the Place of Safety Order, probably for both Kimberley and Z. And we have the strong impression that many a magistrate would not have hesitated to grant the Order, at least for a short period. But we think it just as reasonable for Mrs. Swinburne and Ms Streeter to have concluded that there was insufficient material for them to have reasonable cause to suspect an imminent risk of child abuse. If the Carliles' lies had been capable of being nailed that evening, we think that the balance in favour of an application would have been decisive. It is clear from the notes compiled by Mrs. Swinburne that evening - after office hours - that the immediate action for Monday's Duty Officer was: a) to ring the Court Welfare Officer to ask when she last saw the two younger children (in fact she had not seen any of the Carlile family, and never did); b) to ring the health visitor and ask her to visit and see the two children "as soon as possible"; and c) to ring Wingfield Primary School again and "re-check behaviour of X and Y in school. Kimberley is on nursery waiting list".

In rejecting the idea of applying that evening for a Place of Safety Order, the two social workers were clearly deferring a decision about that step being taken. Once the checking of the two verifiable facts had taken place, the issue of the appropriate action would have instantly to be reviewed. That would be done by Mr. Ruddock on the Monday morning. The delay in seeing a child cannot wait for such punctilious attention to determining parental explanations. We think that a call to the Standby Duty Officer that evening should have been made, if only to alert him or her to the fact of an unseen child, following an incomplete investigation into a case of suspected child abuse. We do think, also, that it would have been sensible to inform the police. At least the police might have kept a weather-eye open on the Ferrier Estate, including possibly checking up on the anonymous caller. If anything were to crop up, the police had their own powers to detain and remove the child to a place of safety.

It is a little difficult to understand why the police were not contacted, because there appears to us to have been, and still is, a very close and helpful relationship between Social Services and the police in Greenwich. (We would hope that similar good relationships operate in all areas of the country). Police forces occupy a unique, supportive role in the investigation of child abuse. They share, together with general practitioners and hospital authorities, the distinction of having the likeliest early knowledge of violence in the family, and in particular about physical injuries to children, inflicted by their parents. Over and above that, the police exclusively possess optimum access to a range of information about the criminal backgrounds of individuals that can be invaluable to those statutorily obliged to investigate cases of child abuse. Indeed, the police can often supply information about a household, which social workers are intending to visit unaware of the likely reception of the householders. Mrs. Swinburne noted that there had been "violence in the past". To dispense with the expertise of police officers is, generally, to indulge in self-denial of assistance, although at this stage it might not have been unreasonable to forego any help that the police might render. Where anonymous calls from neighbours are involved, however, there may be particular help that the police can give in tracing and even interviewing the caller as well as accompanying social workers.

Ms Streeter told us that she and Mrs. Swinburne did think about calling the police to come down to the house on the visit, but thought that the best course of action was to defer such a consideration until the Monday, when further inquiries would be made. That decision was made in the context of the absence of knowledge about the availability of the power under Section 40 of the Children and Young Persons Act 1933. She would feel bound now, under the new child abuse procedures, to apply to the magistrate for a warrant to authorise the police to search the premises for a child at risk of abuse. Mrs. Swinburne said that she did not contemplate involving the police before going on the visit, because if there had been any question of removing the child she would have applied to a magistrate for a Place of Safety Order without the assistance of the police to execute it. She thought that the question of police involvement would have come up for consideration after the visit, on the following Monday. She added that it was not the practice in Greenwich of using the police as a means of persuading parents to let a social worker see the child. The 'procedures' for child abuse in Greenwich refers to the role of the police only in connection with their participation at case conferences. **We recommend that this should be amplified to include police involvement, where and when appropriate, in the investigative stages**. The procedures require that information should be sought from as many places as is consistent with speedy action. A check list of agencies is provided, but no reference is made to the police. This is a serious omission; both Mrs. Swinburne and Ms Streeter are entitled to point to this omission as some excuse for not having at least checked with the police about what (if anything) was known about the Carlile family.

Likewise, we think that the general practitioner for the family might usefully have been contacted. Mrs. Carlile had visited the doctor's surgery on the Ferrier Estate in November 1985 and had seen Dr. Mahesh in respect of Kimberley's speech problems (see Chapter 5). Five days after the visit by the two social workers to the Carliles' home, on 12 March, Ms Barbara Peacock who was the duty social worker for Area 4 that day, called the doctor's surgery to enquire whether the Carlile family was registered with the general practitioners. She was told that the family was registered, and that Kimberley was last seen on 11 November 1985, although she did not discover what Kimberley was suffering from. But the fact that the doctor would probably have been unobtainable on a Friday afternoon, at least for the purpose of supplying confidential information to a social worker, would explain a failure to contact the general practitioner. But we would stress that, as with the police, the general practitioner occupies a unique position in the child protection service, since it is he who will frequently be the first to be made aware of any signs of child abuse occurring within the family, and thereby able to trigger off the protective services. Dr. Mahesh possessed a vital piece of information, if only it had been extracted from his records, and passed on.

## Conclusion

We perceive that the visit of 7 March discloses a general problem, that in many social workers there lurks a lack of confidence about their duty to insist on seeing a child in the parents' home, when access to that child is being determinedly refused. This lack of confidence stems partly, we think, from an uncertainty about the nature and extent of the powers granted to social workers in pursuance of their investigative duties in relation to child abuse. Without the backing of precise statutory powers, it is not surprising that social workers are hesitant about intervening to protect a child at risk. It is for these reasons that we are recommending, in Chapter 25, a clarification and extension of the legislative provisions authorising intervention in the rights of parents, where children are suspected of being abused. The lack of confidence also in part, springs from a healthy respect for parental rights. But when it is the safety of a child in its parents' home, parental rights must yield to child protection.

Given the uncertainty of legal powers and lack of confidence in social workers, faced by obdurate parents protesting against the invasion of their privacy in the face of an accusation of suspected child abuse, it is not surprising that children suspected of being abused go unseen.

# CHAPTER 18

# THE INDICATORS OF CHILD ABUSE, 10/11 MARCH 1986

Mr. Ruddock was away from Area 4's office on the afternoon of 7 March, attending a meeting with officers of the Education Welfare Service (EWS) to discuss cases where the EWS was contemplating court proceedings in relation to truanting children, thus indicating the diversity of Mr. Ruddock's work.

He was first made aware of the previous Friday's visit to the Carlile home by Mrs. Swinburne and Ms Streeter when he came to work on the Monday morning, 10 March. His immediate reaction was to express dissatisfaction that the two younger children had not been seen, and he was sceptical, even incredulous, of the explanation of a 4 year-old sleeping in the middle of the day. His suspicions were instinctively aroused, to the extent that he proceeded to treat it as a case of child abuse, and communicated that approach to others.

He made contact with the Court Welfare Service and learned the nature and extent of the request from Wigan County Court for a report on the home situation of the Carliles. He was told that Mrs. Carrigan had never visited Mrs. Carlile, although an attempt had been made and a visiting card left. The first lie, about regular visits from the Court Welfare Service, had thus been nailed. Mr. Ruddock then made contact with Wingfield Primary School. From the headteacher, Mr. Hayter, he received no further information, but was told of Mr. Hayter's continuing concern about X.

There were two telephone discussions with the health visitor,Miss Reader. Earlier that day she had formally consulted her superior, Mrs. Henlin. Mrs. Henlin said that the issue about a joint visit was not discussed. Miss Reader recorded in her notes on the family that the Carlile case was discussed with Mrs. Henlin, and told us that she did seek approval from Mrs. Henlin of her stance on the request for a joint visit. Mrs. Henlin does agree that she would have endorsed Miss Reader's refusal to go on the visit. Both were adopting an attitude that reflected the traditional training, practical experience and attitudes of a health visitor asked to accompany a social worker to investigate the truth or falsity of an anonymous telephone call indicating suspected child abuse.

Miss Reader then rang Mr. Ruddock to find out the outcome of the Friday evening visit. She was told that Kimberley and Z had not been seen. Mr. Ruddock's note of the conversation indicates that Miss Reader was not intending to visit the Carliles until the next developmental test was due, which would be when Kimberley was four and a half in May 1986. Mr. Ruddock's note goes on to record Miss Reader's concern about the unseen children but that she was "not wanting to jeopardise her relationship with the family", a factor that had in part prompted her disinclination to be involved in the investigation of child abuse. Miss Reader's note adds "?? Whether Case Conference to be called". To whatever extent the question of a case conference may have been discussed, we are confident in saying that the calling of a case conference should have been uppermost in the minds of both Mr. Ruddock and Miss Reader. That one was never called is a matter of fact. That one should have been called, either that day or at least within the next 48 hours, is beyond doubt. Mr. Ruddock fully admits that he cannot now defend this omission. Likewise Miss Reader accepts that she should have insisted on a case conference being convened.

A further discussion between the two took place when Mr. Ruddock outlined his plan to carry out a home visit himself later that day, in which he would advise the parents to bring both Kimberley and Z either to the health clinic or to their general practitioner for medical examination, failing which he intended to inform the Police Juvenile Bureau and possibly apply for a Place of Safety Order. He indicated that he would keep Miss Reader abreast of events. These discussions have to be interpreted against the background of a system that placed the duty to investigate suspected child abuse exclusively on Social Services and did not impose any shared responsibility between Social Services and Health Authorities. Moreover, there was no power vested in Social Services to require assistance of Health Authorities. Joint action depended on the willingness of the two agencies to collaborate to the fullest extent.

Before embarking on the home visit, Mr. Ruddock had an informal discussion with his Area Manager, Mr. Neill. They both thought that, as part of the investigative process, it was imperative that the two younger Carlile children should be seen. Mr. Ruddock told us (and it was confirmed by all the social workers in the Social Services Department who gave evidence) that Mr. Neill was entirely approachable at any time. He practised an open-door policy, encouraging his colleagues to consult and discuss with him any team issues. What passed between the two men never fulfilled the proper function of supervision. It was, of course, quite exceptional for them to be discussing an individual case which was being handled by Mr. Ruddock as a fieldworker. The dislocation of line management, however, could not absolve them from applying the proper function of supervision, a subject we deal with in some depth in Chapter 30.

Before he left the Area 4 office for the Ferrier Estate, Mr. Ruddock drafted a letter which he took with him and deposited at the Carlile home when he found no one in. We reproduce the letter opposite.

While the letter might have been couched in more emphatic language - the Greenwich Child Abuse Procedures Guide states weakly that if there is evidence of injury "then the family should be formally advised to take the child immediately to their doctor" or to the hospital - it did sound a note of urgency, and included a threat of police involvement. But, it contained two drawbacks. First, it might have precipitated more abuse; in practice, it had the effect of inducing contact of the Carlile family with Social Services. Second, abusing parents are not very likely to take their abused child for a medical examination. They have to be taken to the doctor. Instead of writing the letter, the better practice would have been for Mr. Ruddock to make an appointment with the doctor and take Kimberley for the appointment.

It is a paradox in the handling of the Carlile case that, at that moment, Mr. Ruddock wrote the letter and recognised, with blinding clarity, the role of the police in child abuse, yet from then onwards, he never thought of

**GREENWICH**
People and Services First

DIRECTORATE OF SOCIAL SERVICES
**LONDON BOROUGH OF**
# GREENWICH

MARTIN MANBY
DIRECTOR OF SOCIAL SERVICES

AREA OFFICE No. 4,
1a BIRDBROOK ROAD,
LONDON SE3 9GA
01-856 0011
(AREA OFFICER: D. NEILL)

YOUR REF.

MY REF.

DATE March 10th 1986

Dear Mrs Carlisle,

As you were told on Friday 7 March, Social Services recieved an anonymous call stating that local people were concerned about screams from one of your children, thought to be Kimberly.

On Friday, you were visited by 2 social workers from this department, but refused to allow kimberly or Z* to be seen. Given that our job is to ensure the safety of children, I must request you take your children, kimberly e Z* to see a G.P. or Health Visitor by Wednesday evening. If you have not done this, I will discuss the situation with the Police Juvenile Bureau with view to considering further action.

Please co-operate with this request,

Yours Sincerely

Martin W Ruddock — Team Manager
10-3-86

*The name of Kimberley's younger sister has been deleted by the Commission of Inquiry. She is referred to throughout this report as 'Z'.

informing the local police, let alone of carrying out the threat of resort to coercive powers to effect sight of an unseen child suspected of being at risk. Mr. Ruddock was aware of the existence of indicators of child abuse. He was neither ignoring them, nor disregarding them. Indeed, he was giving them full play in the investigative and assessment process. Yet within 48 hours of writing that letter he became distracted from his proposed course of action, and was finally diverted from pursuing a sufficiently rigorous investigation, in which the medical examination of Kimberley was an essential ingredient. The assessment of Kimberley, when he saw her in the company of her parents and three siblings on 12 March, was that she was exhibiting serious behavioural problems. While he now acknowledges that child abuse and behavioural problems are by no means mutually exclusive conditions, his vision of the reality became clouded. The initial picture of Kimberley as "withdrawn, sallow, pasty and still", and her behaviour described by the family, which included "fouling, wetting, eating faeces, screaming and refusing to eat" (all recorded in Mr. Ruddock's notes) was not translated into symptoms of child abuse.

Because the other children presented themselves as lively and healthy looking, Mr. Ruddock seemed to ignore the possibility that Kimberley was the scapegoat of a reconstituted family, in which she was resolutely refusing to relate to her step-father. (We deal more fully with Mr. Ruddock's encounter of 12 March with the family in the next chapter).

We have come to the conclusion that part of the failure to appreciate the psychopathology of the Carlile family was Mr. Ruddock's reluctance to garner the expertise and knowledge of all the relevant agencies within the compass of a case conference. With all the various disciplines contributing their diversified expertise, there can be little doubt that Kimberley would have been placed on the Child Abuse Register, that the case would have been allocated to a named key worker. The case cried out for the convening of a case conference. It was negligent of Mr. Ruddock not to have taken that crucial step. Mr. Neill must share some of the blame, because if he had been supervising in a proper manner he would have had all the information for an objective assessment that would have prompted the calling of a case conference. To a lesser extent Miss Reader was at fault, for not having pressed for action to obtain the medical examination that she knew was urgently needed. And her supervisor, Mrs. Henlin must also accept the responsibility for failing to propel Miss Reader in the direction of insisting on such action.

# CHAPTER 19

# FAMILY APPEARANCE AND FAULTY ASSESSMENT, 12 MARCH 1986

If it was not unreasonable on 10 March for Mr. Ruddock to defer any decision whether to call a case conference, it was a serious omission on his part not to have called one after the events of 11 and 12 March. On the first of those two days there was confirmation of the allegations made by the anonymous telephone caller. Nothing that occurred on the second of those days, when Mr. Ruddock met the family, detracted one iota from the urgent need to set up a case conference. Even Mr. Ruddock's own assessment, that the problems of Kimberley were only "behavioural", could not conceivably have been regarded as unrelated to the other indices of child abuse.

The threat to bring the police into the case may never have been carried out, but it was no idle threat, for it stung Mr. Hall into instant action and made him desperate to find out whether a social worker could lawfully do what Mr. Ruddock was threatening to do. Mr. Hall telephoned the Social Services Department and eventually spoke to Mrs. Armstrong (a senior social worker in the Family Finding Unit[1]). As there was no one in the Child Abuse Section, the call automatically 'tripped' through to the General Office where it was answered by a clerk, who asked Mrs. Armstrong to speak to the caller because of the nature of the call.

If Mr. Hall had merely conveyed the substance of the previous day's letter from Mr. Ruddock that would have sufficed to get his call routed through to the Child Abuse Section. Mrs. Armstrong's handwritten note, however, starts: "A man phoned, refusing to give his name and asking to speak to someone in the Child Abuse Section". An hour-long conversation took place which was highly revelatory, and at times agitatedly emotional on Mr. Hall's part. Mrs. Armstrong made a full, comprehensive note and marked it "**URGENT please** - 1 + 1 on FW116, officer's report sheet", no doubt an instruction to the typist for quick turn-around of the typescript. Although Mrs. Armstrong took no other part in the Carlile case, this piece of information was highly significant. She is to be commended for a skilled piece of professional work which by itself should have induced Mr. Ruddock to call a case conference immediately, as indeed Mr. Bellamy, on behalf of Mrs. Armstrong, submitted to us.

Since Mr. Hall referred to the visit by the two social workers on 7 March, and also read over the letter of 10 March to Mrs. Armstrong, his identity was easily established. Towards the end of the call he handed over the telephone to Mrs. Carlile who identified herself. She wanted to speak to Mr. Ruddock. Mrs. Armstrong agreed to contact Mr. Ruddock and suggested that the Carliles rang back in half an hour's time.

The detailed contents of Mr. Hall's call were important. He admitted that the family was experiencing problems, and that the main problem centred

---

[1] This unit finds and selects suitable adopters and foster-parents.

on Kimberley, thus confirming the singling out of the 4 year-old mentioned by the anonymous telephone caller. The behavioural problems exhibited by Kimberley were said to reflect her unacceptance of Mr. Hall as her stepfather. In the course of the conversation he admitted to having "shaken" and "smacked" Kimberley, although he sought to minimise any injuries by attributing them to Kimberley having fallen down while playing.

Mrs. Armstrong was, not unnaturally, sceptical of this explanation. Although Mr. Hall was insistent that the children were in no danger, the information he was conveying was hard evidence that strongly suggested that the anonymous telephone call was both genuine and accurate. In short, the call indicated that Kimberley was seriously at risk. It could also have been interpreted as a cry for help from someone who had hitherto been stoutly declaring that he and his family wanted only to be left alone by Social Services.

Mrs. Armstrong contacted Mr. Ruddock by telephone and told him of the conversation. He expressed relief at the ready response to his letter. He offered, via Mrs. Armstrong, a home visit on the following day at 4 p.m. Mrs. Armstrong duly received a second call from Mr. Hall, who sounded much calmer. He agreed to the next afternoon's meeting "when he [Mr. Ruddock] can see the younger children". Mr. Ruddock was told of the confirmation to meet with the Carlile family.

The meeting took place on 12 March, but not as planned.

On the morning of 12 March, the duty social worker, Ms Barbara Peacock, was in touch with the health clinic and was told that it was thought that Miss Reader was going to try and visit Mrs. Carlile that day. Ms Peacock left a message for Miss Reader to telephone in the afternoon. Meanwhile she made a call to the General Practice on the Ferrier Estate to learn that all the Carliles were registered there, and that Kimberley was last seen by a partner in the medical practice on 11 November 1985. She was not told that Dr. Mahesh had written a referral note to the Brook Hospital for Kimberley, "for speech therapy". Had this fact been known, another piece of the evolving picture would have assisted towards a correct assessment of Kimberley's deteriorating condition and of child abuse.

## The meeting with the Carliles

Mr. Hall, Mrs. Carlile and the four children arrived unexpectedly between 9.30 and 10 a.m. at the Mini-Town Hall, where Area 4 shares the office accommodation with administrative staff of the local authority. The only space available for interviewing clients were two rooms at the end of a short passage.

To say that the room where the Carliles talked to Mr. Ruddock was incommodious would be to overstate its suitability. Those who sat on chairs at opposite sides of the room virtually knocked knees. There was just enough space for the adults to sit down, with Z on Mrs. Carlile's lap. Kimberley was close to her mother with her arm over Kimberley. So confined was the space that the other children could run about only in the corridor. Nothing could be less suitable for watching and listening to interaction between members

# FRONT SECTION OF KIDBROOKE MINI TOWN HALL
# SHOWING RECEPTION AREA AND INTERVIEW ROOMS

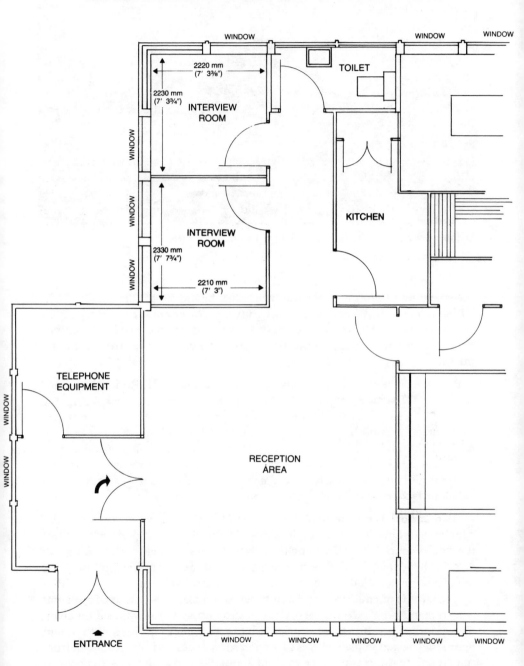

WINDOW

WINDOW   WINDOW

2220 mm
(7' 3⅜")

TOILET

2230 mm
(7' 3¾")

INTERVIEW
ROOM

WINDOW

WINDOW

KITCHEN

INTERVIEW
ROOM

2330 mm
(7' 7¾")

WINDOW

2210 mm
(7' 3")

TELEPHONE
EQUIPMENT

WINDOW

RECEPTION
AREA

WINDOW

WINDOW

ENTRANCE

WINDOW   WINDOW   WINDOW   WINDOW   WINDOW

An interview room at the Kidbrooke Mini Town Hall.

of the family. Even Diogenes could not have displayed greater contempt for the amenities of professional social work than he did for the amenities of life, by living in a tub. **We recommend that urgent consideration be given by Greenwich Borough Council to providing its Social Services Department with proper facilities for interviewing members of the public**.

Partly because of these wholly inadequate conditions, Mr. Ruddock misread the signs. Whatever antennae Mr. Ruddock possessed for picking up the messages of suspected child abuse, they were desensitised by the physical environment. Doubtless, Kimberley was wearing clothing that covered up most of the body which might have revealed the signs of physical abuse; there was no possibility for any examination beyond the most cursory and anatomically limited. Clearly, he did not see bruises or marks on Kimberley's hands or face.

He did, however, note that she was "withdrawn, sallow, pasty and still", which might have triggered off thoughts of failure to thrive, particularly since the "behavioural problems" included such grotesque matters as eating her own excrement. As the interview wore on, Kimberley brightened up. The initial impression that she was exhibiting "frozen watchfulness" - the tell-tale syndrome of children who have suffered trauma at the hands of a parent and stare in a paralysed manner when confronted by that parent - dissipated. The evident cheerfulness and brightness of the other children, with whom Kimberley began to play with evident pleasure, distracted Mr. Ruddock from concluding that this was a case of child abuse. He had at the outset explained the role of social workers in relation to child abuse, the powers of social workers and their primary concern for the welfare of children.

It never seemed to occur to Mr. Ruddock that this was a newly reconstituted family that, even were it parented by highly mature and well-balanced adults, would face enormous problems of settling down to normal life. He was aware that Mrs. Carlile was pregnant and due to have the baby before the normal period of gestation, since she had a record of premature child-birth with the other four. Any mother with 5 children, three of them below the age of 5 would find the going hard, without help and some support. A woman, such as Mrs. Carlile, fatally attracted to violent co-habitees, was highly vulnerable to the acuter problems of child-rearing. None of this seemed to form part of Mr. Ruddock's calculations. To be fair, he did at least adhere to the importance of Kimberley being medically examined.

After the interview he communicated this particular concern to the health visitor, Miss Reader. He set in train arrangements for Wingfield Primary School to offer a nursery place for Kimberley. That at least would have provided the daily monitoring and school health examination. The thoughts running through all Mr. Ruddock's deeds over the next ten weeks were the necessity for a medical examination of Kimberley. It was a theme shared by Miss Reader. But neither managed to achieve that desideratum.

Mr. Ruddock concluded the meeting on an optimistic note. He thought he had reached agreement with the Carliles about the seriousness of Kimberley's unhappiness and maladjusted behaviour. They agreed to discuss the problem further on 3 April. That much could be gleaned from the cheerful letter which Mr. Ruddock wrote the following day to both Mrs. Carlile and Mr. Hall. It began : "It was good to see you all yesterday, and pleasing that a meeting in such difficult circumstances was able to be so constructive". He had been impressed, he told us, by the initiative the parents had taken in coming to him, instead of waiting for the home visit by him. The irony of that observation, then and now, is that in fact the Carliles were coming to him, and not him to them, in order to conceal, rather than to reveal. If he had by then switched his thinking from child abuse to behavioural problems, Mr. Ruddock was still not ruling out the former. His letter went on : "Because of my concern I have requested [note, not "ordered"] that the health visitor considers arranging a medical examination". Whatever favourable signs came out of the meeting, there could be no excuse, at least, for not having seen the child undressed.

Mr. Ruddock's written statement to us said this :

> "At the end of the session I walked with the family to the door of the building and watched as they walked across the road to where their old car was parked. I still have a clear mental picture of the way in which they all walked across the road and got into the car, parents holding children by the hand, children leaping around in the car as they got in, laughing, shouting and playing happily with each other. It was almost an archetype for a happy family scene ... I therefore could not have been more reassured by the family dynamics than I was by this overall display on this occasion".

Far from being reassured, Mr. Ruddock should have been alive to the risk of being manipulated. Plainly, he had been deceived - to some extent, self-induced. Mr. Ruddock sounds the warning to those who come after him :

> "The huge disparity between these very powerful and compelling presentations of positive behaviour and what we now know to have been the underlying reality is difficult to explain or analyse, and my experience here may be a useful lesson to others faced with this type of problem".

Our conclusion is that Mr. Ruddock was in part handicapped by the circumstances of the venue for the meeting, and in part by his inability to isolate Kimberley from the other children, and thus to focus on her. But his reading of the family situation left much to be desired in terms of good social work practice.

Four messages ring out from this episode. First, those working in the field of child abuse must always be on their guard against the risk of seeing what they want to believe. Second, at any meeting with the family, it is vital to talk directly to the children themselves (always assuming that the children are capable of understanding). Third, if child abuse is suspected, the parents must be confronted with that suspicion. And fourth, where the suspicion is denied, the parental explanation for suspicion being unfounded must be put to the test. In all four respects, Mr Ruddock's work was flawed.

CHAPTER 20

# THE UNSEEN CHILD, 14 APRIL 1986

Upon the conclusion of the Carlile family's visit to the Area 4 office on 12 March 1986 Mr. Ruddock was far from being satisfied that his inquiries into a case of suspected child abuse were complete, or were no longer necessary. He told us that the "assessment was in any event unfinished". On the following day he recorded in a letter to Mrs. Carlile and Mr. Hall his observation of Kimberley's unusually withdrawn and pallid appearance, and he noted the parents' description of her behavioural problems, which by any standard were gross. His response was to set in motion arrangements for Kimberley to be medically examined, and he arranged a further meeting with the Carliles for early April. Thereafter, his demonstrable worries were never wholly allayed. Yet while Kimberley was never wholly out of his mind, Mr. Ruddock failed to pursue his duty to investigate the case and to employ the device of the case conference as an aid to appropriate action to resolve the observed need for Kimberley to be medically examined. Apart from possibly one occasion, on 14 April, Kimberley was never seen alive again by anyone from the welfare agencies, and no advance was made in any dialogue with the parents over Kimberley's behavioural problems. Nor were the parents spurred into taking her to the health clinic or to the G.P. Mr. Ruddock's self-acknowledged failure to pursue the case is clear. If the failure is explicable as fully revealed to the Commission of Inquiry, it remains inexcusable.

It is not as if the case went dead. Mr. Ruddock simply adopted a policy of drift. Agency involvement over Kimberley's case continued. A week after the Carlile family visit, Mr. Ian Scott, the Duty Officer on that day, recorded a message from Wingfield Primary School to the effect that the offer of a nursery place for Kimberley had not been taken up by the family. Mr. Neill wrote a note to Mr. Scott (in the absence of Mr. Ruddock on leave) suggesting a contact with Miss Reader asking her if she would call and see if everything was alright. Miss Reader was away on holiday. When she returned on 25 March she phoned Area 4 to say that the two youngest Carlile children had *not*, as was expected by her, attended the clinic.

Meanwhile two other agencies involved in the case were communicating information of their actions. On 13 March Mrs. Carrigan, the Court Welfare Officer, had telephoned Mr. Ruddock to ensure that Greenwich Social Services knew of the Wirral Social Services' involvement with the family. She was told of the anonymous call of 7 March, and offered to assist in any way by furnishing additional information. This communication was not recorded by Mr. Ruddock; nor was a discussion between himself and Mr. Neill reduced to writing. Mr. Ruddock explains the deterioration in the quality and thoroughness of his record-keeping as reflecting a general decline in the quality of his work at that time. Given that there was an acute problem of under-staffing around that time, we are not surprised that Mr. Ruddock's work suffered as a result. But, of course, the ultimate sufferer was Kimberley Carlile.

When Mrs. Carrigan spoke to Mr. Ruddock about the Wirral involvement she was unable to fill in the gaps of Mr. Ruddock's knowledge of the nature and extent of that involvement. She presumed - as, we think, she was fully entitled to presume - that Wirral had passed on all its extensive information about the Carlile family to Greenwich. She herself did not ask for, or receive any information from Wirral. Mrs. Carrigan wrote to Mrs. Carlile on 19 March to arrange a visit on 11 April; the following day she wrote to Mr. Ruddock telling him that she was going ahead with the preparation of her report. She invited Mr. Ruddock to discuss the case with her on his return from leave.

On 24 March Ms Gregory spoke to Ms Roper, a social worker in the Ferrier team operating out of the neighbourhood office at Ebdon Way, and told her that Kimberley had not attended the nursery at which a place had been arranged. That too was on file for Mr. Ruddock to see on his return on 30 March from his two-week holiday. Nothing up to that moment calls for any adverse comment, save to say that there were powerful reasons for initiating a case conference, immediately following the 12 March visit.

On 1 April, on his return to the office, Mr. Ruddock received a message cancelling the forthcoming arranged meeting with the Carliles. The explanation for the cancellation was that the family would be "in Liverpool for Easter returning 10th or 11th". Mr. Ruddock wrote the following day to the Carliles thanking them for their telephone call "from Liverpool". It did not occur to Mr. Ruddock that this may have been yet another lie told by the Carliles. He seems to have assumed that the call came from Liverpool. He should not have been as trusting in the receipt of information from parents who were suspected of child abuse. In proposing a re-arranged meeting for 14 April, Mr. Ruddock repeated the urgent need for Kimberley to undergo a "thorough medical examination" and added, pointedly, "though that decision is not mine to take". By this Mr. Ruddock meant that the decision was for the doctors "and was not something which I could order them to do". Simultaneously on 1 April Miss Reader rang and spoke to Mrs. Carlile. She received a similar reply that the Carlile family was that very morning going away to Liverpool until 11 April. Miss Reader said she would arrange a home visit on the family's return. On 10 April Mrs. Carrigan telephoned Mr. Ruddock to discuss the problem before making her arranged visit of the following day. (A record of that discussion, too, does not appear on Mr. Ruddock's file). Mrs. Carrigan's visit to the Carlile home on Friday, 11 April was abortive. There was no reply.

By the end of the second week of April there was still no medical examination of Kimberley, she had not been seen for a month, and her place at the nursery had not been taken up. Contact between Social Services and the other agencies was maintained but it did not advance the investigation of the case. Mr. Ruddock accurately described the situation as one in which his concern regarding child abuse "was in no way diminished...but they were not inflated either". In short, the investigation was still very much under way but desultorily making no progress.

# 14 April visit

When Mr. Ruddock arrived at the Carlile home Mr. Hall was clearly expecting the visit as he opened the door. From the outset his demeanour was not so friendly as on the occasion of the 12 March meeting. Mr. Ruddock was ushered into the living room on the first floor; no-one else was present. Mrs. Carlile, who was then 3 or 4 months' pregnant, was said to be asleep upstairs, and so was the youngest child, Z. The other children were also upstairs, playing quietly. Mr. Hall was quick to re-assert his hostility to Social Services and his desire to want from social workers nothing more than for the family to be left alone. He went on to express strong feelings about the involvement of all the agencies. He was not angry; he was not emotional; his talk was not aggressive. But he was insistent, to the point of uncompromising emphasis that the family was quite capable of coping with its own problems and in their own good time. Mr. Ruddock concluded in his statement to us: "Overall I would describe his demeanour as assertive rather than angry or intemperate". Having ourselves seen and heard Mr. Hall, we think that "assertive" is too mild. We think that many people in Mr. Ruddock's position would have found Mr. Hall intimidating. But he apparently did not.

Mr. Ruddock adopted the technique of recalling the earlier, more constructive meeting with the family, reminding Mr. Hall of their acknowledgement that Kimberley's behavioural problems called for professional help. The discussion veered away from the need for Social Services to have Kimberley medically examined, and reverted to the question of official intervention. Mr. Hall was testing the strict legal entitlement of Mr. Ruddock to impose himself on the family for the protection of children. The discussion degenerated into repetitiveness. The angularity of Mr. Hall's stance sharpened, rather than softened. He became unyielding to the point where it was being made clear that access to Kimberley (or any of the other children) was being stubbornly and unreasonably refused. Towards the end of the visit Mr. Ruddock was permitted to peep through the small glass panel at the top of the door to one of the children's bedrooms. Two children were on the floor, between the beds, with their backs to the door. All that could be seen was the back of one young head and the top of another, one smaller than the other. That was all that was visible of either child. Reflecting now on the incident, Mr. Ruddock cannot even be sure that the younger child was in fact Kimberley. The two children could have been X and Y. Even if the younger child was Kimberley, to all intents and purposes she was still an "unseen" child. Like a little glow-worm glimmering in the dark, Kimberley's body provided no more than the barest glance.

Mr. Ruddock, while acknowledging the total inadequacy of his sighting of Kimberley for the purpose of ascertaining signs of child abuse, explained that he was positively reassured by the fact that he was allowed to look through the glass window by Mr. Hall who could not have known in advance how much of Kimberley (if it was indeed her) would be seen. Mr. Ruddock argued that Mr. Hall must have realised that there was a good chance of a good look at Kimberley, and that would have defeated all his efforts at concealment of Kimberley's wounds. We are frankly unimpressed by this explanation. Assuming that Kimberley was one of the two children in the room - and we assume the fact only for the purpose of answering Mr. Ruddock's point - we do not think that Mr. Hall was endangering his concealment of Kimberley's bruising and battering by allowing a look through the glass window of a door sealing off the onlooker from the children. Even if Mr. Ruddock had obtained a frontal view it is unlikely that he would have observed any signs of child abuse. After all, when he saw Kimberley in the flesh, at close distance and over a lengthy period of time on 12 March he did not observe any signs of physical injury on her. His observations were limited to the colour (or rather discolourment) of her skin and her demeanour. We are confident in saying that Mr. Ruddock was in no position to draw any inference from the permission to gain a glimpse of Kimberley other than to conclude that he was being hoodwinked. All that we have said at the end of the last chapter applies with like force to the visit of 14 April. Even at the risk of being accused of indulging in boring repetitiveness, we repeat that, when investigating a case of child abuse, the child *must* be seen.

Not only was Kimberley left unseen. No arrangements were made for further contact, though Mr. Ruddock believed that he would be contacted "if they reconsidered the situation". What basis there was for thinking that there would be a change of heart on the part of the Carliles is hard to imagine. Anyone reading that note on file might be forgiven for thinking that Mr. Ruddock was signing off or putting the case on the shelf. When coupled with a final manuscript note of "N.F.A. at present" that conclusion appears compelling. Indeed, that was the core of a restrained submission made to us by Mr. Roger Titheridge Q.C., on behalf of Mrs. Henlin. His thesis was that April 24 was the day of final assessment, when Mr. Ruddock arrived at the decision that the sole problem in the case was the untoward behaviour of Kimberley. Not only do we reject this argument as being fundamentally unsound, because it is based on a view that child abuse and behavioural problems are mutually exclusive diagnoses, but also because the facts do not warrant any such conclusion. It is our view that, while there was a temporary lull in further investigation or work with the Carlile family ("N.F.A. *at present*") there was no discarding concern for Kimberley's welfare. The case was allowed to drift, disastrously so.

Mr. Ruddock had a discussion with Mr. Neill immediately following the 14 April meeting, although once again this was not recorded on the file. Mr. Neill seemed to concur with Mr. Ruddock's view that since the receipt of the anonymous call (7 March) the family had voluntarily presented themselves (including Kimberley) to Social Services (12 March): "this vitiated and undermined the force of the anonymous telephone call"[1]. We think that this was a wholly erroneous judgment. Nothing that had happened displaced in any way the continuing need to investigate the case. If anything, the events of 7-12 March had tended to verify the caller's information. Mr. Ruddock concluded that the position was "one of stalemate". But the position was not one in which Mr. Ruddock, who was next to make a move, had no allowable move open to him without being check-mated. There were several moves that he could have made. He could have arranged for a medical examination, and accompanied the child to it. He might reasonably have broken the

---

[1] This is quoted from Mr. Ruddock's written statement to us.

apparent stalemate by applying for a Place of Safety Order. He now had evidence of abuse (Nigel Hall's own admissions of 11 March *plus* an unreasonable refusal of access to Kimberley). Although he would have obtained an Order from a magistrate, we do not blame him for thinking that an Order, which did not allow a medical examination without parental consent, was inappropriate. He did not think of seeking a warrant under Section 40 of the Children and Young Persons Act 1933, simply because he did not know about it. But the situation cried out for a case conference. No reliance needs to be placed on hindsight for us to conclude that that omission was a serious error of judgment. For this failure Mr. Neill, as supervisor, must share the blame.

Reverting to the chronology of events, we are satisfied that on 15 April Mr. Ruddock telephoned Miss Reader. (We take this from her record and evidence to us, since, yet again, Mr. Ruddock made no note of it). Her note is a terse summary of what happened at the visit of 14 April, and ends: "? may arrange meeting - to discuss further". Miss Reader discussed the matter with her supervisor, Mrs. Henlin, on 16 April, when it was noted that Miss Reader would "try and make further contact in 1-2 weeks". We think that, whatever Mr. Ruddock was proposing to do or not to do, Miss Reader and Mrs. Henlin should have, at the very least, taken some active steps. Either Miss Reader should have visited the Carlile household forthwith, no matter what reception awaited her, or Mrs. Henlin should have insisted to Mr. Neill that a case conference should be convened immediately. The discussion between Mr. Ruddock and Miss Reader does not support, however, the view that inaction was to take over in the case of Kimberley Carlile.

## 24 April - day of decision?

Mr. Ruddock's manuscript notes on the fractious and fruitless visit of 14 April came back from the typist on 23 April. He signed the notes on the following day, when he proceeded to take a number of steps. He telephoned Mrs. Carrigan and was told that her visit of 11 April was abortive. Mr. Ruddock informed her about what happened on his visit of 14 April. He learned that she was planning to visit on 9 May and would keep him informed. A discussion took place in which Mrs. Carrigan raised the question of applying for a Place of Safety Order. Mrs. Carrigan told us that she accepted Mr. Ruddock's view that there was insufficient evidence. After all, she recognised Mr. Ruddock as the person handling the case and who possessed most information upon which to exercise a proper judgment. We think that her advocacy for a Place of Safety Order was mollified only by an assurance that the assessment of the case would continue. That that assurance was forthcoming is supported by Mr. Ruddock's other contacts of that day.

He telephoned Wingfield Primary School and spoke to the Deputy Headteacher, Mr. Cox. He recited to him the event of 14 April, and requested that the school continue "to observe family situation and contact Social Services if concerned". Mr. Ruddock then rang Miss Reader. He brought her up-to-date and learned that "she will try to visit but has not been welcomed recently". This referred to a less than friendly talk over the telephone with Mr. Hall, when Miss Reader rang to speak to Mrs. Carlile.

Miss Reader's notes indicate that she had told Mr. Ruddock of that conversation on the morning of his proposed visit. Mr. Ruddock has no record of that call. He does not dispute that it took place, but he is confident that it happened *after* the visit. We think that the timing is unimportant. But the message, communicated on 14 and 24 April, was how reluctant Miss Reader was to become embroiled in a situation where the Carlile family had begun to treat her with the degree of hostility normally reserved for social workers.

As at 24 April there was no question of the curtain falling on the Kimberley case. Social Services were to remain in play. But for the time being there was to be no direct action to enforce the request - nay, demand - for Kimberley to be brought to the health clinic for a medical examination. There was some slight activity on the educational front in the last days of April. Area 4 was told by Wingfield School that X and Y were being transferred to Henwick School. Mr. Ruddock made contact with both schools. In early May the Headteacher at Henwick agreed to monitor the Carlile children and to inform Social Services if Kimberley attended, or if Kimberley came with either parent to pick up her sister. It was suggested to us that, whatever else may be said about action at this time, the idea of child abuse had totally disappeared from the thoughts of anyone in Area 4. Yet on 12 May Mr. Ruddock telephoned the Department's Child Abuse Co-ordinator. That conversation has assumed a degree of importance in the Inquiry that we deal with in the next chapter. While we think it was given undue prominence, we attach significance to the mere fact that the call was made. Why would Mr. Ruddock initiate a call to the Child Abuse Co-ordinator if he thought that the Kimberley Carlile case no longer presented a case of suspected child abuse?

# CHAPTER 21

# A LOST OPPORTUNITY: CONSULTATION WITH THE CO-ORDINATOR, 12 MAY 1986

One of the principal functions of a Child Abuse Co-ordinator is to act as a consultant to individual practitioners carrying child abuse cases. The consultant must not, under any circumstances, have line management responsibilities for staff holding such cases, in order to remain free to act in an uninvolved, consultative and advisory capacity. There is, in particular, a sharp distinction to be drawn between the role of the consultant and that of the supervisor. The consultant should never seek to supplant the supervisor, but should supplement supervision by providing specialist advice and guidance, based on the perception and analysis of the case by the person seeking consultation. It is the function of the consultant to probe the inquirer and to make sure that all the relevant information is retrieved from the files in order that proper advice and guidance can be given.

Mr. Ruddock "consulted" Mrs. Jean Gabbott, the Child Abuse Co-ordinator in Greenwich since 1983, on the telephone on 12 May 1986, to discuss the Kimberley Carlile case with her. It is clear to us that there was a lack of appreciation on both sides as to the basis for that discussion; and the discussion itself proved unsatisfactory, both in its content and in the ensuing inaction.

For a start, it seems incomprehensible to us that Mrs. Gabbott had not been contacted much earlier in the case. One of the ways in which Mr Ruddock had allowed the case to drift after the meeting with the Carlile family at Area 4's office on 12 March, and again after the abortive visit to the Carlile home of 14 April, was to have foregone, for far too long, the advice of Mrs. Gabbott. And Mrs. Gabbott herself colluded, perhaps unwittingly, to the drifting attitude to the case, when she suggested during the telephone conversation that if Kimberley was not seen by the end of May, action should then be taken in the form of a case conference. The state of affairs in the Carlile household had been sufficiently worrying since mid-March for that action to be taken forthwith. Twentyfour hours may be crucial in a child abuse case. To be inactive for weeks is to put such a child daily, if not hourly at risk. Whatever the reason for the drift, Mrs. Gabbott should, there and then, have put a stop to Mr. Ruddock's predisposition to wait and see. That she did no more than endorse Mr. Ruddock's actions to date and support the convening of a case conference only at the end of May, if necessary, was due in no little part to the context of the consultation. But we think that she ought nevertheless to have been more probing than she in fact was.

The first thing that was wrong about the consultation, apart from its excessive tardiness, was the manner of its initiation. The discussion took place over the telephone. The use of the telephone as a means of communication is always a potential recipe for misunderstanding - particularly, if the communication is not tape-recorded and only a contemporaneous or subsequent, scribbled note is made of the conversation. The process of consultation about a child abuse case is far too important to be conducted over the telephone. No doubt, most of the referrals to Mrs. Gabbott came in that way, but such contact should not constitute the consultation. It should be used only as a means of gaining a quick sense of the nature of the referral, and then to arrange a face-to-face meeting, with the file available for instant reference. Alternatively, the file could be sent to the Child Abuse Co-ordinator for quick perusal. Only in either of those two ways can suitable advice and guidance be given.

Mr. Ruddock conveyed to Mrs. Gabbott a situation that represented the case as being far less serious than was warranted. One issue of disputed fact discloses that Mrs. Gabbott clearly did not get the full flavour of a serious situation over a child at risk, unseen for eight weeks. Mrs. Gabbott was adamant that Mr. Ruddock did not mention to her the details of the hour-long telephone conversation on 11 March between Mr. Hall and Mrs. Armstrong. All that she knew about that conversation was that it had been prompted by Mr. Hall's reaction to the threat in Mr. Ruddock's letter of 10 March, to involve the Juvenile Bureau or the police, if Kimberley was not taken for a medical examination by 12 March. Had the contents of Mrs. Armstrong's full and revelatory note of Mr. Hall's admitted treatment of Kimberley, together with his recital of the gross nature of Kimberley's behaviour problems been communicated to Mrs. Gabbott, we are confident that she would have responded forcibly by urging instant convening of a case conference. Although the mere fact that Mr. Ruddock was consulting the Child Abuse Co-ordinator indicated that he recognised the case as one of suspected child abuse, he was still mesmerised by the favourable view he had taken of the family on 12 March and no doubt that view was conveyed to Mrs. Gabbott. Despite the incident on 14 April and his avowed worries on 24 April, Mr. Ruddock was culpably dallying. That he was not contemplating a case conference before "early June" shows only too clearly his state of indecision. The fact that he and Mrs. Gabbott differed as to the date when the case conference might be held - she was firm in her view that she had said that it should be the end of May - is not germane to our deliberations, since it is manifest that a case conference should have been called weeks before then. The fact that Mrs. Gabbott was also perceiving the case as one that could be approached leisurely serves only to emphasise that there was no sense of urgency at either end of the telephone.

This episode was probably the last but one of the many tangible opportunities to protect Kimberley, any one of which, if properly handled, could have averted her death. The fact that the "consultation" was not properly handled was, as we have said, due to the lateness of its initiation, the unsatisfactory mode of communication and the content of the material conveyed.

**We recommend the section on Child Abuse Consultants at pp. 27-29 of the BASW publication, The Management of Child Abuse, should be revised to take account of the matters to which we have alluded. We also recommend that Social Services and Health Authorities should take note of what we have said about the proper function and role of child abuse co-ordinators or consultants.**

# CHAPTER 22

# FAILURE IN CHILD HEALTH ASSISTANCE, JANUARY - JUNE 1986

The last six months of Kimberley Carlile's life unfortunately coincided with the delayed effect in Greenwich of the reorganisation of the National Health Service in 1982. Greenwich Health Authority inherited a health visiting service that had for many years been under-funded, under-staffed and under-managed. Caseloads of health visitors were heavy. The turn-over of staff was high, and morale low. Inevitably, development of an effective service became stultified at a time when the number of child abuse cases calling for health visiting action was increasing. The improvement in child health care that is now discernible began, moreover, only with the appointment of Mrs. O'Connor as Director of Nursing Services in October 1985 and of Dr. Gervase Hamilton as Locum Specialist in Community Medicine.

For more than a year before Mrs. O'Connor's arrival in Greenwich the health visiting service was headed by a part-time Director, working a 15 hour week. In this limited time, a review of the service was undertaken, and an incomplete child abuse procedures guide had been produced; this was operative during the whole of the period of the work with the Carlile family.

It is against this unpropitious backcloth that two aspects of the health visiting service in Greenwich, which played significant parts in the failure of the child abuse system to protect Kimberley Carlile, are to be judged. The first aspect concerns the health visitor's misguided inaction in respect of ensuring a medical examination of Kimberley, and endorsement of that inactivism by the Nursing Officer as supervisor. The second aspect revolves around the state of the medical records at that time in Greenwich, and the faulty distribution of those records within Greenwich Health Authority.

## Health Visitor and Nursing Officer

Miss Marilyn Reader, who had been a health visitor in Greenwich since September 1982, first became acquainted with the Carlile family when Mrs. Carlile came to the Kidbrooke Clinic on 18 November 1985. (We have dealt fully with that early encounter in Chapter 15). It was not until the New Year that Miss Reader had contact with the Carlile family on her delayed "removal-in" visit. The visit had been prompted by Social Services, when a request came from Area 4, consequent upon the incident at Wingfield Primary School involving X. The visit left a favourable impression on Miss Reader, a factor that weighed with her in her attitude to the case and persisted until mid-April. Mrs. Carlile visited the clinic with Z on 22 January 1986, which served to reinforce the favourable view of Mrs. Carlile.

Miss Reader's direct involvement in the attempted process to protect Kimberley Carlile arose on the evening of 7 March when she was asked by Social Services to go on a joint visit for the purpose of seeing Kimberley. We have dealt with this incident in Chapter 17 and do not need to repeat it here. Miss Reader accepted before us that there can be valid reasons for a health visitor going on a joint visit. She acknowledged that where there is a clear need for the health visitor to intervene in order to protect a child at risk she should not flinch from acting accordingly, either on her own or jointly with Social Services personnel. Where there is a clear health visiting objective, or where for some reason Social Services are unable to act, the health visitor should appropriately step in.

Miss Reader did consult her nursing officer, Mrs. Henlin, on the Monday, 10 March, after she had declined to go on the visit, and received support for her action. We think that Mrs. Henlin was wrong, but that attitude was of little consequence, after the event. We are more critical of Mrs. Henlin for not having herself investigated the situation and ensured that Miss Reader followed up the case with a sense of urgency. Miss Reader did speak to Mr. Ruddock on that day and was told of his immediate plans, which included getting Kimberley Carlile medically examined. Two days later, after Mr. Ruddock's meeting with the Carlile family, he conveyed to Miss Reader his assessment of Kimberley. He reported that the parents were agreeing to have Kimberley medically examined in respect of her "behavioural problems". The stage at which the case had arrived fitted in with the favourable, but wholly mistaken view that both Mr. Ruddock and Miss Reader, jointly and separately, were taking of the Carliles.

Mr. Ruddock has acknowledged that his assessment was ill-judged. For her part Miss Reader, who took her cue too readily from him, accepted her share of the responsibility for that faulty assessment. She should have been much more questioning of Mr. Ruddock's assessment. And, although she was handicapped by limited information about the Carlile family, she should have brought to bear her independent judgment of the case. Knowing that the prime aim was to see Kimberley and have her medically examined, Miss Reader should have pursued that objective. It is the essence of the multi-disciplinary approach that professionals from the different disciplines should contribute their own expertise in the handling of child abuse cases, for the very reason that only by pooling all the relevant expertise can a realistic assessment be made.

Miss Reader went on holiday from 14 to 25 March. She arranged for her colleagues at the Kidbrooke Clinic to cover the Carlile family in her absence. Miss Reader genuinely thought that Mrs. Carlile would be bringing Kimberley to the clinic for the medical examination. Miss Reader should have left instructions that Mrs. Carlile was to be reminded of her need to attend the clinic. On her return from leave, Miss Reader discovered that Kimberley had not been examined medically. She told Mr. Ruddock and she arranged to pursue the matter. On 1 April she telephoned the Carlile home with a view to making an early appointment, only to be told that they were going to Liverpool. She once again spoke to Mr. Ruddock.

Miss Reader accepted that her response to this situation at the end of March and the beginning of April was inadequate. Kimberley had still not undergone the medical examination that was urgently needed. Miss Reader was too easily fobbed off by assurances from Mrs. Carlile that Kimberley would be taken to the doctors, assurances (some of them by implication) that had been given and had remained unredeemed ever since the home visit of

16 January. Miss Reader lacked that "well-developed professional scepticism" that Miss Willis, Assistant Secretary of the Health Visitors Association told us about, which is so vital in the handling of a child abuse case.

Miss Reader's view of the Carlile family changed, following a hostile reception she received from Mr. Hall in a telephone conversation of 14 April. She was clear in her own mind that the Carliles were no longer willing to seek and receive help over Kimberley. But instead of turning to positive action, Miss Reader became infected with the occupational disease of drift and inaction, fed by Mr. Hall's hostility. Miss Reader told us that she was upset by Mr. Hall. She added that the idea of visiting the Carliles was "the sort of event that you would put off for a day when you are feeling particularly strong and able to cope with it". Such natural feelings are the ingredients of drift.

On 15 April Miss Reader again discussed the case with Mr. Ruddock. That was the day following his visit to the Carlile house (which we have described in Chapter 20). When he came to sign his notes of that visit on 24 April, Mr. Ruddock concluded that there should be no further action "at present". He doubtless communicated that conclusion to Miss Reader, who gained the understandable impression that Mr. Ruddock would be consulting his supervisor. On the following day, 16 April, Miss Reader had a "formal supervision" with her supervisor, Mrs. Henlin, who advised that Miss Reader should put off any visit to the Carlile family for another week or two.

Miss Reader accepted before us that she should have initiated the convening of a case conference. That she failed to do so was due mainly to the fact that her supervisor failed to promote urgent action, by way of a case conference or an immediate visit by Miss Reader to the Carlile house. Such action was imperative. Mrs. Henlin's endorsement of the procrastination provides some excuse to Miss Reader. They must share the blame for inaction, but the larger share is Mrs. Henlin's. Having heard her in evidence, we think that she misconceived her role as supervisor, by not having engaged in a proper survey of Miss Reader's work with the Carliles. The "supervision" was more like a consultation, in which all the questions were asked by Miss Reader - e.g., "Do I go on a visit today?" - and no questioning of Miss Reader's work came from Mrs. Henlin. There is some explanation for Mrs. Henlin's faulty supervision, in that she was new to her post and relied on Miss Reader as a highly competent health visitor who had recently been acting as nursing officer.

Miss Reader's inaction was further endorsed on 24 April when in her conversation with Mr. Ruddock she concluded that Social Services could do little more than monitor the situation for the time being. Mr. Ruddock's drift continued to infect her conduct. She did nothing on the case until 29 May 1986. If she failed in early April to exercise her independent, critical judgment (as she did fail), she was doubly at fault in not re-assessing the position by the end of April. She accepts now that the Carlile parents should have been given, long before that event, an ultimatum, or that the police should have been employed. And it was up to her to argue powerfully with Mr. Ruddock that that was what was needed.

Miss Reader's responsibility for her inaction is mitigated to some extent by three factors. First, at this time she was becoming overwhelmed by a dramatic increase in her work. She told us that during the period from mid-April to the end of May she had 5 families with thirteen children on the child abuse register (Kimberley was not on the register). She made eighty home visits, sixty of which called for careful preparation. She attended ten clinics, three case conferences and one case review. Second, she was powerfully affected by the most recent response from the Carliles, in particular Mr. Hall's verbal agression on 14 April. It induced a wish to postpone dealing with it, and she knew that Mr. Ruddock was handling the case for Social Services. Third, she still had not received much of the essential background information about the Carlile family. Had the medical records arrived from Wirral and been efficiently processed in Greenwich, Miss Reader would have possessed a great deal of information that would have made her take some action; any inaction on her part would then have been wholly inexcusable.

## Medical records

Miss Reader made her request to Greenwich Health Authority for the medical records of the Carlile family promptly, following Mrs. Carlile's visit to the Kidbrooke Clinic on 18 November 1985. She made a second request by telephone early in December 1985 and a further written request on 13 December. Although the records department of Greenwich Health Authority was told that there were no records for Kimberley at the London addresses given by Miss Reader - those being the addresses given misleadingly to Miss Reader by Mrs. Carlile on 18 November 1985 - this information was not passed to Miss Reader. The request forms were sent back to Miss Reader without any message or note whatsoever. Not suprisingly, Miss Reader did not know that her requests had drawn a blank.

The medical records for Kimberley Carlile eventually arrived, in dribs and drabs. Kimberley's main school record - she had attended a nursery in Wirral - arrived on 17 February 1986 and her immunization details arrived on 27 February 1986. Miss Reader assumed that other records would follow on. At that stage she still did not know of the Wirral connection, although Greenwich Health Authority did. She now accepts that she should not have assumed that these further records would come, unsolicited, and she should have made an urgent request for them, at least by the time of the anonymous call of 7 March; and Mrs. Henlin should have spotted this fact and insisted on the records being provided. There was thus no impediment for receipt of the records, save for human inaction. Greenwich Health Authority accepts now that it must take responsibility for failing to realise at least by the end of February, that Kimberley's records must have been in Wirral. But the responsibility does not end there.

Greenwich Health Authority divides - as do many other health authorities - its records department between pre-school (personal) health and school health. Given the volume of uncomputerised medical records, and the staff resources available, the system for obtaining records did not permit the clerical staff to do more than perform a perfunctory, administrative task. That situation made it all the more necessary to maintain a procedure for cross-referencing information between the two divisions whenever there was a request for, or receipt of medical records. But cross-referencing or liaison was inoperative in Greenwich. We note that the National Standard Child Health (Computer) System will in future accommodate the cross-referencing of all health records.

The problem arose in this case, that the records received in Greenwich in February 1986 came to the School Health Division, and did not percolate through to the Pre-School Health Section. The Senior Medical Officer responsible for children aged 0 to 5, Dr. Govender, did not even know of Kimberley's existence until after 8 June 1986. Had Dr. Govender been aware of the Kimberley Carlile case, she would have been alerted to Kimberley's medical history. She would instantly have instigated either a medical examination by the general practitioner or a developmental assessment. And she might well have asked Social Services to convene a case conference. It is a thousand pities that Dr. Govender was never informed of Kimberley's existence. We think that this failure stemmed from the assumption that Kimberley was attending Wingfield School and would come under the aegis of the school medical service. If that assumption was not unreasonable, the question remains whether Dr. Hooper, the Senior Medical Officer (School Health), on receiving the limited records on 14 and 27 February 1986, read them sufficiently carefully to have alerted Dr. Govender.

Dr. Hooper says she did not see all the records. We find that the clerk, Mrs. Linda Allen, gave all of them to Dr. Hooper. The only direct evidence of what Dr. Hooper in fact did read came from Dr. Hooper herself. She recalled receiving the records. Since she acted on them, by asking Dr. Kamalanathan to see the children at Wingfield School, we have no hesitation in accepting her word for it. The fact that she asked for a medical examination of all three children at Wingfield School supports her assumption that Kimberley was at the school, as well as X and Y. Dr. Hooper clearly thought that the school medical records and the summaries of the case conferences represented the totality of the records available. Dr. Hooper's choice of the school route was the correct one for X and Y. If Kimberley had been in the nursery section of Wingfield School, the child was clearly under Dr. Hooper's aegis, but she should have checked whether Kimberley was in the nursery section of the School. Even if Dr. Hooper's assumption that Kimberley was at the school had proved correct, she should nevertheless have communicated with her opposite number, Dr. Govender.

The remaining issue is: how did Dr. Hooper go about seeking the medical examination of all three children? She wrote a note - it was in fact undated - for Dr. Kamanalathan on 3 March 1986. The request to Dr. Kamalanathan was plain enough. The trouble was that Kimberley was below school age and was not attending the nursery. She was, therefore, not available to Dr. Kamalanathan for medical examination. It is true that he knew of the two case conferences - at least he was able to, and did read the summaries of them. But it was unreasonable to expect him to realise that Kimberley needed a developmental assessment, or that he should make enquiries about Kimberley and her social circumstances. He communicated to Dr. Hooper that he had examined X and Y, and told her that he knew nothing of their social circumstances. He made no mention of Kimberley. On receipt of that information Dr. Hooper took no action, which is surprising, having regard to her request that the *three* children should be medically examined.

Ought she now to be criticised for not having shared the information which she alone had, and which might have altered the course of events? She had initiated the process of intercepting "bulky" records. We find it hard to understand her distinction between bulky and slim records as a means of identifying cases which cause concern. That she did not appreciate the full significance of what was absent from the records that arrived in mid-February is not disputed. Would it be overly critical now - deciding the matter with hindsight - to blame her? Her failure to promote further inquiries and to alert Dr. Govender was the kind of error that was ultimately the product of a defective system. Records are records. There is no place in any information system for sifting out and separating the component parts of a unitary organisation's documentation. Records on all the children of a family should pass through the one system, irrespective of the welfare service appropriate to each one of the children. On balance, because she was working within such a system, Dr. Hooper is not to be censured.

# CHAPTER 23

# ENCOUNTER AT KIDBROOKE CLINIC: THE LAST CHANCE, 4 JUNE 1986

Four days before Kimberley Carlile died, her step-father, Mr. Hall, had taken Z, the youngest child of the family (a girl, then aged 19 months) in the afternoon of that day to the Kidbrooke clinic on the Ferrier Estate for a measles injection and for her 18 month developmental assessment. Miss Reader, the health visitor, was on the clinic premises that afternoon. She did not, however, know that Mr. Hall had attended the clinic until after he had left. She telephoned Mr. Ruddock later that day to tell him of the visit. Mr. Ruddock's note on file states that Miss Reader "had seen Z at clinic who was fit and healthy. Mr Hall defensive and no mention of Kimberley". Some of this information - the noting of Mr Hall's defensiveness and the lack of any reference to Kimberley - came originally to Miss Reader from Dr. Mary Spencer who was the clinical medical officer on duty and had administered the immunization to the child and conducted the developmental assessment.

Dr. Spencer has worked for health authorities in Greenwich for the last 17 years; she has specialised in obstetrics, child health and community health. Mr. Hall and the child were taken by the clinic nurse, along with the appropriate documentation, from which Dr. Spencer observed that there were three older children in the family, none of whom was Mr. Hall's. Nevertheless, she noted that he handled the child very competently, and she complimented him on this approach to fatherly duties. The ensuing dialogue did not match the friendliness of the initial encounter. Dr. Spencer asked questions about the other children. Mr. Hall was uncommunicative, insisting that the eldest child was at Wingfield School, which in fact was no longer true. When he was asked about the second child he was wholly unresponsive. No questions about Kimberley were asked. Dr. Spencer was keen not to create a barrier that would lead to members of the Carlile family absenting themselves from the clinic in the future. Dr. Spencer carried out the immunization and, without more ado, an unsmiling and graceless Mr. Hall left the clinic with the child.

At the end of Dr. Spencer's session, around 4 o'clock, she spoke to Miss Reader, whom she had known as an excellent health visitor for over 4 years. There is some disagreement between the two as to whom first brought up the subject of the "problem" within the Carlile family. Dr. Spencer told us that she told Miss Reader about Mr. Hall "putting up the shutters" on being questioned about the family, and asked "what's the problem?" Miss Reader claims that it was she who initiated the discussion about Kimberley being the one member of the Carlile family who was causing concern to herself and to Social Services because she and the social workers had not been able to see Kimberley. We do not find it necessary to determine who said what, and at what point in the conversation. Suffice it to say, Dr. Spencer was made aware of the fact that for some time Miss Reader and social workers had failed to gain access to the Carlile home for the purpose of seeing Kimberley in the flesh, and for arranging for her to undergo a medical examination. But

Dr. Spencer was probably told no more about the case other than the continuing concern of Social Services and Miss Reader for Kimberley's welfare.

Dr. Spencer said she was mystified about the "unseen" child, but added that she had no reason to suspect child abuse, although she had an unpleasant feeling that all was not well. She concluded then, as she told us, that since Social Services were clearly involved, together with Miss Reader, she "took it that everything was under control". And there, as far as Dr. Spencer was concerned the matter rested. Miss Reader very properly reported the incident immediately to Mr. Ruddock. She had been watching out for a visit to the clinic by Kimberley (as well as Z), because on 29 May she had telephoned Mrs. Carlile to learn that Mr. Hall would shortly be attending the clinic with Kimberley and Z. The knowledge that Mr. Ruddock acquired from Miss Reader of yet another failure to get Kimberley medically examined provided positively the very last opportunity to save Kimberley. The opportunity afforded by this incident was not seized, even though it coincided with the time-table agreed by Mr. Ruddock and Mrs. Gabbott for convening a case conference. Had the practice of delay and drift not been adopted by Mr. Ruddock, the incident would have prompted instant action.

Dr. Spencer made no note of the disconcerting behaviour of Mr. Hall; nor did she make any note of the discussion she had had with Miss Reader. And even when Dr. Spencer heard a few days later of the shattering news of Kimberley's death, she still did not commit to paper the events of 4 June 1986, knowing (as she must have done) that there was bound to be some sort of inquiry, internal or external, in which she would be asked to recount the encounter of that afternoon at Kidbrooke clinic. We think that Dr. Spencer ought to have made a note, recording the sequence of events that, on the face of it, touched on an issue relating to the safety and protection of a child. Such recording must become part of an information system in the child protection service (see Chapter 26).

What troubled us more than the venial failure to record the incident of 4 June 1986 was Dr Spencer's total reliance on action being taken by Social Services. Initially, we thought that she might have taken some positive action. We think that it is of the essence of the multi-disciplinary approach to the management of the child protection system that all agencies involved must act in collaboration with each other. Still more, it is bad practice for any of the other agencies - be it, health services, education, general practitioners, police and lawyers - to assume that, because Social Service Departments of local authorities are the only bodies with the statutory duty to investigate cases of suspected child abuse, all decisions and actions pursuant to those duties can properly be left to Social Services.

Under Section 22, National Health Service Act 1977 there is a duty on local authorities and health authorities to co-operate. In *A Child in Trust*, the Panel of Inquiry recommended that in the context of child protection the duty should be more specific, to include the duty to consult and the duty to assist by advice and the supply of information so as to help the management of child abuse cases. Such a duty would, it was argued, operate as a positive and practical step to promote multi-disciplinary working, particularly at the stage of identification of abuse. *A Child in Trust* was published in December 1985, and we would have hoped that, in advance of legislation, those personnel in local authorities and health authorities would have taken this recommendation on board as a professional or public duty. In paragraph 43 of the White Paper, the Government has indicated that it intends to make legal provision for co-operation between statutory and voluntary agencies in the investigation of harm and protection of children at risk. Subject to what we say in Chapter 24, **we recommend that any such legislative provision should include a specific duty on the health authorities in this context to promote the welfare of children, in terms similar to Section 1, Child Care Act 1980.**

We think that it would, however, be overly critical for us to say that Dr. Spencer should have taken some positive action. In fact we acquit her of any fault, given the absence of any statutory duty on her to do more than respond to some request from Social Services to take some action, and there was no request to do anything in relation to Kimberley. She had, after all, passed on her worries to Miss Reader, whom she knew was in direct and frequent contact with Area 4 officers.

We conclude, however, that often the protective or preventive role of community and child health is optimally achieved through crisis intervention. Health services personnel must in the future acknowledge and accept that on occasions, in collaboration with Social Services, they must take the first step of intervention. This may be particularly appropriate when what is needed urgently is the medical examination of an unseen child.

# A CHILD IN MIND:
## PROTECTION OF CHILDREN IN A
## RESPONSIBLE SOCIETY

# PART IV

## GENERAL ISSUES

# CHILD ABUSE IN PERSPECTIVE

Although child abuse and child neglect are depressingly common occurrences in our society, *deaths* resulting directly from parental abuse or neglect (or, as in the case of Kimberley Carlile, a combination of both) are relatively infrequent. There is, however, a marked tendency in the public's mind both to ignore this fact and to display a heightened perception of the incidence of such deaths. This is not altogether surprising. The death of a child at the hands of those most responsible for the care and protection of a child is regarded as an abhorrent act.

Parental abuse of children almost invariably takes place in the privacy of the home, without independent witnesses. Suspicious child deaths, where the parents deny having caused the injury and where there is insufficient evidence for a criminal prosecution, are normally recorded by the coroner as open verdicts. Such deaths are recorded as "injury undetermined whether accidentally or purposely inflicted", according to the International Classification of Diseases, Injuries and Causes of Death (ICD). They could not be recorded as "homicide and injury purposely inflicted by other persons".

The Registrar General's figures for child homicides over the last decade have fluctuated from 72-105, an average of 85 per annum. This figure probably represents only a fraction of the actual child abuse deaths. Recognition of this "tip of the iceberg" statistic has led researchers to produce estimates based on extrapolations from their own studies. The figure of 300 pre-school deaths per annum, quoted in the First Report of the Select Committee on Violence in the Family, and 700 child deaths per annum reported in 1975, were based on such studies. The problem about such extrapolations, as Adelstein and others pointed out in a study published in 1982, is that they are based on very small actual numbers which can lead to wide fluctuations in the final estimate. They concluded that "estimates as high as 700 deaths a year in England and Wales are exaggerated". They also drew attention to those "natural deaths" of children where the child's resistance to infection is weakened by abuse or neglect. They analysed a sample of children's death certificates, and identified a number of cases where the underlying cause of death was non-violent, but where violence had contributed to the child's death.

The NSPCC has recently published a revised estimate of child deaths' based a) on the Adelstein study; b) the Registrar-General's figures for "homicides" and "injuries undetermined whether accidentally or purposely inflicted"; and c) the small number of potential, mis-diagnosed cot deaths (Creighton, 1985). This estimate produced a figure of 200 child deaths per annum either caused, or contributed to by abuse or neglect. Parents of those providing regular care of children were considered to be responsible for between 150 and 170 of those deaths.

This refined figure does not, however, represent a major cause of child mortality. By comparison, the number of children killed accidentally -

whether in the home or on the roads or streets of this country - is about 1000 a year. Compared to the widespread concern about child abuse deaths, the waste of children's lives due to avoidable accidents receives much less public, or even professional attention. Such selective public response is not easy to explain. Particularly puzzling is the explosion of public outrage when a child dies in care of a local authority, or when an agency of the welfare state appears to have failed to prevent a child suffering abuse or neglect. Verbal abuse of social workers, bordering on the hysterical, abounds in the popular press; threats of violence have not been uncommon. Social workers have not found it easy to cope with such saturating media coverage devoted to each successive child abuse case. We detect less of the recrudescence of moral panic that has accompanied earlier child abuse inquiries, and sense that there are, at last, some glimmerings of public awareness that the problems of protecting children from abusing parents do not yield readily to simplistic situations. When child abuse is put into proper perspective we are confident that a more rational public debate than in the past can usefully take place. That perspective is the aim of this introductory chapter.

With recent advances in understanding child abuse, it has been possible to develop our knowledge of those familial factors associated with child abuse. The NSPCC register research, for example, has provided evidence of those factors which social workers consider to have created stress in families precipitating the abuse. The factor which was recorded most often for the registered children was "marital problems". Other factors indicated as likely to cause stress in families included "inability to respond to the maturational needs of the child" and "unrealistic expectations of the child". These "predisposing" factors may act as warning signs, but they will not predict abuse in any particular case. We remain far from a knowledge of what causes a caretaker to kill his or her child. And without a cause we are unlikely to find a remedy, remembering that all the available evidence points to multiple causal factors.

In Kimberley's case we can suggest a few factors that might have contributed to her death: a clash of strong wills, a child's behaviour and feeding problems, adults damaged by their own experiences, parental inexperience and immaturity, a new "marital" relationship having to assume sudden responsibility for four children, with another on the way; the need to find a scapegoat for what is wrong with life; familiarity with violence; social isolation; and possibly the effects of drink. Many who read the details surrounding Kimberley's life and death will have their own items to add to this list, but even at the end of the Commission's detailed deliberations it has not been possible to identify precise causes for the way Mrs. Carlile and Mr. Hall behaved towards the hapless child. We have to accept that, given our current state of ignorance, and the fallibility of human beings and the imperfect world we live in, children will continue to be killed by their parents. This acceptance does not come easily, and part of the outcry that greets the more publicised cases might be due to our despair. It may be an expression of our collective guilt in failing to protect our children. With Victor Hugo we might want to rage:

"Is it children we are killing now? My God,
What are we? Savages?..."

and want to ask:

"Why was he killed? If only someone could explain".
("A recollection of the night of the 4th").

As we have said, child abuse is uncomfortably close to our own domestic scene, and all too common an occurrence in our society. But we cannot claim to know whether the phenomenon of child abuse is on the increase. As L.C.A. Knowles has observed: "Englishmen are always despondent about their own times, and it would be easy to quote contemporaries in every period so that this testimony would show we had gone downhill ever since the time of the Norman Conquest". We have little from the past to compare our existing knowledge with, and few countries keep reliable national statistics. **We recommend that active consideration be given to the systematic recording and publication of cases of child abuse.** What is urgently needed is a national survey, much like the British Crime Survey of 1982. What we do know is that the *reporting* of cases of child abuse has risen rapidly in the last decade, with the dramatic increase of reported cases of child sexual abuse being the latest feature in the trend. While it is common to interpret increases in reported cases of child abuse as an actual increase, there is no basis for such a deduction. The increase of reported cases does, however, have at least three desirable features. First, it suggests a growing concern for our children and a willingness to express this. The increase in reported sexual abuse could be reflected in a rise in moral standards, leading to us no longer being prepared to accept that children should be on the receiving end of the kind of behaviour that has been accepted (or condoned, or ignored) before. Second, the increase provides us with the opportunity of building up a true picture of what is happening to children. Third, cases of suspected child abuse, if reported, provide at least the opportunity for helping children at risk.

This brings us to the question of why the system established to protect children sometimes fails to do so. Such failures need to be put in perspective. Many of them are well publicised, while the children successfully protected remain unknown. The Association of Directors of Social Services, following its survey of child abuse registrations, "noted that Social Services Departments are protecting nearly 30,000 children who have been determined, at multi-disciplinary case conferences and in court hearings, to have been seriously injured, or who are at risk of serious injury". This represents between 2 to 3 for every 1,000 children population. We are circumspect in accepting that the incidence of *serious* injury is as great as that implied in these figures. However, if one considers the vulnerability and size of this group, and one looks at it alongside the performance of other services concerned with the safety of other vulnerable groups, the child protection system might bear favourable comparison. We do not suggest for one moment that the child protection system cannot be improved, and indeed the very purpose of this Inquiry has been to make suggestions how this might be achieved. We trust that we will have made a small contribution to it. What we do want to suggest is that the record of the child protection service be

135

judged fairly. Casualties of any lack of perspective in reporting cases of child abuse tragedies include both the loss of public confidence in the service and the loss of confidence in those frontline practitioners, the social workers who are trying to help children.

One of the less publicised reasons why the child protection system fails is that risk is an inherent feature of the system. We would have fewer failures if society supported greater intervention by the welfare agencies. If a case of suspected abuse always led to a child being removed from home, or if social workers always resisted attempts to work towards returning children to their families following an allegation, a few more children might be spared parental abuse. The fact is that most children who are the subjects of referrals concerning their welfare do remain with their families. Society, rightly in our opinion, is not prepared to tolerate too heavy-handed disruptions to family life, and expects careful judgment to be exercised in deciding on the appropriate action to be taken in any particular case. This more flexible approach offers some security to families. But, given that human judgment is fallible, society must tolerate occasional failure. Staff who follow up suspicions of child abuse are not creating these risks. They are inheriting the risks, and are accepting them on our behalf.

What we have to prevent at all costs is that those taking responsibility for these decisions should become a kind of collective scapegoat for what goes wrong in a system, in the way that Kimberley, on the smaller scale of the Carlile home, became the scapegoat for what went wrong in her family.

# CHAPTER 24

# TOWARDS A CHILD PROTECTION SERVICE

We have been led to tackle the large scale subject at the heart of this chapter by an attempt to understand the circumstances surrounding Kimberley's death in their fullest sense, and by an awareness that previous inquiries have repeatedly come up with the same kind of recommendations as ours.

The incomprehensible maltreatment inflicted on so many children by their parents - the very people who should offer comfort and protection - has always presented a profound challenge to civilised society. For a long time the phenomenon of child abuse was so unpalatable that eyes were averted from the problem, and society palpably failed to establish any kind of child protection service. Indeed, in this country until late in the nineteenth century, both Parliament and the public were unconcerned with the way in which parents treated their children, regarding the most barbarous cruelty as beyond public intervention, since children were still not regarded as citizens in their own right[1]. In contemporary Britain a child has rights against its parents. Legislation concerned with children since 1925 has declared the welfare of the child to be the first and paramount consideration, but it is only since 1971 that the principle has become universally applicable. When Parliament finally could no longer ignore a pressing social problem, it was uncertain about the appropriate method of official intervention to adopt. Should the responsibility for ensuring that children at risk are properly safeguarded and, if necessary, removed from their parents, be handed exclusively to a single governmental agency? Or should a child protection system be managed by all the agencies relevant to a socio-medical problem which calls not just for multi-disciplinary input but composite responsibility? We examine first the statutory framework to discern which, if at all, of the two approaches the legislature has adoped. Our examination focuses on the ways in which official intervention is authorised to safeguard the welfare of children.

## The Statutory Framework

Historically, there are two ways in which a child who is at risk may be put in the care of a local authority. One is voluntary, a term in common usage (indeed used by us) but not entirely accurate. This was introduced in the Children Act 1948 which imposed a duty on the local authority to receive a parentless child into care if it appeared that certain grounds for reception exist - where the child is an orphan or has been deserted, or where the parent is permanently or temporarily incapacitated by mental or physical illness, "or infirmity or their incapacity or any other circumstance" from providing the child with proper accommodation, maintenance and upbringing. In any case the local authority's intervention must be necessary in the interests of the child's welfare, and the child must be kept in care so long as the child's welfare requires it and the child has not attained the age of 18. The voluntary

---

[1] Pinchbeck and Hewitt, Children in English Society. Vol II P611 ff.

aspect of care is demonstrated by the duty being placed on the local authority to secure the resumption of parental care if a parent desires it and such resumption of parental care is consistent with the child's welfare. If a local authority seeks to resist the resumption of parental care, it may exercise a power to pass a resolution, vesting in the local authority "the parental rights and duties with respect to that child". Alternatively, it may apply to a Magistrates' Court for a Care Order, or invoke the wardship jurisdiction of the High Court. The voluntary method, which involves the local authority Social Services exclusively in its duty to *receive* children into care, was preceded by the compulsory method.

The Children and Young Persons Act 1933 (itself a consolidating enactment) empowered a juvenile court to commit a child or young person "to the care of any fit person". The fit person into whose care the child or young person was committed had the same rights, powers and liabilities as if they were the parent. The child or young person committed to care continued to remain in care, notwithstanding any claim by the parent. The Act provided for the committal to the care of a local authority.

The Children and Young Persons Act 1969 repealed those provisions. It left intact, however, the provision for the issue to any constable of a warrant from a magistrate for removal of a child to a place of safety. This provision, which is to be found in Section 40 of the 1933 Act, has become little used since the provision of the Place of Safety Order in Section 28 of the 1969 Act (a replacement of a similar provision in the 1933 Act). But Section 40 remains, to indicate a wider involvement than local authorities in the task of protecting children. The 1969 legislation constitutes the existing law for the *taking* into care of a local authority of children in need of care and control. A Care Order is an Order committing the child to the care of a local authority which alone has the duty to receive and keep the child in care, notwithstanding any claim by the parent during the currency of the Order. The conditions specified as justifying the making of an Order include that the child's proper development is being neglected, or his or her health impaired or neglected. Parental rights vest in the local authority; those of the parents are overridden, but not extinguished.

These provisions would seem to indicate a high preference for the exclusivity of intervention by local authority Social Services. But the process by which legal intervention is actually effected discloses an involvement of other agencies and persons. If a local authority receives information suggesting that there are grounds for bringing care proceedings it has a duty to cause inquiries to be made into the case, unless satisfied that such inquiries are unnecessary. While only a local authority has the duty to bring proceedings, a constable or an authorised person - only the NSPCC has been authorised - may initiate care proceedings, in which case notice must be given to the local authority. The NSPCC, which carries out extensive investigations of child abuse, has given an undertaking that it will consult the appropriate local authority before bringing care proceedings, and invariably does so.

Although in practice application to a magistrate for a Place of Safety Order is almost invariably made by social workers employed by local authorities or the NSPCC, Section 28 of the 1969 Act empowers any person to apply for authority to detain a child or young person and take him to a place of safety if he satisfies the magistrate that he has reasonable cause to believe that one or more of the primary conditions for a Care Order is satisfied. The Order is made *ex parte*, and lasts up to 28 days. Likewise, any person can apply to a magistrate on information on oath that a police warrant be issued to remove a child suspected of being at risk. This is the 1933 Act provision. The police possess a separate power to detain a child in a place of safety without recourse to a magistrate, for a maximum period of 8 days.

The White Paper, *The Law on Child Care and Family Services*, of January 1987, recognising the limits of the duty of a local authority to investigate, proposes that the law should impose a more active duty to investigate in any case where it is suspected that the child is suffering harm or is likely to do so. Enquiries by social workers will be made such as are necessary to enable the local authority to decide what action, if any, to take. The White Paper, recognising also that the performance of such a task calls for the co-operation of the health authorities, proposes to include a duty to consult and a duty to assist by advice and the supply of information. These proposals are an acknowledgement of the need for co-operation between statutory organisations in pursuance of the multi-disciplinary approach to the management of the child abuse system.

## The Law in Action

Given the ambiguity of the statutory framework, we proceed to consider the two principal ways in which a child protection service could be rationally established, and to examine how far the existing management of the child abuse system reflects either one or other of the two ways. In approaching these two ways we are only too aware that our descriptions are brief and superficial. Firmer definitions would require a far wider and more thorough analysis than we have been able to undertake. Nevertheless, we should be able to answer the question: Who is responsible for child protection in this country? Any confusion in answering that question will be translated into the work with children, and will cause the kind of problem we experienced in knowing where to direct our more general recommendations.

The first way is to entrust the overall responsibility for the management of the system to one authority. This could be achieved either through establishing one statutory child protection authority employing all the relevant staff and doing all the work, or by assigning to one authority the overall responsibility for the child protection service and giving it power for this purpose to require the assistance of professionals working in other agencies. Given that the first model, despite its clear-cut appearance, is probably too radical to gain support, we concentrate on the second version of the single authority. This will not mean all the work involved being carried out by the single authority, but to function well the system will require the full co-operation of the public, and of all relevant professions and agencies. Case conferences would remain the crucible of the system, and it would continue to be possible to appoint key workers, but these key workers and all involved in the case would have to be answerable to the controlling authority. This authority, if it is to avoid responsibility without power, would need to be empowered to demand action, within their competence, of all contributors to the system. For the purpose of managing the child protection system, all participants would thus be answerable to the controlling authority. This structure has the advantage of making accountability clear. It has the advantage of being intelligible to the outside world. More conscientious and determined action may also follow if overall responsibility is not diffuse. It has the disadvantage of separating child protection from other areas of child care and child health, unless the one authority is a massive children's agency. It also has the disadvantage of cutting across existing organisations and professional hierarchies, thereby making change unlikely, particularly if the authority were to be placed under local, rather than central government.

The second way is to make the management of the child protection system a multi-disciplinary responsibility. This would entail something more than all the relevant agencies working together. It would mean more than contributing knowledge, skills and professional competence: such "contributing" is more likely to belong to the single-authority structure. The second structure requires that overall responsibility for the *management* of the system is shared, although it would be possible for specific parts of the responsibility to be formally delegated. The multi-disciplinary structure has the advantage of leaving people accountable within their own hierarchies. It has the advantage of sharing an awesome responsibility. It has the disadvantage of inducing ambiguity in accountability and leaves the door open for confusion, conflict and inter-agency hostility to enter if something goes wrong. It has the disadvantage, given the number of agencies involved, of creating a body with many heads, and would need all agencies to be equal in authority while some, in reality, might reckon that he who shares honey with the bear has the least part of it. Accountability could be made clearer, and management possibly more effective and efficient, if a governing body was appointed by the contributing agencies. This body would need to have executive powers, in contrast to existing Area Review Committees.

Major improvements have undoubtedly been made to the existing system for protecting children. We have much to be proud of in the service provided for children, and many organisations, as well as individuals, have worked long and hard to achieve those improvements. Anyone familiar with the findings of the various child abuse inquiries will be aware, however, that the same flaws in the system have been repeatedly exposed. While the relevant organisations, and the front-line staff, will continue to strive to raise their standards and improve their practices, we doubt if a big step forward can be achieved without a fundamental review of the structure of the child protection service. **It is this review we seek to inspire and recommend should take place.**

We think that it is unclear what kind of child protection service society wants, and what system we have in fact established and operated. We seem, in many ways, to have travelled far down the road towards a shared, multi-disciplinary responsibility, while retaining features of the one authority system, with Social Services Departments of local authorities the primary, although not exclusive authority for the entire system. The role of the Area Review Committee is ill-defined and, while it remains unfunded, cannot

140

exercise real authority. Its influence, moreover, varies from one area to another. Certainly, when disaster strikes, and blame is to be apportioned, shared responsibility is conspicuous by its absence. Social Services, as the authority carrying the legal burden, is instinctively blamed.

Indeed *any* managerial responsibility for the system is usually absent, with the brunt of the criticism borne by individual practitioners, often low in the employment hierarchy, as if they acted as independent professionals.

If this analysis is accurate, one should not be surprised if it is remarkably difficult to bring lasting improvements to the system. One would expect inquiry reports, such as ours, to repeat over and over again the same kind of recommendations, simply because they are either never implemented or their impact lessened by the fissiparous nature of the system. Problems in areas of inter-agency and inter-departmental co-operation would prove to be especially intractable. Also to be expected would be a lack of urgency about getting things right, and a fatalistic attitude on the part of those most likely to be at the receiving end of public criticism, even though much of it could be dismissed as ill-informed and ill-motivated. We believe these symptoms can easily be detected in current practice.

This is not merely a sterile exegesis of inter-organisational responsibilities, for, if the argument is right, we are likely to see the imprecision and ambiguity in the structure constantly reflected on the ground. We suggest that shadow is precisely what can be seen in Kimberley's case, and other reported cases.

Mr. Ruddock's activities are, we think, intelligibly understood only when seen as an attempt to mobilise a multi-disciplinary system. Knowing that Mrs. Carlile and Mr. Hall were hostile to intervention by Social Services, and believing insufficient legal grounds existed for imposing such intervention whether they liked it or not, Mr. Ruddock tried to involve other agencies and professions - the health visitor, the primary school, educational welfare service and the general practitioner (although, surprisingly, not the police).

However, the response of many of these professionals and their agencies, whether contacted by Mr. Ruddock or not, was not to get involved beyond their own professional remit, or to define their involvement in very limited terms. For example, should the health visitor involve herself in a joint visit to the Carlile home? Ironically, the reason often given for the lack of initiative was that Social Services were thankfully dealing with it. Comments included: "As Social Services were involved, I took it everything was under control"; no contact with the family "since Social Services were actively involved"; "did not feel it was my role to follow through such allegations, therefore stated that Social Services should visit and act accordingly".

The principal device for achieving multi-disciplinary co-operation is the case conference. A case conference would have overcome the lack of response from the other agencies concerned with Kimberley, but a case conference cannot be called at an early stage with every referral of suspected child abuse, so the collaborative relationships must be in place all the time. Also the responsibility for making sure a case conference is called (as distinct from the practical responsibility of organising the conference) must be defined by the child protection system. Some people involved with Kimberley never

141

thought of suggesting a case conference. Others told us that they thought they could have required a case conference to be called, but did not, although with hindsight they obviously wished they had. Thus the failure to hold a case conference might itself have been symptomatic of confusion and lack of clarity between agencies about their respective responsibilities.

Mr. Ruddock was demonstrably operating on the basis of child protection being a multi-disciplinary responsibility. Others in the network were operating on the basis of it being one authority's responsibility, namely, Social Services; they were at best mere auxiliaries within their own disciplines. Thus Mr. Ruddock was like a puppeteer, where none of the parts responded to the strings he was pulling. An arm was perfectly prepared to be an arm, but was not going to be part of a body, and most definitely was not going to answer the tugging of some higher authority. The child protection system as a whole is less than the aggregate of its several parts. It is a puppet with no-one to pull the strings. While many decisions concerned with child abuse make the practitioners feel like they are setting themselves up as God, the system would benefit from a layer of temporal authority in between.

Whatever decisions are made in the future they must help all those participating in the system to make the child's safety the first and foremost consideration of their work.

## The Problem of Change

We approach the problem from the present position of the two existing, quite separate services: child care and child health. Under existing legislation it is the child care service which alone has a statutory duty to investigate cases when information is received indicating that there are grounds for taking the child into care, either voluntarily or compulsorily. Except for the NSPCC, only the local authorities' Social Services are in practice empowered to bring care proceedings before the courts, since it is they who will carry the responsibility for the execution of a Care Order or a Supervision Order.

The Government's White Paper proposes that the child care service should have a more active duty to investigate in any case where it is suspected that the child is suffering harm, or is likely to do so. While this will underline the investigative role of child care, it may at the same time serve only to reinforce the separatist situation. In recognition of this, the White Paper further proposes to strengthen the collaborative efforts of the child health service. The duty on local authorities or health authorities to co-operate, expressed in general terms in Section 22, National Health Service Act 1977, is plainly insufficient in practical terms. The proposal, therefore, is to buttress the duty to collaborate in the investigation of child abuse and in the protection of children, by specific duties to consult, to assist by advice and the supply of information, and to promote the management of child care cases. We think that, in its attempt to give greater practical effect to the multi-disciplinary approach to the management of the child abuse system, the proposals do not go far enough. At the very least the specific child health contribution of health authorities concerning the child's health will have to be spelt out in statutory form.

142

If that were the right way forward, it would require a management group, each member of the group being responsible for his or her own part of the service. One of them would be in the lead but all of them would accept responsibility for the service as a whole. Individual practitioners would be responsible for their own item of specialist service, the key worker in the lead, but all accepting responsibility from the point of view of their own discipline. That would still fall short of a *shared* responsibility. While we think that such a structure would be an improvement in the present haphazard nature of collaborative effort, we remain unconvinced that it is the right structure to accept. Nothing short of a joint organisation incorporating child care and child health will suffice. We note that in Northern Ireland there exist joint Social Services and Health Boards, but we have not been able to examine how they work.

A single controlling authority would need to employ its own staff, or be able to command the services of those with expertise in child care and child health. It would have the exclusive investigative function (save for the NSPCC) and the duty to protect children through the taking of care proceedings. It would have to control all the professional staff necessary to perform its statutory functions. The controlling authority - the Child Protection Service - would be answerable to a Minister of the Crown. The Child Protection Service could operate regionally through the structure of local committees which, funded nationally, would exercise the delegated powers and duties of the Child Protection Service.

Despite the major improvements achieved within the current child protection system, and the valiant and effective endeavours of many individuals working to serve children, we do not believe the present mixture of child care and child health services, functioning separately, and not always in harness with each other, will provide the protection that children in our society are entitled to expect. In reaching this conclusion, we know we are close to concerns that have been expressed before. Indeed, the Report of the Care of Children Committee in 1946 was worried that confusion in the management of services for children was "acute and dangerous": "The local authority for one purpose, e.g. child life protection, may be different from the local authority for another purpose.... This may lead to a position in which no one feels actively and personally responsible for the welfare of the individual child, and in which... there may even be wrangles between committees... while the child is left without proper care". (Paragraph 438).

Whatever the way forward, whether it is towards a single authority or toward a genuinely shared managerial responsibility, the issues involved should not be avoided on the grounds of their scale and complexity if the safety of children demands that they should be addressed. Only then can we be sure we are making the same demands of the structure as we are of those working within it - to put the interests of children first. We should not demand that individuals from the relevant professions continue striving to improve their performance, and continue bearing the responsibility for their work, unless we are satisfied they are working within an overall framework that maximises their skills.

CHAPTER 25

# RIGHTS OF ACCESS,
# EMERGENCY PROCEDURES
# AND POWERS TO EXAMINE MEDICALLY

## General principles

At the heart of our Inquiry have been the acute problems that social workers constantly face in the course of investigating allegations of child abuse. Mindful of the dilemma facing social workers, between the duty to pay full respect to family life and to observe scrupulously the rights of parents to bring up their own children without unnecessary interference from authority, and the duty to protect children from risk of abuse by their parents, we have paid particular attention to the fine balance that needs always to be maintained between the two. Here we are not considering the consequences that flow from a Care Order, in which a child is in trust to a local authority to protect the child, even, if necessary, by overriding the rights of natural parents. Here we are at the crossroads of competing social policies - parental rights and the interests of children.

The initial difficulty we have is to know what precisely is incorporated in the concept of parental rights. The difficulty is not dispelled by the recent House of Lords' decision in *Gillick v West Norfolk and Wisbech Area Health Authority*[1] in which Lord Scarman described the law relating to parents and children as "the beginning, not the conclusion, of a legal development".

Parental rights are, rightly, given great prominence in our law, but it seems that they are rights conferred on parents ultimately for the benefit of their children. A doctor does not have a right to examine a child or give it medical treatment, except in the case where the child is old enough and capable of appreciating the nature and consequences of the medical examination and treatment. For that reason, we think that the Place of Safety Order, as presently framed in Section 28(1), Children and Young Persons Act 1969, probably does not permit the person, who applies successfully to a magistrate to remove and detain a child, either by himself or anyone else, to examine the child medically. The most that could be done lawfully is for the detainer to observe the child's body in the course of daily caring for the child at the place of safety. Apart from the comprehending child and from the case of an emergency, the parents' rights will prevail, subject to any abandonment of parental responsibilities and to court orders.

None of this provides, as Mr. Richardson pertinently submitted to us, any clear legal framework for the social worker investigating allegations of child abuse. In this state of affairs we have had to construct for ourselves the principles upon which we base our attitude to the existing powers and to the powers that Parliament might hereafter enact. We think that in the current

[1] [1986] 1 A.C.112.

144

debate insufficient weight is given to the interests of the child. This is particularly so in the case of children under the age of 5 who are not subjected to compulsory schooling and, therefore, come under the School Health Service. For under-fives, we think that the law should be more sensitive to the need for protection of the child, and give marginally less play to the claims of parents to be left alone.

The principal duty of parents, as Trollope's Doctor Thorne observed, is to make their child happy. If the parent fails in that regard, there can be no legitimate objection to the welfare authorities coming in to act for the child against the defaulting parent. While acknowledging fully the proper claims of parents, and not in any way desiring to see intrusion by social workers on any scale more than is strictly necessary to protect children, we would like to see a shift - not a dynamic change, but a significant shift - towards the interests of children. This has led us to recommend certain new limited powers to buttress the existing duties of social workers to investigate cases of child abuse. We think that, while they bear the mark of infringement of parental rights, they are designed to improve the protective element and to interfere in family life only minimally. Indeed, we think that, armed with new and clearly defined powers, social workers are likely to go about that difficult task with greater confidence. Confidence, in its turn, breeds security in coping with parents who are unwilling to co-operate. We think also that the relationship would soon become one in which the persuasive power will supersede the coercive power. In short, there should be less reliance on strict enforcement of the law and more on promoting predilection among parents for protection of their children.

## The existing law

The statutory powers available to social workers are three-fold. The most widely used is the Place of Safety Order, obtainable on an application to a magistrate, in which the social worker must have reasonable cause to believe that the child is at risk of ill-treatment or neglect. If it is considered that force will be needed to secure entry to premises or gain access to the child, a warrant must be sought from a magistrate, under which a police officer is directed to search for, and may in certain circumstances (but need not) remove the child to a place of safety.

This power, which exists under Section 40, Children and Young Persons Act 1933, was virtually unknown to all our social worker witnesses, until their attention was drawn to it in a "Dear Director" letter issued by the Chief Inspector, Social Services Inspectorate of the DHSS, Mr. W.B. Utting, just before our Inquiry began at the end of June. Our expert witnesses were aware of its existence, but told us that nationally the Order has been little used in recent years, particulary since the 1969 Act. If speed of action is necessary to save life and limb, the police are empowered to effect entry without a warrant, under Section 17(1)(e), Police and Criminal Evidence Act 1984. Woman Police Sergeant Tullock told us that she knew of instances where this relatively new power had been used, adding that in her experience (and that of her colleagues) persuasion of parties to allow access to a child

145

happens in 75% of cases. We shall describe briefly each of these powers, pointing out the problems that each of them presents.

*Place of Safety Orders*

The existing power is a repeat of a provision in the Children and Young Persons Act 1933 which largely reflects the 19th century legislation, with its concentration on the poor, and therefore the most vulnerable to official intervention. Section 28, Children and Young Persons Act 1969 enables the police, the NSPCC, social workers and others concerned with the welfare of children, to remove them to places of safety, although only the police can act without authority of a magistrate.

The Act provides:-

"28. **Detention of child or young person in place of Safety**

(1) If, upon an application to a justice by any person for authority to detain a child or young person and take him to a place of safety, the justice is satisfied that the applicant has reasonable cause to believe that-

(*a*) any of the conditions set out in section 1 (2) (*a*) to (*e*) of this Act is satisfied in respect of the child or young person; or

(*b*) an appropriate court would find the condition set out in section 1 (2) (*b*) of this Act satisfied in respect of him; or

(*c*) the child or young person is about to leave the United Kingdom in contravention of section 25 of the Act of 1933 (which regulates the sending abroad of juvenile entertainers),

the justice may grant the application; and the child or young person in respect of whom an authorisation is issued under this subsection may be detained in a place of safety by virtue of the authorisation for twenty-eight days beginning with the date of authorisation, or for such shorter period beginning with that date as may be specified in the authorisation.

(2) Any constable may detain a child or young person as respects whom the constable has reasonable cause to believe that any of the conditions set out in section 1(2)(*a*) to (*d*) of this Act is satisfied or that an appropriate court would find the condition set out in section 1(2)(*b*) of this Act satisfied or that an offence is being committed under section 10(1) of the Act of 1933 (which penalises a vagrant who takes a juvenile from place to place)."

The scope of the legislation has increased in application, but in spirit and phraseology it reflects the child-rescue philosophy of the late 19th century. The circumstances where removal or detention is permitted are identical to the conditions that justify the making of a Care Order, with the exception of delinquency. Children subjected to a Place of Safety Order are not legally in local authority care; no parental rights or powers are transferred to, or vested in a local authority. Nevertheless the children become the responsibility of local authority Social Services by virtue of Section 73(1)(a), Child Care Act 1980.

An Order under Section 28(1), Children and Young Persons Act 1969 gives authority, under magisterial order, for the child to be detained and taken to a place of safety. The maximum period is for 28 days, but increasingly in recent years, magistrates are making Orders for much lesser periods. Eight days is now the most common period. Under Section 28(2), the police possess the power to take a child to a place of safety for up to a maximum of 8 days. That power is challengeable, on application by the parent or child, under Section 28(5). At the hearing the police are entitled to be present and to adduce evidence why the detention should be continued for the whole period.

The Place of Safety Order does not give authority for premises to be entered and a search made for the child. If that is thought necessary, the application should be for a warrant under Section 40, Children and Young Persons Act 1933. (see below). There has been a considerable body of research evidence that the Place of Safety Orders have been misused; whereas Parliament intended the Order to deal with emergency situations, social workers have used the Order as a holding operation pending the launch of care proceedings.

The stereotype of the "child rescue" situation is that of the dirty, undernourished child, neglected or ill-treated by a mother from whom the child is wrenched screaming and kicking. Such a picture, drawn by the mythologists of the media, are the most exceptional. The circumstances in which Place of Safety Orders are applied for, in fact, range across a whole spectrum of society, with the exception of the middle and upper classes, who by virtue of their comparative affluence and social skills are able to fend off the attentions of welfare authorities who are often intimidated by verbal dexterity and threats of complaint.

*The Tyneside scheme*

We wish to add here a few words about a scheme that is operative in the Newcastle-upon-Tyne area. The clerk to the local justices, Mr. C. Paton Webb, very kindly explained the scheme which he has established in conjunction with the local Social Services.

Whenever a social worker wishes to apply for a Place of Safety Order he is not permitted to apply direct to a magistrate, whatever the time of day or night it is. He must initially contact the justices' clerk or one of his deputies. The clerk then arranges for a suitably qualified magistrate to be made available to hear the application, at which the justices' clerk will be present. It is the practice of the clerks to make every endeavour to make contact with the child's parents, and to arrange, if at all possible, for them to be present at the hearing of the application. While the motive for this practice is highly commendable, we are not at all sure that Parliament intended that a parent should know in advance that an application for a Place of Safety Order was to be made, let alone be present at the hearing.

We think there is every reason why the application, being an emergency procedure, ought not to be jeopardised by any prior knowledge on the part of the parents. The effect of such knowledge might be to put the child severely at risk, because the parents may take evasive action. It may be that the Newcastle experiment has not disclosed any untoward effect as a result of prior notice, but we think it nevertheless has that dangerous potential. **We positively do not recommend a replication of the Tyneside experiment. Our recommendation is that the legislation should provide redress to the parents only after the Place of Safety Order has been made**.

*Section 40, Children and Young Persons Act 1933*

Since this power is grossly under-used, if indeed its existence is known, we need describe only its legislative features. The section provides:-

> "40. **Warrant to search for or remove a child or young person**
>
> (1) If it appears to a justice of the peace on information on oath laid by any person who, in the opinion of the justice, is acting in the interests of a child or young person, that there is reasonable cause to suspect -
>
> (*a*) that the child or young person has been or is being assaulted, ill-treated, or neglected in any place within the jurisdiction of the justice, in a manner likely to cause him unnecessary suffering, or injury to health; or
>
> (*b*) that any offence mentioned in the First Schedule to this Act has been or is being committed in respect of the child or young person,
>
> the justice may issue a warrant authorising any constable named therein to search for the child or young person, and, if it is found that he has been or is being assaulted, ill-treated, or neglected in manner aforesaid, or that any such offence as aforesaid has been or is being committed in respect of him [to take him to a place of safety, or authorising any constable to remove him with or without search to a place of safety, and a child or young person taken to a place of safety in pursuance of such a warrant may be detained there] until he can be brought before a juvenile court.
>
> (2) A justice issuing a warrant under this section may by the same warrant cause any person accused of any offence in respect of the child or young person to be apprehended and brought before a court of summary jurisdiction, and proceedings to be taken against him according to law.
>
> (3) Any constable authorised by warrant under this section to search for any child or young person, or to remove any child or young person with or without search, may enter (if need be by force) any house, building, or other place specified in the warrant, and may remove him therefrom.
>
> (4) Every warrant issued under this section shall be addressed to and executed by a constable, who shall be accompanied by the person laying the information, if that person so desires, unless the justice by whom the warrant is issued otherwise directs, and may also, if the justice by whom the warrant is issued so directs, be accompanied by a duly qualified medical practitioner.

(5) It shall not be necessary in any information on warrant under this section to name the child or young person".

The warrant, which can be applied for, on oath, by any person acting in the interests of a child, may direct a police officer to search for and remove the child to a place of safety. Or it may simply give the police officer some discretion, to the extent that the child need be removed only if it is apparent that the neglect or ill-treatment has taken place. This discretionary power of removal becomes useful where there has been a refusal on the part of the parent to allow anyone access in order to examine the child. The existence of the power can be, and is apparently a powerful persuader to the parent to comply with a request that the child be seen.

The person who applies for the warrant may accompany the police officer, who alone is empowered to execute it, and a doctor may be brought in as well. Thus there is in effect, by implication of the statutory provision, a power to effect a medical examination within the confines of the home. (No such indication is provided in the Place of Safety Order). But it would appear that the parent would have to consent to anything more than a mere observation of the child's body. Even if the removal power is exercised, it is probably not permissible to examine the child medically at the place of safety to which the child has been removed, beyond observation in the course of caring daily for the child.

## Section 17(1)(e), Police and Criminal Evidence Act 1984

This power of the police to enter and search any premises without a warrant for the purpose of saving life or limb is restricted to the case of dire emergency where gross physical child abuse is imminently threatened or is taking place. This statutory power is part of the common law power which the police have always possessed.

# Proposals for Change

We trust that we have sufficiently indicated in outline the limited scope of Social Services' power to back-up their duty to investigate cases of suspected child abuse. It is our concluded view that the present powers are inadequate. We make our proposals for change in an ascending order of interference with parental rights.

## Power to Enter and Inspect

Section 40, Children and Young Persons Act 1933 (as we have indicated) enables social workers to apply to a magistrate for a warrant authorising a police officer to search for a child, and, if the child is found to be ill-treated or neglected, take him to a place of safety. Social workers have felt reluctant to use this power - even if they have been aware of its existence, which many have not - except where they are absolutely certain that such a step is necessary. Since there is an unwillingness often to involve the police, social workers will tend to use their own indirect power of removal and detention of a child via the Place of Safety Order. We do not quarrel with their preference, except that we would wish that social workers more frequently, at an early stage, inform the police of any case of suspected child abuse.

It has been represented to us that what is needed is a power of first resort, as part of the local authority's duty to investigate suspicions of child abuse. Social workers, as was the case of Mrs. Swinburne and Ms Streeter on 7 March 1986, need to cross the doorstep, in their own right and without having to go to a magistrate, for the purpose of seeing the child. We have given careful consideration to this question, since it involves an invasion of privacy. We recall Mr. Hall mouthing the old adage, in relation to his repulse of Mr. Ruddock on 14 April when he was seeking access to Kimberley, that an Englishman's home is his castle. *Sotto voce*, we muttered to each other, that the Carlile Castle contained a dungeon in which Kimberley was the tortured prisoner. Whose rights were being protected in that situation? Certainly not Kimberley's rights. Her right was to expect help from the welfare authorities who alone could supply the requisite protection from the unspeakable assaults upon her body.

To provide for a power to enter and search (including the power to interview and examine) - but *not* to remove, other than by way of a Place of Safety Order (or its proposed successor) - would not be a novel departure in our law. Such a provision exists in the mental health legislation. Section 115, Mental Health Act 1983 (replacing, in substance, Section 22, Mental Health Act 1959) provides that an approved social worker of a local authority may at all reasonable times enter and inspect any premises (other than a hospital) in the area of the local authority in which a mentally disordered patient is living, if the approved social worker has reasonable cause to believe that the patient is *not under proper care* (italics supplied).

The rationale of that power may be that a mentally disordered patient needs to be protected from the potential danger to himself or to others living in the same household, which is the basis of any compulsory admission to a mental hospital. But since the power is designed to ensure that the mentally disordered patient is being properly cared for, the rationale of the power must be for the protection of vulnerable, dependant persons, such as the mentally disordered. It is that latter concept that applies, with like force, to other vulnerable, dependent persons, such as children at risk of abuse. We, therefore, see no objection in principle to a similar provision in the child care legislation, subject to certain specific safeguards.

We think that the safeguards should be : a) only a social worker designated by the local authority as a child care officer should have the right of entry, and we think that only field social workers who have been more than 2 years in post should qualify; b) the social worker must produce, if asked to do so, some authenticated document indicating that he or she is a designated social worker; c) that the parent of the child is entitled to be present at any interview or examination (which shall not include anything more than an observation of the child's body); and d) that the test for exercising the power to enter and inspect should be a stringent one. We would add that the power should exist automatically if the child is in the care of the local authority, but is home-on-trial, or is under a Supervision Order. Where there is no statutory power in relation to the child, we are more hesitant about the right of access to a child suspected of being abused. We incline towards the conferment of the right, but **recommend that there is a process of consultation before**

**legislation is proposed**. We set out below a draft of the clause, based on the mental health provisions, that we think Parliament might find helpful. **We recommend also that the Secretary of State should, in any future legislation, be given the power to extend the right of access to officers of the NSPCC.**

## Clause 1: Power to Enter and Inspect

A social worker of a local Social Services authority who is designated a child care officer may at all reasonable times after providing, if called to do so, some duly authenticated document showing that he is such a social worker, enter and inspect any premises (not being a hospital) in the area of that authority in which a child or young person is living, and interview and examine such a child or young person, if either the child is in the care or supervision of such local authority, or if such a social worker has reasonable cause to believe that the health, safety or welfare of the child of young person is seriously at risk.

## Clause 2 : Obstruction

(1) Any person who without reasonable cause -

(*a*) refuses to allow entry and inspection of any premises; or

(*b*) refuses to allow access to, interviewing or examination of any child or young person by a person authorised in that behalf or under the previous clause; or

(*c*) refuses to produce for the inspection of any person so authorised any document or record the production of which is duly required by him; or

(*d*) otherwise obstructs any such person in the exercise of his function;

Shall be guilty of an offence

(2) Without prejudice to the generality of sub-clause (1) above, any person may insist on being present, and cannot be requested to withdraw by a person authorised by or under clause 1 to interview or examine a person.

(3) Any person guilty of an offence under sub-clause (1) above should be liable on summary conviction to imprisonment for a term not exceeding three months or to a fine not exceeding level 4 on the standard scale, or to both.

*Emergency Protection Orders*

The Government's White Paper, The Law on Child Care and Family Services proposes (paragraph 46) that in place of the present Place of Safety Order, lasting up to a maximum of 28 days, there should be an Emergency Protection Order for 8 days only. In exceptional circumstances, an applicant would be permitted to apply for an extension of the Order for a further period of up to 7 days, to provide continued protection for the child. On that occasion, the law will provide an opportunity for the parents or the child to challenge the extension, such a challenge being based on the ground that there is no risk to the child which justifies an extension. The existing provision for a Place of Safety Order contains no specific right to challenge the Order. It is made by any person *ex parte* - usually by a social worker or NSPCC officer to a magistrate, out of court hours and in the magistrate's private residence without the presence of a justices' clerk. (We have described earlier a system that operates in Tyneside, which, while no doubt admirable in conception, we do not think is appropriate for nationwide application).

The Place of Safety Order (and its proposed replacement) is indisputably severe in its effect. It sanctions the removal and detention of the child for the period of the Order, with no ostensible redress to the child, or more particularly to the parent. The physical separation, even for the most limited period of 8 days, is potentially traumatic. It is certainly an infringement of liberty that would hardly be tolerated in the criminal justice system without adequate judicial safeguards. It is, of course, intended to meet a drastic situation urgently, in order to protect a child from serious risk from parental abuse.

There can be little doubt that a Place of Safety Order is susceptible to habeas corpus proceedings, in which the applicant for the Order and the magistrate would have to sustain its legal validity. And there are good grounds for thinking that judicial reviews would lie to challenge the making of the Order. But these procedures are limited to ensuring the legal validity of the Order; they also have to be brought in the High Court.

Recently, the High Court entertained an application for judicial review by a Chief Constable, for an order that he was entitled to be present at the hearing of an application by a parent against a police Place of Safety Order under Section 28(5) Children and Young Persons Act 1969. It is a truism that judicial review is primarily a safeguard against procedural impropriety, and will not ordinarily permit the court to review the decision on its merits, but is confined to ensuring that procedurally the decision was made lawfully, reasonably and fairly. There is some scope for a review on the merits, in the very limited sense that it must not be a decision which no reasonable tribunal could make.

The mischief of the present law - and its perpetuation under the proposed Emergency Protection Order - is that the child can be whisked away from its parents and home without the parents being able to argue the case for non-removal. The test which the applicant has to meet, it is true, is a severe one: Has the applicant-social worker "reasonable cause to believe" that the criteria for removal and detention are satisfied? The statutory provision would seem to require not only that the applicant has reasonable cause to believe, but also that he or she actually does believe[1].

This has two important consequences. First, an applicant who is in doubt whether the test has been satisfied on the evidence before him cannot, properly, put such evidence before the court and ask it to make the judgment whether the child is at risk.

This was the very reason Ms Streeter gave to us for discarding the idea of applying for a Place of Safety Order on 7 March; and we think that she was

---

[1] Halsbury's Statutes, 4th Ed., Volume 6, p.27 cites, in a footnote, cases to support that proposition.

behaving most correctly in concluding that if (as was the case) she was not satisfied that she had reasonable cause to believe that Kimberley was in danger, she could not ask a magistrate to substitute the court's view for hers.

Second, although the test for applying is stringent (perhaps overly strict), we think, having heard expert witnesses on the research into Place of Safety Orders (which has revealed considerable evidence of misuse of the Order), that some applicants will apply rather more readily than the strict letter of the law allows.

Both these considerations are worrying, in circumstances where the parent is remediless to reverse the making of the Order. We note that in the Beckford report it was stated that the Place of Safety Order, like any other Order of a court made *ex parte* - that is, in the absence of the party whose rights and interests are affected - can be discharged, on application to the court which first made it. Whether this statement is correct or not depends upon the construction of Section 28(1), Children and Young Persons Act 1969 which provides the power to any person to apply for a Place of Safety Order without giving any notice to the parent (or child, if it is old enough to understand).

The legislation is silent. It clearly gives no right of appeal: From which it would be argued that, by implication, the decision should remain unchallengeable. That would appear to be the view of the Government, when in the White Paper it declares positively that under the new Emergency Protection Order the initial Order would be unchallengeable, but that any extension of the Order would be susceptible to challenge in the courts.

Fairness, we think, demands that the party whose rights are affected should be entitled to be heard, immediately after the Order has been made and the child removed to and detained at a place of safety. **We recommend accordingly, that the new provisions for an Emergency Protection Order should contain a requirement that on obtaining the Order the applicant must forthwith give notice of the Order to the parent (and child, where appropriate) and indicate the right to ask the court to review the grounds of the application.** (The new Emergency Protection Order will, it seems, carry with it specific obligations to notify the parents, but without any right of redress to the parent). We agree with the White Paper (paragraph 45) that the Emergency Protection Order should be made where the magistrate is satisfied that the applicant had reasonable cause to believe that the child's health or well-being is likely to be impaired unless the child is immediately removed to, or detained in a place of protection for the duration of the Order.

We would endorse what the Beckford report said, that where the child is already in a place of protection (such as a hospital) no Emergency Protection Order should be made unless the magistrate is satisfied that there is reasonable cause to believe that, without the Order, the parent would be likely to remove the child from the place of protection.

### Child Assessment Order

The White Paper acknowledges (para 47) a powerful suggestion, made to the Government during the consultative process of its Child Care Law

Review, that a new type of Order is appropriate in circumstances where removing the child would be too drastic a step, but where there is nevertheless serious, although not urgent, concern about the health and well-being of the child - for example, where there is difficulty in gaining access to see the child. The Government thought that such lesser Order than the power to remove and detain could consistently be encompassed by the Emergency Protection Order. A child need not in fact be removed under the Order if, when seen by the applicant for the Order, this proves to be unnecessary. We do not agree that the lesser intervention in the child's life is catered for within the confines of the Emergency Protection Order. The case under our Inquiry discloses the desirability and need for a separate and distinct Order, which we call a Child Assessment Order.

A new and separate Order would meet all the difficulties experienced with the Place of Safety Order. First, its prime virtue would be that it would partake of none of the coercive nature of a removal and detention of a child from the child's parents and home. It would be an Order, obtainable from a magistrate, that the parent bring the child, within a very short period of time, to a clinic or to a general practitioner.

We think that it should not only be for medical examination but also for a developmental assessment in the case of a child under the age of five. We shall indicate hereafter how we would see the Order working in practice.

Second, since the Order would not physically order the detachment of the child from its parents, there should be no question of family trauma. The test for such an Order could, therefore, be less stringent than that for the Emergency Protection Order.

Third, there would be none of the inaptness of the Order that has emerged from misuse of the Place of Safety Order in the past. The only worry that we entertain is whether there might not be a kind of bureaucratic magnetism about the lesser Order. What we fear might happen is that social workers would too readily opt for the Child Assessment Order in circumstances where their clear duty would be to apply for an Emergency Protection Order. This real danger can be countered by Social Services Directorates issuing clear instructions about the proper use of the two discrete orders. So long as social workers understand the different functions, there ought not to be any confusion about their use.

The fourth matter pertains to the purpose of the Child Assessment Order. All our witnesses (with some qualification from Mr. John Pickett of the NSPCC) and all the parties before us (again with a mild reservation from BASW) were adamant in saying that such an Order, if it had existed in 1986, would have been exactly what was called for to deal with the case of Kimberley Carlile.

From 10 March onwards both Mr. Ruddock and Miss Reader were striving to persuade Mrs. Carlile to get Kimberley seen (and, to some extent Z) either by the GP, the health visitor or at the health clinic. They thought then that their only means was either persuasion, or a Place of Safety Order. (The initial threat of involving the police fell away, and there was at that time total ignorance within Greenwich Social Services of the power to apply for a police warrant to search and inspect the Carlile home under Section 40, Children and Young Persons Act 1933). And in Greenwich at least, there was an opinion - which we think is correct - from the legal department of the Borough Council that a medical examination could not be effected as an adjunct to a Place of Safety Order. We have dealt earlier with our view that unless mere observation of a child's body (including undressing) as an adjunct to caring for a child in a place of safety, is permissible, anything more by way of examination - X-rays, blood tests or the like - would not be lawful, without the parent's consent. We think that it is unfortunate that such an important power in the process of child protection should be riddled with doubt.

We are clear that the new Emergency Protection Order should contain a specific provision allowing for a medical examination, including a developmental assessment. But we think that there is still room for the separate Child Assessment Order.

We think that the criterion for making a Child Assessment Order can properly be broader and more interventionist in its scope. The applicant should simply have to satisfy the magistrate that he or she believes that the health, safety or welfare of the child may be at risk, coupled with a single refusal to produce the child on request for such examination. To translate that into practical terms, in relation to the case of Kimberley Carlile, we think that Mr. Ruddock would have been in a perfect position to apply for such an Order at any time after 10 March, had such a legal power existed. It could even have been obtained by Mrs. Swinburne and Ms Streeter after their failure to see Kimberley on 7 March.

We have considered carefully whether, like the Place of Safety Order (and its projected successor, the Emergency Protection Order) *any person* should be able to apply. Because the Child Assessment Order will be more readily obtainable and relates to attendance within the Health Authorities' purview, we think that there should be a restriction on the persons who can apply. Rather than name them in the statutory provision, as with the nomination of the NSPCC as an authority that can apply for a Care Order, **we recommend that the Secretary of State should authorise, by regulations under the statute, the classes of persons who could apply.** We would suggest that they be social workers, designated as child care officers, health visitors, officers of the NSPCC, a police officer not below the rank of inspector, and a medical practitioner.

**We recommend that the Order should be specific as to the time and place of examination.** It should permit X-rays, blood tests and intimate examination - this particularly in view of the emerging worries over child sex abuse. Such intimate examination would be allowable only after the parent has had an opportunity to make representations why no intimate examination should take place. If the parent objects to such an examination, such objection should be overridden only in exceptional circumstances.

We do not see why, in the case where the only question is whether the child has been sexually abused (and there is ordinarily no urgent need for an intimate examination) there should not be some special arrangement for a hearing before a magistrate.

The Child Assessment Order would have to be served on the parent of the child. We think it should be served on the parent by the police. Failure to comply with the Order will inevitably lead to either an Emergency Protection Order or the lesser Order contained in Section 40, Children and Young Persons Act 1933.

If the examination discloses a case of child abuse, the Health Authorities should have power there and then to detain the child in a place of protection and either they or Social Services would be under a duty to apply for an Emergency Protection Order and, if not already done, convene a case conference with a view to applying for a Care Order.

*Section 40, Children and Young Persons Act 1933*

We think that it is desirable to retain this power, over and above the Child Assessment Order. It provides a convenient option to Social Services and Health Authorities, short of a complete removal of the child, where a Child Assessment Order is not complied with, or where the medical examination can conveniently be conducted in the home and without the necessity of the child being taken to a clinic or doctor's surgery. We have noted that, in practice, warrants are often executed under Section 40 by the police accompanied by a medical practitioner.

There is nothing in the statutory provision indicating one way or the other whether such a power to examine medically exists. **We recommend that the law should provide that when issuing the warrant a magistrate should be empowered to authorise a medical practitioner to conduct a medical examination**. It would be desirable if on such occasions the medical practitioner had some expertise in child health.

We think that the Order should indicate whether that examination includes an intimate examination of the child's body: in which case the parent must be told that he or she may object to such intimate examination. If it is decided to not permit such an examination, the matter must come back to the magistrate for an *inter partes* hearing. The magistrate alone can override the parent's objection.

## Conclusion

In summary, **we recommend, in ascending order of interference with rights, a bunch of Orders relating both to the investigation of cases of child abuse and to immediate action where child abuse is suspected:**

(*a*) A power to enter and inspect premises (including a right to interview and examine the child) where a child is living and is thought to be at risk, coupled with a right to see the child.

(*b*) A Child Assessment Order for the production of the child at a clinic for medical examination.

(c) A warrant to search for or remove a child - a re-enactment, with amendment, of Section 40, Children and Young Persons Act 1933.

(d) An Emergency Protection Order, to replace, with modifications, the Place of Safety Order.

(e) A police officer's right of entry and search without warrant under Section 17(1)(e), Police and Criminal Evidence Act 1984 to safe life or limb.

We do not forget that there is always available the ability to make a child a ward of court, by initiating action in the High Court.

# CHAPTER 26

# INFORMATION SYSTEMS AND INTER-AUTHORITY SOCIAL SERVICES' RELATIONSHIPS[1]

The Department of Health and Social Security (DHSS), in its booklet, *Child Abuse* (1981) declared that "efficiency in recording, transmitting and sharing information is an essential and integral part of professional practice". Two years later, the British Association of Social Workers reported that a "rapid reappraisal of recording systems in social work is needed". In spite of both these authoritative sources emphasising the need for an efficient information system, the report of the Panel of Inquiry into the circumstances surrounding the death of Jasmine Beckford in December 1985 showed clearly that no system of exchanging information among the relevant agencies existed in the case of the Beckford children; from the evidence given to that Inquiry it could be inferred that no system existed at all. The DHSS draft circular of April 1986, *Child Abuse: Working Together for the Protection of Children*, declared that the Secretary of State regarded the statutory duty in Section 22 of the National Health Service Act 1977, for Health Authorities and Local Authorities to co-operate, as requiring the staff of those authorities to consult appropriately and to assist as necessary in the supply of relevant advice and information. The statutory duty is framed in such general and imprecise terms that it does not instinctively compel the degree of collaboration that is clearly required.

Throughout this report we have pointed to a number of instances where the principles of an information service were breached. We think it is opportune to underline the pressing need to establish and maintain an efficient information system for the child protection service, and to indicate what principles apply.

It is relatively easy to identify the organisation pursuing the commercial objective of profit; the individual company is readily understood and accepted. Organisations pursuing social objectives are not only more difficult to identify, but are also often not accepted as being subject to the same criteria. We think that, while the defined objective of a group is social rather than economic, the same organisational criteria apply, the more important element being the information system which must serve the organisation's objective.

An information system is simply stated. It is the manner in which both facts and ideas flow through the organisation. The flow of the information must be both osmotic and symbiotic. It must be diffused through every part of the organisation and it must be shared through co-operative effort. The facts and ideas may emanate from outside the organisation or be introduced by any of the component parts within the organisation. An information

---

[1] For the writing of this chapter we have relied heavily on an essay, *Information Systems in Child Care* by Mr. Ron Pluck, lecturer in the Department of Social Policy, Royal Holloway and Bedford New College, in a policy paper, *After Beckford?*, published by that Department.

system that might profitably be constructed in the organisation of child protection would contain the following stages: a) the initiating report – anonymous telephone calls, hospitalisations, reports from police or general practitioners or through the school health service; b) the investigation – by Social Services Departments of local authorities, NSPCC or the police; c) action – Social Services and the other agencies; and d) control – by Social Services and the courts. For the system to be efficient, information must continue to circulate at each stage of the process of protection and to all the agencies involved, until a conclusion is reached by the attainment of the child's safety. It is obviously unsatisfactory if any component of the organisation is not in full possession of all the available information at an early stage of the process until a satisfactory conclusion is reached. The only limitation on complete disclosure of information is the material that may attract confidentiality, and for the reasons we gave in Chapter 2 we do not think even this presents any great difficulty.

All information systems require four main elements. First, there must be a precisely defined objective, clearly understood by everyone within the ambit of the child protection service (the organisation). In the management of the existing child abuse system the objective is clear – the safety of the child. In the Beckford case there emerged an objective which was related to the restoration of the family unit by returning the children to it. This proved to be disasterous to Jasmine Beckford. We do not think that there can now be any doubt that the focus will be primarily on the child.

Second, the components of the child abuse system must be clearly identified, and their existence as part of that system must be fully recognised and accepted by all the other components. This must include awareness by individuals that they are a responsible part of the system. A teacher, a general practitioner or a police officer is as much involved in child protection as are the more centrally involved social workers and health visitors; the former must feel that they are an integral part of the system. That applies at every stage, and not just within the case conference setting.

Third, the structure of the system which links the component parts together must also be clearly defined. This is necessary in two respects: a) to create a hierachy in order to demonstrate who initiates what kind of action; there was, at least, a hierachial arrangement, in that Greenwich Social Services was the main repository of information from October 1985 – June 1986; and b) to ensure that all information flows freely and quickly throughout the system, and is readily available to all components. In this case the information did not always flow freely – for example, the incomplete information from the general practitioners to Greenwich Social Services on 12 March 1986 about the visit of Kimberley on 11 November 1985. It also did not flow quickly, as, for example, the transfer of health records from Wirral Health Authority to Greenwich Health Authority in early 1986 demonstrated. By no means was all the information that had been assembled in one or other of the component parts shared among all the component parts.

Fourth, related to the third main element is the behaviour of the system, that is to say, how the system responds to the input of data and to its environment. Doctors, health visitors, and social workers have a professional relationship with their patients/clients. It is important to know exactly how they interpret their individual professionalism in the context of a case of child abuse. So long as some agencies have no statutory duty in relation to child protection, it is important to know whether a suspected case of child abuse will result in action by the agency without statutory responsibility, with regard to the welfare of the family, either directly or indirectly, or by returning and passing information to the component that does bear a statutory responsibility, such as a local authority. One example suffices to make the point. Dr. Mahesh did not notify any other agency of the referral on 11 November 1985 of Kimberley Carlile to the Brook Hospital "for speech therapy".

Information systems exist in some form in every organisation. It did exist, in some ill-functioning form, in the case of Kimberley Carlile during the period from October 1985 - June 1986. It existed in a similarly defective form in the case of the Carlile family for the period, May 1982 - October 1985. It was virtually non-existent in respect of two components of a child protection service - namely, as between Wirral Social Services and Greenwich Social Services with respect to pre-October 1985. **We recommend that urgent consideration be given to the establishment of a child protection information system as between Social Services Departments of all local authorities in England and Wales.** We exclude Scotland and Northern Ireland, because we are insufficiently conversant with the child care and child health systems in those two parts of the United Kingdom to feel competent to pronounce in respect of them. But we would urge that those responsible for those two parts of the United Kingdom do join in the discussions for an information system.

The creation of an information system is necessary for the organisation within its own sphere of operation. It can be established in the stages of analysis, design and implementation. We think that this is a task eminently suited to the role of Area Review Committees. **We recommend that each Area Review Committee undertakes forthwith, under the auspices of the DHSS, a study of the needs in its area, with a view to establishing an information system.** The studies should cover both manual techniques and mechanical and electronic aids. The principles we have outlined for an information system can be followed by all individuals without any specific aids. But computerised methods should relieve some of the pressures of work.

# CHAPTER 27

# AREA REVIEW COMMITTEES

Following the Maria Colwell Report in 1974 it has been Government policy that a multi-disciplinary approach to the management of the child abuse system was essential. To that end, much emphasis has been placed on the need to ensure that relevant information about abused children, or those suspected of being abused, should be brought together for the purposes of assessment and planning intervention. In giving effect to these purposes, the DHSS recommended the establishment of Area Review Committees, where they did not already exist. Among their tasks, these Committees were charged with the duty of advising on the formulation of local practice and procedures to be followed in the detailed management of cases, and to approve written instructions defining the various duties of all personnel involved with any aspect of these cases. From their inception, the Area Review Committees have included social work managers, community health paediatricians, GPs, health visitors and nursing officers, educationists, NSPCC officers, police officers and lawyers.

Area Review Committees thus represent the only part of the present management of the child abuse system which is a formalised, constant feature of the multi-disciplinary function. Since we have received evidence about the functioning of the Greenwich Area Review Committee, which came into separate existence in 1981 after being part of the Greenwich and Bexley Area Committee, we have felt able to come to some conclusions about the value and effectiveness of an Area Review Committee.

We were encouraged to study the workings of the Greenwich Area Review Committee, since in June 1986 the Social Services Inspectorate of the DHSS, in a report to the London Borough of Greenwich, made an adverse comment. The report stated:

"Although it has not been possible to discuss the matter with the key people involved, the Area Review Committee *seems to be a passive group, without any clear strategy* [emphasis supplied] and with initiatives being mainly as a result of individual drive - particularly through the Child Abuse Co-ordinator".

We have heard evidence from the Child Abuse Co-ordinator at the relevant time, Mrs. Jean Gabbott. We endorse the view, expressed by Mr. Devaux (who was Chairman of the Area Review Committee from 1981 until a few months ago, when he stepped down from the chairmanship to attend to the preparations for our Inquiry) that "without her support it would have been very difficult for us to do the things we have done during the past four years". He listed the delicate issue of participation of parents in case conferences, the study of procedures preparatory to an update of the child abuse procedure which was last issued in 1982, and making contact with the medical authorities about disseminating the work of the Area Review Committee.

The Social Services Inspectorate noted in its report that "Social workers were aware of the Child Abuse procedures issued by the Area Review

Committee in 1982". But that was not the case in respect of other disciplines. Dr. Mahesh, the general practitioner, said he was "not aware of the Greenwich Area Review Committee". Mr. D.F. Lacey, the Acting Administrator, Greenwich and Bexley Family Practitioner Committee, told us that any copies that had been supplied to him would have been distributed to general practitioners, but he could not say whether every G.P. now had a copy. The school nurse said she had not seen the Area Review Committee's procedure guide. Neither it seems had the Education Welfare Officer, although the procedures guide states that "when a possible case of abuse is brought to the attention of the Education Welfare Officer he/she should ensure above procedures have been carried out, advising teachers on aspects if need be". Yet the introduction to the procedures guide contained a statement from the Chairman : "All principal agencies have collaborated in the production of the guide, and it is hoped that workers in the field will find it of great benefit. I should be grateful if you would ensure that the guide is kept in a prominent position and is readily available to all staff".

From the evidence, it would appear that not everyone who should be in possession of the procedures guide in fact had a copy or had seen it, or was aware of its existence. We did not explore the question of where in the system management responsibility for this failing lies. But **we recommend that when the revised procedures guide is published in the near future (as we are assured it will be) the Area Review Committee should take steps to ensure its efficient dissemination among all relevant personnel.**

We have little doubt that part of the problem about distribution (as indeed there is about all other activities of the Area Review Committee), stems from the lack of funding for the operation of the Area Review Committee. We have been told that in the early years of the Area Review Committee a child abuse news sheet was published. There were annual reports issued until 1984; and several other activities, such as a publicity campaign and consultative papers, were undertaken. All of them suffered in some way from lack of financial resources. The newsletter ceased to be issued, and there have been no recent annual reports. A revised and updated version of the procedures guide was held up, in part due to lack of funds.

We sympathise with Mr. Devaux who described, with justified feeling, his frustration in having to go cap in hand for money to finance as crucial a document as the procedures guide, let alone for the other variegated activities. If the Area Review Committee is going to perform the pivotal role in the management of the child abuse system it is imperative that it is properly funded. **We recommend that Health Authorities and Social Services should include in their budgets an item appropriating sufficient funds for the Area Review Committee to carry out its functions.**

The current procedures guide is dated March 1982. It is long overdue for revision. Some thought was given in 1984 to revising it, but since that date there has been a huge amount of fresh thinking about child abuse. There has been the DHSS's Child Care Law Review in 1986 (followed by the White Paper), the Beckford Report (*A Child In Trust*) and the BASW procedures in 1985. Greenwich was itself the subject of inspection by the Social Services

Inspectorate in 1985/1986. The mere delay in time might appear to reflect muddled incompetence. We acquit the Committee of any such charge. Like the Social Services Inspectorate, we have not heard the key personnel in the Area Review Committee (except, of course, Mr. Devaux and Mrs. Gabbott, both of whom displayed a keen awareness of the limitations that they worked under and a consequential handicap in what could be achieved). We do not, therefore, feel able to pronounce upon the efficiency or effectiveness of the Area Review Committee. But we should be less than fair if we do not say that we feel the Inspectorate was a little harsh in its verdict. We did not gain the impression of pure passivity on the part of the Area Review Committee, although we readily acknowledge that it has not performed its pivotal role in the management of the child protection system.

We have given some thought, however, to the future of Area Review Committees. We note that in the draft circular from the DHSS of April 1986, *Child Abuse: Working Together for the Protection of Children*, it is recommended that, with a view to improving the effectiveness in the formal arrangements for policies and procedures for inter-agencies co-operation, the Area Review Committees should be re-designated Joint Child Abuse Committees which would be accountable to the Joint Consultative Committee for the area. The Joint Consultative Committee is a creature of the legislation providing for the National Health Service, and is composed of those engaged in supplying Health Services and Social Services. To make the Area Review Committees accountable in matters calling for joint planning between the health and local authorities will, in our view, do nothing more than impose another layer of unproductive consultation and advice. It will not strengthen the multi-disciplinary management of the child abuse system. To do that it will be necessary to provide some executive power. And that means beginning with the Area Review Committees.

We have indicated in Chapter 24 that we favour either a single statutory authority - a child protection service - or a shared responsibility. If the latter is the preferred choice, it could conveniently be organised around an Area Review Committee which had allocated to it the responsibility for organising the child protection service in its area, ensuring that all the agencies carried the legal responsibilities for investigating cases of child abuse, for taking appropriate action and for executing the orders of the courts.

# CHAPTER 28

# ROLE OF OTHER AGENCIES

## Health Visiting Service

At present there is no statutory definition of the role of the Health Visitor. The former statutory body for health visiting, the Council for the Education and Training of Health Visitors, (CETHV), defined the function of a health visitor as: "The prevention of mental, physical and emotional ill health and its consequences; early detection of ill health and surveillance of high risk groups; the recognition and identification of need and mobilization of appropriate resources where necessary; health teaching; provision of care including support during periods of stress, and advice and guidance in cases of illness as well as the care and management of young children". It is still a valid definition. It reflects the traditional view that health visiting is pro-active and oriented towards prevention and education. It does not reflect a reactive and crisis intervention role. We explain why, sometimes, health visitors are required to abandon their traditional function, in order to protect a child at risk.

Suitable, experienced post basic-qualified nurses compete for health visitor training in colleges or universities. Although there is a national syllabus, training institutions are given a considerable degree of freedom regarding the course detail. Child abuse is not specified as a separate subject, but it is implicit in the main subject areas. Relatively few institutions impart much knowledge of child care law. **We recommend that all health visitor training courses provide students with training in child protection as a separate subject**.

Theory and practice are integrated during practical placements throughout the academic year and are then consolidated during a final three months when students work with a small caseload under supervision. All nurses have a responsibility to keep themselves up-to-date in their sphere of work. However, child abuse is a complex subject, and its management requires a multi-disciplinary approach. **We recommend that employing authorities take on board the need to ensure staff have adequate knowledge of the subject and of the importance of inter-agency co-operation, possibly by shared learning**.

Health visitors are concerned with all individuals and families within a geographical area of GP practice list, but have no right of entry to households and depend on the consumer's perception of a friendly relationship for their ability to gain access and discharge their duty. A routinely authoritarian stance would be counter-productive to the acceptance of advice, and would change the whole ethos of primary prevention. Apart from meeting health visiting objectives, home visiting allows explanation in informal surroundings of what families may expect from the service. Miss Willis, Assistant General Secretary to the Health Visitors Association, neatly described the risk of over-dependence on a relationship: "A relationship which does not allow an explanation of the less attractive and more sensitive areas of the health visitor's role is illusory and may be an impediment which blunts that critical faculty of perceiving the true situation rather than what is presented".

A well developed professional scepticism is healthy, even essential. It must be recognised that in cases of child abuse, members of the household can be very manipulative and plausible in their explanations of non-accidental injuries to children. Miss Reader was diverted from the prime objective of ensuring the immediate safety and well-being of Kimberley, by attaching undue importance to the preservation of her future working relationship with Mrs. Carlile who was expecting another baby.

It is well documented that the events during a child's early years have a lasting effect and set the pattern for adult life. This fact influences priority being given to ante-natal mothers and children under 5 years old - *all* children, not just those with problems. The emphasis of health visiting is on health surveillance, prevention and education. Such a wide remit does not permit health visitors to undertake substantial, intensive casework. Time spent on unplanned and crisis work detracts from the routine nature of their duties and disables them in fulfilling their professional obligations to unabused children.

Every professional person who is involved with children has a duty to intervene to protect a child. Health visitors are in the unique position of visiting all homes with young children. They must be alert to the possibility of child abuse and refer potential and actual cases appropriately. Communication must extend at least to Social Services, the medical officer, the nurse manager and the family doctor who has overall responsibility for the health of the child. This does not breach the requirements of confidentiality, and is covered by the statement of the United Kingdom Central Council for Nursing, Midwifery and Health Visiting (the successor to CETHV), that "information must not be divulged unless judged necessary to discharge her [the nurse's] professional responsibility to the patient/client".

To practice effectively, health visitors must have a clear understanding of their own role and responsibility and those of other workers to enable appropriate information to be communicated, understood and acted upon. Health visiting advice is not intended to be aimed exclusively at the carers of children; it must be extended in the form of sharing and interpreting information with other agencies and include a professional opinion on the future course of action. Ongoing work with cases of suspected and actual child abuse must be in collaboration with other agencies, particularly Social Services who bear the statutory duty and exercise the statutory power in relation to child care. Regular health surveillance, including developmental assessments with the plotting of vital measurements on centile charts, is essential. The latter is not a luxury, but forms a permanent basic record of a child's progress.

The fact that a child is under the supervision or in the care of another agency does not displace the continuing need for health surveillance. Indeed, it should be the signal for a heightened level of service, as there must have been sound reason for the disruption of the family. Apart from attending the two case conferences in 1984, following Kimberley's first reception into care,

Wirral health visitors appear to have made no effort to see her, or verify her health status at any time after March 1984.

Health visiting practice demands assessment of need and the formation of child care objectives. This involves actively seeking out known health and social records to provide a history, and analysing the information. Following assessment, a health care plan must be recorded with an accompanying timescale. Ongoing surveillance enables evaluation of the care given, and necessary modification to be made to the plan. This also serves the purpose of drawing attention to any deflection from the pre-set aims and objectives. No health care plan was ever made for Kimberley.

Initial suspicion of child abuse should automatically necessitate a medical examination and the starting of a "concern sheet" which will form a composite picture. It is obligatory that accurate pertinent records are kept and the health status of individuals and their levels of functioning within the family detailed, as well as being descriptive of the home and social environment.

Health visitors, as we have indicated above, are not in a position to be key workers, since intensive case work would distract them from work with non-abused children and from other aspects of health visiting work. In the interests of the child, however, where other agencies are not acceptable to the family, she may be the prime worker. More commonly, a social worker is allocated to the case, and the health visitor must collaborate by sharing information, reporting changes, advising on possible courses of action and participating in joint visits, where and when there are immediate health implications. Attendance at case conferences provides the opportunity to share and appraise critically each others' information and perception of the family under discussion.

Full inter-agency co-operation, which is a reality and not just a concept, is vital to the protection of children. And that means that on occasions a health visitor may have to engage in crisis intervention. Any definition of health visiting should include this aspect of a child protection service as part of the health visitor's preventive function.

## School and education welfare services

Greenwich schools are within the jurisdiction of the Inner London Education Authority (ILEA) where the incidence of social deprivation, assessed by the density of population, range of different native languages, number of single-parent familes, is higher than the national average.

The local housing policy results in many people who have been homeless in London being re-housed in Greenwich, so causing a concentration of vulnerable people living in the area. This exerts exceptional pressure on the statutory agencies, including that of education.

Due to the high proportion of lone parents, and of children aged under 5 years, ILEA has appointed a pre-school development officer who is working closely with Social Services, looking at the siting of nursery provision. Mr. Hayter, Headteacher of Wingfield School, told us that he used to do some direct teaching, but the time which he allocated to this has now been taken up with dealing with social problems. The weekly visit by Ms Gregory, education welfare officer to Wingfield School, was extended with a meeting with staff, and included Ms Roper, social worker, once a month, as an acknowledgement of, and an attempt to grapple with the social issues. This has proved to be a valuable liaison link between the school and Social Services. The medical officer at the time these meetings were set up was unable to accept the invitation to participate, due to his other commitments; and Dr. Kamalanathan told us that, although he was unaware of the meetings, he would not have been able to attend anyhow. The invitation was not extended to the school nurse, but this is now being considered. Each member of this liaison group raises children about whom they are concerned. The outcome of the ensuing discussion is taken back by the participants to their respective organisations.

A nurture group within Wingfield School provides concentrated teacher-attention to a very few children at a time, when they have behavioural or academic difficulties. X was originally included in such a group because of his immaturity and attention-seeking ways, but after his allegation on 9 January 1986, that he was thrown across the room by his stepfather, it also provided better opportunity to observe him more closely and to give him the chance to talk more freely.

Both Wingfield and Henwick Schools have a nursery class. When Mr. Hayter was requested by Social Services in March 1986 to provide a place for Kimberley, he did so directly, in spite of a long waiting list. We were glad to hear that a second nursery class is to be opened in his school in the autumn of 1987. Two invitations offering a nursery place for Kimberley were sent to the parents, but there was no response. Education authorities do not have the right to enforce attendance of children under the age of 5 years. When X and Y were moved at their parents' insistence to Henwick School, Mrs. Gatehouse, Headteacher, also offered a place for Kimberley, but this too was rejected.

After X had spoken of the incident of 9 January, he was included in the internal monitoring system in school. There were about 15 children being monitored at this time for a variety of reasons, including possible child abuse. Monitoring - an elusive word that means different things to different people - included making a daily record of any unexplained significant changes in the child's physical appearance and attitude, and being receptive to his conversation. In relation to X, the staff were also being watchful of Mrs. Carlile and Mr. Hall when they came to deliver the children to school, or to collect them, with regard to their attitude and the relationship between them and X.

Although we were told that the education welfare services and Social Services were always informed of the decision to monitor a child, in this case it did not happen until 6 days after 9 January, when the information was shared at the next liaison meeting. Just one piece of information, seen in the context of the whole family situation, could be the keystone to planning the future course of action. A delay such as occurred could have been crucial.

Neither the school doctor nor nurse was present at the meeting, so they did not hear of the incident then, and were not informed of it subsequently. Mr. Hayter clearly did not attach value to a medical opinion in the circumstances, and told us that school doctors do not provide "that sort of medical examination". We disagree. As new entrants to the area and one of its schools, medical examinations were carried out on X and Y on 3 February. Although Mrs. Carlile indicated that she wished to be present, she in fact did not attend, but neither did she refuse permission for the examinations to take place.

Prior to the medicals, a fairly detailed but simple questionnaire is sent by the school nurse to the class teacher asking for information about the child's appearance, co-ordination, vision, hearing, speech and social development. It then goes on to ask if there are any other relevant factors and if the teacher would like to speak to the doctor.

Mrs. Coker, school nurse, told us that a form is not used for 'older' children. So X, being over 7 years, did not qualify for the benefit of his teacher's opinion being considered when he had his medical examination. It seemed to us that X was examined in a vacuum - no previous medical records, no knowledge of his immaturity, attention-seeking behaviour and tendency to fantasize, of his inclusion in the nurture group, of the possible child abuse allegation, or the fact that he was being monitored.

Within Wingfield School, communications between education and health staff were usually conducted through Mr. Hayter and Dr. Kamalanathan meeting after the latter had completed his medical sessions. It was on one such occasion, during the lunch hour after completion of his medical session, that Dr. Kamalanathan wanted to get information from Mr. Hayter about X and Y. Mr. Hayter could not recall any such specific occasion but was quite prepared to concede that it did take place as Dr. Kamalanathan described it. We are confident that Dr. Kamalanathan did positively seek the information on X and Y; we think that it does not matter who initiated the discussion on that occasion. If there was a need to seek information *between* medical visits, the Headteacher would inform the education welfare service who would inform Dr. Hooper at the headquarters of Greenwich Health Authority, who would presumably inform Dr. Kamalanathan.

Mrs. Coker gave evidence that if she was in the school at the time that a concern was discussed, she would probably be told about it. She does not receive direct referral from the teachers; these come to her via the Headteacher or his deputy. There was virtually no contact between the school nurse and Ms Gregory, the education welfare officer, although their roles are identical in many aspects. This was not surprising, as we heard that if Mrs. Coker did want to contact the education welfare office, this would have to be via the Headteacher or the Community Administration Office of the Health Authority.

Teachers who are anxious about the health or development of a child rightly report this to the Headteacher. He then decides what action is to be taken and, if appropriate, communicates with the school nurse, or the education welfare service who, if they consider it appropriate, inform Dr. Hooper and/or Social Services. As a result of the good relationship between Mr. Hayter and Area 4 social workers, Mr. Hayter was in frequent, direct contact with them.

Historically, the main role of the education welfare service is to supervise school attendance, and this was the understanding of many of our witnesses, including Miss Rouse, X's class teacher. Ms Gregory told us that she had responsibility for Wingfield School and the homes in a fixed geographical area. Her work was centred on dealing with problems which inhibit children from benefiting from their education. Referrals were labelled a "school" case when the focus of need was in the school and she reviewed each week their academic progress and well-being during her visits to check the register for attendance. Those who generated a higher level of concern, or where the difficulties encountered in the school were thought to emanate from the home, were classed as a "home" case. Rather misleadingly, a "home" case did not mean that there would be home visiting.

Ms Gregory first heard of the Carlile children at the liaison meeting of 15 January. As part of her regular reporting to her senior, she relayed to Ms Nuaimi the information about X's allegation. It was decided that X should be classed as a home case, as the previous history of voluntary care, reunion in a reconstituted family, and their understanding that X was frightened of his stepfather, aroused some concern. Neither they, nor teaching staff felt that the incident should be referred to the education welfare service designated officer for child abuse.

Apart from Mr. Hayter expressing concern on 10 February about Mr. Hall having an aggressive demeanour, which made staff feel uneasy, there were no other significant reports until March.

The anonymous telephone call of 7 March to Social Services triggered off a 3 week period of communication between the school and education welfare service, one of the few instances of good interchange of information. All these communications were expressing concern for Kimberley, or were concerned with attempts to arrange her attendance at nursery school and the need for continuing vigilance of X and Y. Ms Gregory was updated on the current situation at her weekly meeting at the school.

On 28 April, Mr. Hayter informed Social Services of Mr. Hall's intention to transfer the children to Henwick School immediately. This knowledge also awaited the liaison meeting before being shared with the education welfare services.

Henwick School, with which Wingfield School communicated satisfactorily, was visited regularly by Mrs. Gibbs, another education welfare officer. Her only record of note was on 22 May when she learnt from teaching staff that X was scruffy and often late. This was in marked contrast to previous reports, but does not appear to have been communicated to anyone else.

Ms Nuaimi, senior education welfare officer, explained to us the changes which are occurring in the education welfare service in accordance with the ILEA 1984 and early 1985 guidelines. A new structure is being implemented for the service, and there is a change of emphasis in the work carried out by it and by the schools, particularly in the context of child protection.

School staff continue to be watchful for signs of abuse, but refer anxieties to the education welfare service which acts as a filter and co-ordinator in the ensuing identification and management of cases. This includes seeking information from other agencies, compiling a file and notifying Social Services, if this is thought appropriate.

In our opinion, filtering of even minor concerns of possible abuse and referring only the selected cases to Social Services, may lead to several agencies having some information and none of them possessing the whole picture on which to assess the situation. Another danger of indirect referral is the modification of the message by the perceptions of the receiver, which may ultimately convey a false impression and cause inaccuracies.

We heard and saw obvious examples of message distortion - X thrown "across" the room or "about" the room; X frightened of his stepfather, or not. The statement which Miss Rouse made to the police soon after Kimberley's death stated that X had been frightened, but in evidence to us she denied this strongly. Ms Gregory also recorded that X was frightened, and believes that she was told this at the school, but it may understandably have been her expectation that that would be his reaction. All other education witnesses commented on the casualness of X's declaration.

Any suspicions about child abuse must be reported direct to Social Services. The education welfare service has a designated officer for child abuse, to whom any school, or any of its own staff, can refer to for advice. An Abuse at Risk register is maintained, consisting of children who are being monitored by the service because of possible abuse but are not on the formal At Risk register.

We do not doubt the good intention of ILEA to assist in the management of the increasing number of referred cases of school children being the subject of abuse. ILEA's proposals must not, however, either muddle the procedures agreed by the Area Review Committee or confuse communication between a worried teacher and those who have the duty to protect a child.

## Court Welfare Service

In mid-February 1986 Mrs. Deborah Carrigan, a Court Welfare Officer attached to the Royal Courts of Justice and employed by the Inner London Probation Service, was allotted the task of preparing a report on the Carlile family for Wigan County Court in a dispute between Mr David Carlile (who was living in Bristol) and Mrs. Carlile over access to the child, Z. That task involved an assessment of the family, including the three other children. She wrote to both parents seeking a visit. Her visit to Mrs. Carlile on the Ferrier Estate was arranged on the telephone to take place on 5 March. That visit never materialised. There was no one at home when Mrs. Carrigan called, but she left her visiting card, which was shown to Mrs. Swinburne and Ms Streeter when they made their visit on 7 March (see Chapter 17). Thereafter Mrs. Carrigan was sporadically in touch with the Carliles by letter or telephone; on one occasion there was a conversation with Mr Hall when he rang in early May to say that Mrs. Carlile had gone to Liverpool with the two younger children. Thereafter, in consultation with her senior officer and with Wigan County Court, Mrs. Carrigan discontinued her efforts.

From early March until mid-May she was often in touch with Mr. Ruddock, exchanging information and indicating a readiness to assist Social Services. In a telephone conversation of 24 April she relayed to Mr Ruddock the fact of her failed visit of 11 April, whereupon she suggested an application for a Place of Safety Order, but was persuaded that there was insufficient evidence. (We have dealt with this episode in more detail in Chapter 20). It is unnecessary to deal with Mrs. Carrigan's efforts to perform her allotted task. We are more than satisfied that the chronicle of events, as revealed by her activities, discloses the required mutuality in the sharing of information between the two agencies. Mrs. Carrigan embarked on her assigned task expeditiously and executed it, so far as she was able to, in a professionally competent and thorough manner.

She clearly perceived the case as one of potential child abuse, and communicated her undoubted worries to Mr. Ruddock. She was more than willing to engage in a case conference, and clearly thought that there ought to have been one in March or April. We would commend her in particular for her assiduity. Indeed she acted well beyond the call of duty, manifested by her frequent attendance at our Inquiry, both before and after she had given her evidence.

One aspect of her work attracted our attention. It appeared to us that, partly perhaps due to a lack of understanding of the function of a Court Welfare Officer, Mrs. Swinburne and Ms Streeter were not alive to the lie told to them by Mrs. Carlile on 7 March. Some reliance was placed by those two social workers on the contact between Mrs. Carrigan and Mrs. Carlile when the idea of a Place of Safety Order was considered and rejected by them as a means of achieving a sight, and medical examination of Kimberley. Mrs. Carlile, using the visiting card, had conveyed the impression that Mrs. Carrigan had been visiting the Carlile family regularly.

Even when the truth of Mrs. Carrigan's unavailing attempt to visit and lack of any personal contact with Mrs. Carlile had been uncovered, we think that the implications of Mrs. Carlile's lie was insufficiently considered by Mr. Ruddock as a clear indication of the manipulative capabilities of the Carlile couple. We also think that insufficient attention was paid in the months of April and May to the evidence from Mrs. Carrigan about the Carlile family's hostility to, and unwillingness to co-operate with Greenwich Social Services and other agencies. Mrs. Carrigan's experiences with the Carliles should have significantly altered the assessment of the situation.

Those experiences would have made their impact more forcibly, had there been a case conference, which we have found ought definitely to have taken place at some time during this period.

We revert to the simple issue of the lie told to the two social workers on 7 March. Regular visiting, or acting as a social worker, is incompatible with the role and function of a Court Welfare Officer. Because we suspect that it is not uncommon for social workers to lack understanding about the function of court welfare officers compiling reports for the courts, we think it useful to describe shortly the aim and purpose of the Court Welfare Service.

The role of the Probation Service in civil law matters has developed considerably over the years since the passing of the Probation of Offenders Act 1907 which established the Service as a court-based statutory agency. When carrying out work with families, a probation officer may on occasions come across a case of child abuse or suspected child abuse. All probation officers are impressed with the need to engage in frequent and open communication with other agencies in the system of child protection.

The Inner London Probation Service's handbook for its officers contains the following guidance:

"Experience has shown the vital importance of frequent and open conversation between the various workers involved with the families of children at risk. It is essential that inter-agency agreements or understandings about their respective responsibilities should be recorded, be endorsed at senior level and be confirmed between agencies in writing."

Probation officers are instructed to attend all case conferences where they have had an involvement with the family under review. They are told that the case conference is the prime vehicle for the exchange of information and as such is the proper forum where decisions and recommendations might be taken to protect children.

We are confident of the keenness of the Inner London Probation Service to participate fully in every aspect of the management of the child abuse system. We wish this to be widely known. We are confident that at both management and field level the liaison between Greenwich Social Services and the Inner London Probation Service (which incorporates the Court Welfare Service) was satisfactory at the time of Kimberley's death, and remains satisfactory to date. **We recommend that both services should give consideration to ensuring that even closer contact, both formally and informally, should be continually developed and improved.**

## Police

At no stage of the handling by Social Services of the case of Kimberley Carlile did the police in Greenwich become involved. They knew nothing of the Carlile family. They received no anonymous calls themselves, and they were not told of the call on 7 March 1986 to Social Services, or at any time thereafter. We note in Chapter 17 that the presence of the police at the time of the anonymous telephone call from the neighbour of the Carliles, and the police availability thereafter, might have contributed to a successful outcome to the investigation of abuse of Kimberley. We do not repeat what we said earlier about why it is important for the police to be directly involved in cases of child abuse. Their importance generally is obvious. What we wish to do is to point to two issues of police powers in relation to child abuse.

*Anonymous calls*

Woman Police Sergeant Tullock, of the Care/Child Abuse Section of the Metropolitan Police Youth and Community Office based at Shooters Hill Police Station, told us that she and her colleagues treated anonymous telephone calls about child abuse that were made to the police very seriously. Such cases are classified as urgent investigations until the child and the child's parents have been seen. In as many as 75% of the cases where the police investigate reports of child abuse, the parents co-operate in letting their children be seen. Where there is an absence of co-operation and potential violence, the police, almost invariably in conjunction with Social Services, exercise their powers under Section 40, Children and Young Persons Act 1933.

Now that Greenwich Social Services and, no doubt similarly, other local authorities are aware of that neglected power - a circular letter of 24 June 1987 was sent by the Chief Inspector to Directors of Social Services reminding them of the available powers to effect access to a child at risk - **it is our recommendation that if a social worker has any difficulty in obtaining access to a child in pursuit of the statutory duty to investigate cases, where information is received which suggests that there are grounds for care proceedings, the police must be informed**. We think that this need not be done before a visit for the purpose of seeing a child. But where, as here, the visit is unsuccessful in gaining access to the child, the police must be told. The police will then investigate, in collaboration with Social Services. Between them a decision will be made whether to re-visit the place where the child is thought to be, or apply for a warrant which is executable by the police. The police may, and often do, in an emergency act on their own accord.

*Place of Safety Orders*

Any police officer may detain a child whom he has reasonable cause to believe is being ill-treated or neglected. Unlike the power of social workers to apply for such an Order to a magistrate (to which we referred at length in Chapter 25) the police act executively without a warrant, and may detain the child for eight days. The police officer making the detention must, as soon as practicable, ensure that the case is examined by a police officer not below the rank of inspector, or by the police officer in charge of a section. On completion of that inquiry, the child must either be released or further detained in his own interests. The parents of the child must be informed of the right to apply to a magistrate for the child's release.

Paragraph 48 of the Goverment's White Paper, *The Law on Child Care and Family Services* suggests that the police should retain the power to detain a child without recourse to a magistrate in a place of protection, but that such power should be limited by law to 72 hours. The prospective legislation will allow for an application to a magistrate for an extension up to 8 days, calculated to start from the beginning of the initial detention. The parents would be notified of the application, and could attend if they wish. The police would no longer be empowered to apply for an interim Care Order, but should hand the case over to the local authority for any further Order. The Metropolitan Police have registered their objection to these proposed changes. They think that 72 hours is insufficient time for them to make proper inquiries, and they do not see why they should not retain their power to apply for interim Care Orders. So far as we can determine, the proposals in the White Paper seem sensible. The new Emergency Protection Order will authorise magistrates to order that removal and detention of children to a place of safety will last for a maximum of only eight days (reduced from 28 days) and there will be a corresponding reduction in the police powers. These proposals are logical, in order to indicate that what is being dealt with is a true emergency. Any extended period can be applied for, if neccessary. These changes will reduce the element of executive power to take a child away from its parents. Since it is the local authority which exclusively has the obligation to administer a Care Order, there seems to be no reason why the police should be able to apply for an interim Care Order.

Under the present law a parent may, during the period of eight days, apply to a magistrate for the child's release. The practice has been for the child's representative alone to be present on the application, in the absence of the police or indeed any other person. Recently, in *R v. the Bristol Justices, ex parte Broome*[1], Mrs Justice Booth held that, on the application for the release of a detained child, the police were entitled to be notified of the application and to be heard and to give evidence. In that case the application was made at a specially convened hearing within 48 hours of the child being detained by the police. The police came to hear of the application and wished to be heard. They were refused by the single magistrate. Hence the subsequent and successful application to the High Court for judicial review. Although it will be rare for a parent to be able to get to court within 72 hours to apply for a child's release, we think that the right to do so under Section 28(5), Children and Young Persons Act 1969 should be retained. We see no reason why a child should be taken away from his or her parents by an executive act for a moment longer than can be justified according to evidence, judically tested. **It will, we think, be sensible if the decision in the Bristol Justices case is statutorily declared.We so recommend**. If the police are desirous of a longer period than 72 hours to make the necessary inquiries, we think that, like any other person, they should apply to a magistrate for a Place of Safety Order for the new, extended period of 8 days. It must be remembered that if there is a risk to life and limb there is always the power in Section 17(1)(e), Police and Criminal Evidence Act 1984 for the police to effect a speedy entry into premises without a warrant.

## General Practitioners

Three general practitioners were on three separate occasions professionally involved in the promotion of Kimberley Carlile's welfare after she had first been received into voluntary care in the spring of 1984. Each of them contributed nothing towards uncovering the underlying failure of Kimberley to develop, due in the main to the absence of information that each might have usefully received and passed on with their own notes of examination and reports.

Two doctors in the Wirral each supplied a medical report to Wirral Social Services; the first shortly after Kimberley's reception into voluntary care on 24 August 1984, and the second on her discharge from voluntary care on 4 October 1985. The reports indicated, respectively, "a happy child" and a "happy, clean, well nourished, well dressed" child. Neither of the two doctors appeared to be aware of the 24-month developmental assessment of 17 November 1983, when the warning signs were revealed by the medical officer at the health clinic. Nor were the two doctors apparently appraised of the clinic's examination and weighing of Kimberley on 24 May 1984.

Developmental screening, including the recording of height, weight and head circumference and their plotting on a percentile chart should be part of

---

[1] CO/1080/86, 28 November 1986.

any medical examination of any child under the age of two, whether the child looks well or is ill; for children up to five, percentile charts should be used where there is some cause for concern. An increasing number of general practitioners are gaining paediatric experience and are participating in child health screening programmes. This is a welcome development and should become widespread. When the child is presented at the surgery, the general practitioner must satisfy himself of the developmental status of the child as well as dealing with the presenting problem. He must liaise with the health visitor so that the home influence can be evaluated. Particular attention should be paid to what parents say about what is wrong with their child's progress. They are usually right, although they may not have been able to identify correctly the real problem or underlying cause of the problem.

When the Carlile family moved into their home on the Ferrier Estate they became registered with Dr. Mahesh. He did not receive the medical records of Mrs. Carlile and her three older children until after Kimberley's death. Mrs. Carlile came to the surgery on 11 November 1985 and Dr. Mahesh gave her a letter of referral to the Brook General Hospital for Kimberley to undergo "speech therapy"; but he could not remember having examined Kimberley and diagnosing some speech problem. We do not think that it is good medical practice for G.P.s to refer a patient to other services without having seen the patient and determined that referral is appropriate. Dr. Mahesh did not follow up his action; in fact Kimberley was never taken to the Brook Hospital, nor indeed to any speech therapist.

The importance of record-keeping, communication within an agency and to other agencies, and collaborative work cannot be over-stressed. It is as important, if not more important in general practice than it is with other disciplines. General practitioners are likely to possess information about more families than any other person in other disciplines.

In relation to the Carlile family, information was not shared between Dr Mahesh and the health visitor and/or Social Services. He did not inform the health visitor of his referral of Kimberley to the Brook Hospital and the lack of response by Mrs Carlile. The health visitor, Miss Reader, did not inform him of her growing concern about the family. She told us of the difficulty in achieving a meeting with the doctor, and that in instances where she persisted, communication was one way only. **We recommend that urgent consideration be given to closer collaboration between the health visitors on the Ferrier Estate and the general practitioners at Telemann Square.**

The two social workers who undertook the visit on 7 March, following the anonymous call, did not attempt to contact the G.P., since they believed they would be unsuccessful in making contact. On 12 March a telephone call was made to the surgery by Ms Peacock, the Duty Officer in Area 4. She elicited the last date on which Kimberley had attended. There is no record of this call in the surgery, nor does it seem to have imparted to the surgery the level of concern felt by the social workers. Dr. Mahesh did not know of this call, and was not informed of the request by Mr. Ruddock in his letter of 10 March 1986, repeated at the meeting of 12 March, for Kimberley to be taken to the G.P or health visitor for a medical examination. Even if Kimberley had been presented for examination at the surgery (which she was not), Dr. Mahesh might not have been forewarned about the possibility of child abuse.

In the absence of family records, information from health visitor, medical officer and social workers, there was no overt reason for Dr. Mahesh to be concerned for the safety of Kimberley. Nevertheless he should have been sufficiently concerned about her development to have passed on the information about Kimberley's need for speech therapy to the health visitor, medical officer, and possibly Social Services.

Dr. Mahesh had not seen a copy of the Area Review Committee's Child Abuse Procedure manual until he came before the Inquiry. The representative of the Family Practitioner Committee, Mr David Lacey, told us that manuals were distributed to all general practitioners as requested by the Area Review Committee in 1982, and that any further action would have been taken only if there had been a specific request to be supplied with a copy. That is inadequate. **We recommend that the Family Practitioner Committee should ensure that all child abuse procedures are currently available to all general practitioners in its area**.

General practitioners need to meet the same stringent standards of practice as other professionals, in order that they may fulfill their important role in the multi-disciplinary system for protecting children at risk.

CHAPTER 29

# SOCIAL WORK TRAINING

The authors of "*A Child in Trust*"[1] apologised to their readers for taking them "somewhat wearily, through the thickets of social work training". Given the controversies and debates concerning social work training that have grown apace since 1985 the thicket is even thicker now than before. Nevertheless we must venture in once more. Social work training is every bit as important a subject now as it was then, and hopefully we are approaching the time when some fundamental decisions will be made about the future of qualifying courses. Issues came up during the Inquiry which once again underlined the importance of good training if we are to establish and maintain high standards of practice. A number of the people involved with the Carlile family expressed reservations about the adequacy of their training. We will not attempt to provide an overview of the current position, as this can be gleaned from other documents. We will comment on three areas of training: basic qualification training, post-qualification training, and training for first line managers.

## Basic qualification training

That all is not well with the state of social work training is perhaps the one point on which all the professionals involved are likely to agree. Mr. Tony Hall, the new Director of the Central Council for Education and Training in Social Work (CCETSW), said that "as Director of CCETSW, I would be the first to admit, as I have, that there is a very great deal wrong with the present structure and pattern of social work training at all levels". The Minister of Health, in a letter to the Chairman of CCETSW in April 1987, also stated that "it is clear to me that improvements are required in the ways in which staff in the Personal Social Services are prepared for their work".

To determine how we came to be in this predicament would probably require a historical study rivalling, if not outdistancing the length of this report! Mr. Robert Harris, Professor-elect of Social Work, University of Hull, in evidence to us, suggested that "it is arguable that CCETSW's relatively laissez-faire attitude to social work course development since 1971 reflects not so much a studied commitment to academic freedom, as a failure of nerve, or possibly a central uncertainty as to the best way forward". He went on to say, however, that CCETSW was not "to be blamed entirely" and that "the conflicting interests represented on CCETSW" and the equivocations "within social work itself" have played their part. Concerning social work uncertainty over its professional training system, Mr. Harris concluded that "CCETSW's present difficulties are a consequence, rather than a cause of this uncertainty". CCETSW in its submission explained that it "gives advice and guidance to courses but it does not regulate detailed curriculum. A significant and important number of courses are taught in

---

[1] The report of the Panel of Inquiry into the circumstances surrounding the death of Jasmine Beckford, Chapter 20, at p.204, published by Brent Borough Council.

Universities which have charters guaranteeing their autonomy". Mr. Hall, in his oral evidence, put it like this: "Although the Council has a statutory duty and responsibility to promote social work courses, to approve them, to set standards, it actually has a very few powers to bring that about. Very crudely put, the only power we've got is to stop colleges running courses of which we don't approve. We can't make colleges run courses because we don't have the resources to do it, and we don't have influence in various sectors of higher and further education. We can't make agencies provide the practice placements which are required to provide the essential opportunities for training social workers to develop their skills. All that we achieve therefore, in the absence of any real powers, is through discussion, negotiation, persuasion in a very political environment".

We were interested to hear Mr. Hall describing the kind of body he would like CCETSW to be, in similar terms to those used by Mr. Devaux when he was talking about Area Review Committees (ARCs). Mr. Hall told us that he "would dearly love to preside over an organisation that had a few more teeth". Mr. Devaux expressed his view that an ARC "not only has to have money, but teeth". In CCETSW and the network of ARCs we have bodies that have a key role to play in raising and protecting the standard of services to children, and yet both lack authority and power, and are under-resourced. (ARCs have no funds of their own). Mr. Hall explained why he wanted CCETSW to have teeth: "to insist and require, as well as support, both agencies and training institutions to do some of the things that we would like to do. We are in a position where we can set very high standards. But if nobody can, or is prepared to meet them, then we would see the numbers of qualified social workers produced every year dwindling, and that is another one of our requirements - that we produce a sufficient number of social workers to meet the needs of agencies. So we really are caught between negotiating our way through a morass of different interests with very few powers to achieve our aims".

A survey of CQSW and CSS courses (*"Protecting Children"* by Elizabeth Ash, CCETSW Paper 25, August 1987) showed the child care content of these courses to be extremely varied. This variety poses a problem for future employers, for colleagues in other professions and for the public because, beyond a level of benign generalisation, the possession of a CQSW cannot be taken as a reliable indication that social workers have acquired specific areas of knowledge, or demonstrated competence in specific areas of practice. As Mr. Hall told us, "the variety within ...training programmes is so enormous that it's very difficult to establish a national view or a guarantee of the minimum quality". Without this, it is impossible to pitch expectations accurately and maybe this is part of the reason why many people seem to have such unrealistic expectations of social workers.

We recognise there has been a venerable debate on the distinction to be made between education and training; we are also aware that many interested parties will be insisting that their particular subjects should be included in courses, but we believe it is possible to work out the content for a course which will be of most help to social workers and their clients. In his letter to CCETSW, the Minister of Health suggested that it would be helpful for the "existing powers of validation" to be used "to create a more common output from the existing range of CQSW courses". We welcome the lead given by CCETSW in its policy statement (Paper 20.8, June 1987) which, in Mr. Hall's words, seeks "to ensure that all qualified social workers will have, at minimum, a core range of knowledge, a core base of essential skills and some demonstrated skills in practice by the time they receive their qualifying award". We were interested to hear that since the writing of the "draft statement of minimum expectations of the social worker at the point of qualification" it had been completely re-drafted. Mr. Hall told us "It's a measure of how quickly things are moving". We hope that this momentum is maintained and **recommend that agreement is reached concerning the minimum expectations of the social worker at the point of qualification.**

## Training in law

With such variety in courses it is hardly surprising that some subjects are casualties. One of these casualties is the subject of law. Mr. Harris assured us that "there is no doubt...that some students are leaving courses without having been assessed in any aspect of the law". In his written statement Mr. Ruddock told us that "in relation to my knowledge of legal powers and procedures I felt far less sure of myself". We have already noted the widespread ignorance of Section 40 of the Children and Young Persons Act 1933. We suspect that part of the problem is that the law is seen, and taught, as a dry subject far removed from the intimacy of the relationship between social workers and clients, or seen as contributing those inpenetrable phrases that appear in quotations within departmental procedures. Instead, the law should be seen as fundamental to the definition of the framework within which the various child protection agencies operate. Legal provisions supply workers with the tools to use when statutory intervention is required. The art is to use the right tool for the job in hand. For this reason we have outlined in another part of this report the kind of legal provisions we think should be available to social workers in child protection. We do not think that training in the law should be restricted unimaginatively to promoting the relevant statutory sections, but should include teaching on the court process and the art of giving evidence. We noted that CCETSW's draft statement of minimum expectations, required students to have demonstrated "knowledge of the relevance and application to practice of social work studies, health studies, policy studies including law and relevant social and behavioural sciences", but we were worried that the legal focus might not be sufficiently clear in the company of such weighty bed-fellows. We want to follow-up the recommendation in "*A Child in Trust*" that "a further study by CCETSW of legal training for social workers should now be seriously considered as a matter of high priority", with the recommendation that **all social work courses should provide their students with a thorough grasp of the legal framework within which they will work, and all students should be assessed as to the adequacy of their knowledge of the relevant legal provisions.** After writing this we were glad to note that CCETSW in its paper, "*Care for To-morrow: the case for reform of education and training*

179

*for social workers and other care staff"* places emphasis on the need to remedy past and present failures of social workers to know their legal powers. (Para 3.1.20, p.15.).

Another theme in this report has been social workers' reluctance to press their requirements in the face of determined resistance from parents. CCETSW's paper number 10, *"Education and Training for Social Work"* November 1978, described the two kinds of mandate for the practice of social work: "The first is derived from society and its values and concerns which may in part be embodied in social policy and legislation. The second comes from the client or users of the social worker's services towards whom the social worker feels a contractual obligation for specific acts of intervention". Although the social work profession has been grappling with the issue for years, we believe the use of authority remains a predicament for some social workers who dislike exerting power over their clients. It is hardly surprising that many of us are worried about interfering with the freedom of fellow human beings or intruding into their family life. Social workers, coming from courses for interviews for their first job following qualification, often deal with the question about making decisions that will involve removing a child from his or her family in words such as these: "Well of course I don't like making those type of decisions, who does? But I expect I will, if I have to". It is this conditional approach that is not good enough in child protection. It implies a reluctance that has to be overcome, without any clarity concerning how this might be achieved. All of us would probably agree that the safety of a child is a compelling reason for having to do something but, as is constantly observed, social workers rarely deal in certainties, and so there are always likely to be features in a case giving support to reluctance, prevarication, drift, outright inaction, and even abandonment. Children at risk need confident and determined social workers.

Dealing with this issue is not entirely a matter for courses, but basic training has a key part to play. Yet again it is a matter of balance. The content of courses should be balanced so as to give proper weight to both of these mandates. **We recommend that CCETSW, in considering the minimum expectations of social workers at the point of qualification makes sure that proper weight has been given to training social workers for taking up their statutory responsibilities.**

We agree with Elizabeth Ash who wrote in her survey that "especially worrying was the fact that some students could complete their CQSW training without having studied or worked with children". In fact we found it not so much worrying, as astonishing. Elizabeth Ash's description of "child abuse teaching", did not inspire confidence: "Child abuse teaching, however, seemed, on the whole, detached from the body of the curriculum. It was agreed that child abuse work demanded supervised practice and post-qualifying training to build up basic professional skills. In reality such post-qualifying training and supervision were not readily available and courses which tried to decide how far to fill the gap sought guidance from CCETSW as to the appropriate levels of skills for newly qualified social workers. Since the reality, though undesirable, is that many newly qualified social workers will be called upon to work with children at risk of abuse (or abused), it is essential that basic training should equip them not only with the ability to recognise and assess risk but also with the confidence to demand the necessary support and supervision in such cases. Longer courses could make such preparation possible".

This inadequate level of teaching of child care in general, and child abuse particularly, has been recognised by CCETSW. In its written submission to us, the Council said that it "recognises and accepts that there is the legitimate concern in the community, in the social work profession, and amongst allied professions and groups about the preparedness of many qualified social workers to deal with complex child care problems". **We recommend that child care in general, and child abuse specifically, should be a compulsory part of all courses offering basic training to social workers. We also recommend that teachers on these courses must be sufficiently up-to-date in their own knowledge and practice to be able to prepare students adequately.**

Elizabeth Ash's study also confirmed that the relationship between courses and Social Services Departments, which will employ most of the courses' students, is not as good as it should be: indeed the relationship seems more like that between distant cousins than between members of a closely-knit family. It is no wonder that staff fall down the gap left between courses and employing authorities. The gap was evident in a number of the responses from courses replying to Elizabeth Ash. For example, "we believe that neither public nor professional concern about child abuse should stampede us into assuming that basic level courses are the appropriate place for training in such demanding work"; and "I hope that all our students going into employment in local authorities will have the opportunity of in-service training in child abuse. I am by no means convinced that this is always the case". Obviously it has to be worked out what is appropriate for basic level training to provide and what should be provided by post-qualification studies, but what concerns us most is that courses and employers make sure that staff receive the training they need. It is a failure on both sides if they fail in the task of all good parents to prepare their charges for the life ahead so that they go out into the work well equipped to deal with the problems they will face.

Another problem, confirmed by Elizabeth Ash's study, is the difficulty in getting appropriate practice placements. She referred to the current position as being "a mini-crisis". Most of the courses "who commented on practice placements were critical". Departments are often reluctant to encourage their staff to offer practice placements and some were reported as having a policy not to allow students to hold child abuse cases. This policy is wrong and contradictory, unless all Departments insist on providing further training before their staff take on child abuse cases. We believe that supervised practice has an important role to play in exposing students to the kind of complex situations they will face as qualified social workers.

In the relationship between courses and employers, the issue of variety in content is not the prerogative of one side of the relationship. We have talked about the variety in the content of courses but we should also note the great variety in the organisation of Departments to which newly qualified staff will be heading. If, within Departments, posts are set up in very different ways and with different responsibilities it is difficult for courses to prepare students for their future work. For example, if some Departments are moving towards establishing a growing number of specialist posts, this will have major consequences for training.

We suspect that, given the parochial nature of local government and given the preoccupation with getting a good return on your investment, it is not easy for many Social Services Departments to act on a commitment concerning the general standard of professional training in this country. However, if progress is to be made, those organising the courses and employers are going to have to work more closely together. Given the lack of any crossover point above the academic world and the various employers of social workers, we have had trouble in formulating a recommendation for future action. We noted that the Minister of Health in his letter to CCETSW suggested that future areas of work could include attempts to "see what can be done to build more widely on the best arrangements currently in existence for securing employer involvement in course planning" and to "see what progress might be made within the existing framework to bring about improvements in both the quantity and quality of students' practice placements". We are also aware of the initiatives that have already been taken in this area by CCETSW, and we believe these problems will have to be resolved if the qualifying diploma in social work is not to inherit the defect of its predecessors. In the light of this, **we recommend that CCETSW should oversee continuing discussions between those organising courses and employers to dovetail their respective responsibilities for the standard of service provided to clients.**

As we write this report, consideration is being given to the length of the qualifying courses for social workers. CCETSW has agreed (in a Council resolution of 20 September 1985) that "the minimum period of education and training prior to qualification in social work should normally be three years"[1]. From what we heard during the course of our Inquiry, we would be surprised if better use could not be made of the existing time available to social work courses. We were also much aware of the concern that, without agreement as to the content of courses, the length of them would guarantee nothing. Mr. Harris suggested, for example, that if some courses were "thirty-three years long" we could not assume "that students would emerge competent and confident in the law which defines their powers and the rights and obligations of their clients". Nevertheless, given the rising expectations of our society, the increased requirements of social workers, the increasingly complex legislative measures, the growing knowledge base, and the general raising of standards, we cannot believe that everything a social worker needs from a basic course can be condensed into the present length of qualifying courses. The exact length required (for example, why not $2\frac{3}{4}$ years or $3\frac{1}{2}$ years?) depends on a precise definition of what must be covered and an accurate assessment of the time it will take. We have already recommended that work should continue on the content of courses and this should lead to

---

[1] The requirement of a minimum period of education and training of three years is re-stated in the recent CCETSW paper of October 1987, *ibid.,* para. 3.2.13. p.20.

firm evidence being available on what is required. Given the present state of the art, we would reckon that 3 years is likely to be the minimum time to do all that is needed and the maximum time for a realistic bid to be made for the required resources. In the chapter on resources (Chapter 11), we have spoken of the different levels of responsibility in the child protection service. It is for central government to make sure that social work training has the resources, in whatever form, to enable social workers to provide a service to a standard that is acceptable to us all. We know that CCETSW and the Minister of Health have been corresponding on this matter, and **we recommend that the DHSS and CCETSW come speedily to a decision on the minimum period of basic training for social workers, and that central government makes the necessary resources available.**

## Post-qualification training

We heard a good deal of evidence suggesting that post-qualification training in Greenwich Social Services Department was inadequate. We know that Greenwich Social Services Department is not alone in having problems financing post-qualification training. The Director of Social Services made it clear to us that progress has been made in Greenwich to increase the training resources available. In a written statement, the Director described how the social services training section grew from 1982 when it was comprised of "a training officer, a full-time study supervisor for students undertaking the Certificate in Social Services (CSS) and some administrative support", to 1987 when the section was comprised of "a full-time child care training officer, a training officer in the race unit, an internal tutor for in-service training programmes and additional CCS study supervisors...a part-time mental health tutor post..." and "...provision for a training officer for pre-school services and a post of training officer...attached to the Greenwich regional child care establishments". Evidence was also provided that between 12 and 20 staff were being sent on secondment each year, and a great deal of use had been made of the Management Development Training Officer appointed in 1984. Also "the Child Care Training Officer has a budget of £3,500 to establish courses. Additionally there is £20,000 now in the budget for consultancy on child abuse and child care which is available to boost the training output".

The Social Services Inspectorate report of 1986 focused, however, on the particular need in Greenwich, and nationally, for increased training, and the Director concluded "it must be the case that more could have been done". With regard to post-qualifying courses, the Director reported that "the experience of field social workers has been that too few courses have been provided by Greenwich to develop their knowledge and skills and too little money has been available to pay for social workers to attend external courses".

Post-qualification training is essential if staff are going to keep up-to-date following their basic training, and if they are to study areas of practice in greater depth. The Seebohm Committee reported that "we assume therefore that students should have the opportunity, by means of optional courses, of taking their studies and/or professional practice to greater depth in certain areas of knowledge and in one social work method and we also recognise the need to provide opportunities for students to develop skills to a higher level in subsequent training". We do not feel the need to argue any further the case for post-qualification training, because we have heard no-one disputing its importance. What has to be urged is that local authority Social Services Departments, pressed for money, give priority to training. One of the troubles is that training is often seen as a discrete budget, separate from staffing and direct services to clients, whereas in reality there is not much point in having staff that are not properly trained, and there is not much point in providing services unless they are of good quality. We doubt if training, as a separate financial item in budgets, will be given the priority it deserves. Instead, following the lead of a number of organisations, **we recommend that Departments should allocate to training a set proportion of their expenditure on staffing**. Decisions are always going to have to be made between the needs of different staff and the importance of different subjects (and of course we want to argue the highest priority be given to child protection) but we believe that our recommendation will lead to a more realistic baseline for training. It would also provide, we hope, a secure footing for discussing post-qualification courses with training bodies, with the expectation that these could be established on firmer bases.

Before we leave the question of social work training, we want to comment briefly on two areas. First, we think it is the task of basic training courses to help students record their work effectively. A good deal of recording that we have seen is of the purely descriptive kind, i.e., "called to visit Mrs. Bloggs, she was in with her 3 children and the dog". Recording needs to start with the purpose of the work, carry on to describe its content and finish with an evaluation of how far the purpose was achieved, and how far it needed to be refined and changed.

Second, there is no need to comment any further on the fact that the provision of an effective child protection service is going to involve a large number of professions. The service requires good relationships between these professions. This is easily said, but very difficult to put into practice. We suspect that major problems in professional co-operation remain to be overcome. One of the ways of helping to achieve this is to make sure that training in child protection, at all levels, is undertaken on a inter-disciplinary basis.

## Training for managers

The last area of training we want to cover is management training. We believe that everyone on becoming a first line manager should have appropriate training to help them with their new responsibilities. In the chapter on supervision we suggest that, in a social work career, the biggest step of all is from being a practitioner to being a first line manager. While practice and management overlap in many ways, team managers, for example, will need help in taking on their new tasks. Although Mr. Neill did provide training and guidance for his new team managers, there was no systematic programme of induction and training. We saw in Mr. Ruddock a man who was having to cope with too much, too quickly, without adequate training and supervision. The Director reported to us that an internal review had "recognised that the

Team Manager directly involved in the Kimberley case had been expected to take on full responsibility for the Ferrier Team with minimal (though useful) induction and preparation. The Assistant Director had made some specific provisions for training and consultation for the fieldwork management team; even so, the re-training opportunities available to the Area Manager were not extensive". Good management training would have helped Mr. Ruddock to establish priorities and objectives for his own time and for that of his team, which in turn would have prevented him personally taking on a workload that he could not cope with efficiently. **We recommend that all new first line managers are provided with an appropriate induction programme and management training**. The content of the training provided for these first line managers, we believe, should concentrate on general management training, employment legislation and industrial relations, leadership skills, team building, setting priorities and attainable objectives, evaluation and how to give good supervision (including knowledge of legal provisions and departmental procedures).

# SUPERVISION

When dealing with the Carlile family Mr. Ruddock was acting as a field worker from the position of Team Manager. Supervision of his work thus devolved on his immediate superior, Mr. Don Neill, the Area Manager. This produced a dislocation of the management structure of the Social Services Department which was never more apparent than in the question of supervision, for it is manifest that Mr. Ruddock failed to obtain for himself the kind of supervision, we believe, he would have expected to provide for a member of his own team carrying a child abuse case. Mr. Neill, the Area Manager, did not recognise that his relationship with Mr. Ruddock in relation to the Carlile family needed to be adjusted, so that his Team Manager received the appropriate kind of supervision. Such adjustment would have enabled Mr. Neill to be clear about his own accountability.

So important generally, and particularly in the Carlile case, is the need for good supervision that we make no excuse for expressing at length our views on the subject. We underline the importance of supervision in social work, and particularly in child care work, if only because in the Inquiry, there seemed to be a lack of understanding about what supervision involves. Supervision applies with like effect to health visitors and nursing officers.

## Accountability

The BASW *"Code of Practice for the Supervisors of Social Workers Dealing with Child Abuse"* makes the point of accountability with clarity: "Although supervisors must allow a degree of professional autonomy in their staff, they remain accountable to their agency for the quality of work by social workers". Understandably, Mr. Neill saw Mr. Ruddock as an experienced and able social worker and allowed a fair measure of professional autonomy to Mr. Ruddock. Nevertheless Mr. Neill remained responsible to his Department for the quality of work in Area 4. Indeed, the effect of the dislocation on the Social Services Department can be seen higher up the managerial line. The BASW code of practice recognised that: "Supervisors of workers dealing with child abuse cases need themselves to have supervision and support in what is a stressful and demanding task". Mr. Neill would no doubt have expected to provide this for his team managers, but it would not have been feasible for the Assistant Director (Fieldwork), Mr. Devaux, to provide this for Mr. Neill for a number of reasons, including their separate offices, their insufficiently frequent meetings and the Assistant Director's other managerial responsibilities and span of control.

We applaud the decision to create another Assistant Director post, and would expect this will relieve the pressures of Mr. Devaux's workload. Nevertheless, we doubt if an Assistant Director can be reasonably expected to provide the kind of time and attention a supervisor of child abuse cases might need from his superior. This is a compelling reason that leads us to **recommend that team managers should not carry child abuse cases**. That will avoid the unfortunate impact of dislocation in management.

# The background

Supervision is as old as social work. This is not the place for a detailed history, but a few details concerning the development of supervision might be helpful as background. It has been the traditional orthodoxy to see supervision as a process that has two parts: "administration" and "teaching"; or "managerial" and "professional". The administrative function is concerned with making sure that work undertaken conforms to standards acceptable to the employing agency. The teaching function is concerned with enabling workers to develop skills commensurate with their potential.

The administrative function probably came first, with organisations recognising the need to ensure that their workers provided the right service to an appropriate standard. From social work's early days, however, social work educators recognised the importance of field training, and sought to place students with experienced workers who could share their experience and help the student to learn at work : to learn by doing the job.

As psychodynamic interpretations of human behaviour became more influential in social work, they also started to permeate theories of supervision. At its worst, this led to a focus which seemed to concentrate more on the worker, or student, than on the work to be done. Some on the receiving end of such supervision complained of being caseworked themselves. (One unintentioned consequence of this approach might have been to give social workers a feeling of what it was like to be on the receiving end of social work. It was not unheard of for supervisees to complain of being treated like a client!). Also, the popularity of "non-directive" approaches in casework was echoed in supervision, with supervisors relying on their supervisees to provide the direction.

As time passed, a more pragmatic approach to supervision concentrated on the tasks to be accomplished, rather than the personality of the worker. Debates continued concerning the administrative and teaching components of supervision, and it was still maintained that the two parts could be antithetical. In 1979 Dorothy Pettes reported that "agencies in Switzerland have developed a practice of divided supervision. The worker is administratively accountable to one person in his agency but is supervised professionally by another whose services may be purchased from outside the agency".

Even if desirable, such a system is unlikely to be developed in this country. We do not pursue this debate, since much of it has been sterile, especially when it has run parallel to the harmful split occurring when attempts are made in practice to contrast the institutional (requirements of the employer) approach with the professional (requirements of the independent practitioner). We believe it is perfectly practicable for one person to perform the task of good manager and good supervisor to the same member of staff. As Dorothy Pettes observes : "The trick is to maintain a mutuality of involvement, with each understanding the other's role in the learning and teaching tasks. With this understanding, the worker may see it as his responsibility to seek knowledge from the team leader, who in turn is responsible for providing learning opportunities for the worker. Thus rather than viewing his ignorance as a confession of failure, it is the worker's right to make it known so that together he and the team leader may devise ways in which he may increase his knowledge and skill. Similarly if the team leader really accepts that both worker and he are engaged jointly in an endeavour to increase the worker's knowledge and skill, he may the more easily and matter-of-factly respond to questions or point to errors as a part of their continuing work of identifying learning needs and deciding what each needs to do as a result". We are aware that this trick is not always performed, and recognise that deficiencies in supervision are not restricted to this case, or to Greenwich Social Services Department.

A National Children's Bureau study (Autumn 1985) by Judi Vernon and David Fruin, "*In Care: A Study of Social Work Decision Making*" (and reported by the DHSS paper "*Social Work Decisions in Child Care*") found that their "experience of practice (in 11 authorities) was that, with only a few notable exceptions, supervision sessions did not occur at the departmentally prescribed frequency and that overall, their content did not correspond to our understanding of what supervision entails". The study also found that : "Overall planning for a case was not a routine consideration of the supervision session. Cases were rarely selected systematically and discussed".

Another finding would suggest that the non-directive approach still has life in it : "The initiative for planning ..... rested with the social worker, with little by way of support in this process from the supervision session, unless directly raised by the social worker".

Not dissimilar findings were made by the Social Services Inspectorate when it inspected 9 local authorities and reported its conclusions in March 1986 in the snappily titled "*Inspection of the Supervision of Social Workers in the Assessment and Monitoring of Cases of Child Abuse when children, subject to a court order, have been returned home*". This paper reported, among other things, that "in all authorities there was a general assumption that supervision is necessary, but no social services department had a clear and explicit written policy statement about the nature of supervision, and no authority prescribed the method of supervision in detail". The Inspectors came to the opinion that supervisors could use their time more effectively if they "resisted the temptation to be drawn into so much reactive supervision and spent more of their time on planned work focused on stated objectives".

The Inspectors reported "a lack of clarity surrounded the position of level III social workers. It was acknowledged everywhere that supervision is equally appropriate for them, but there was confusion about whether this was supervision or consultation, and whether the content should be managerial or professional". (We defer our remarks on the appropriateness of "supervision" and "consultation"). The Paper also provided a picture of a supervision process that lacked planning and proper recording. "It was said that scheduled supervision sessions usually lasted an hour to an hour and a half, but in most places these were subject to interruptions because of crises and the needs of other workers ..... Only a small number of supervisors kept notebooks which indicated the frequency with which cases had been considered and to remind them to discuss particular cases and issues ..... Interestingly there was no evidence of a really effective administrative system to remind workers and supervisors when a case was due for a discussion ..... Inspectors studied the files for any evidence of the supervisory process, and found little written evidence of the supervisor's influence... It was clear that supervisors did not see the records as an important tool to enable their staff to approach their work in a structured and planned way, nor did they see the records as a tool for themselves to use in supervision. Only rarely did supervisors write comments on files concerning workers' practice or define issues relating to accountability. It was unusual for workers to bring their files to supervision sessions, and equally rare for supervisors to read files in advance of discussions".

We agree with the Inspectors' conclusion that "by not seeing records, supervisors missed the opportunity to lay down expectations about recording. They missed the chance to emphasise the importance of records in safeguarding the interests of the child by providing enough information for planning, and in building up information for use in legal proceedings". Although a few books, and a large number of papers and essays have been written on the subject of supervision, we suspect that an up-to-date, definitive work waits to be written. (The subject of supervision does not even rate a separate heading in the index to the Barclay Report). We are insistent in saying that good supervision for all those involved in providing a direct service in the child abuse system is essential, although the nature of the supervision will vary from one professional to another.

## What is supervision?

There is no easy definition of the word. It has become one of those "vogue" words - like "concern", "monitoring", "professional" and "support" - where preciseness is lost in a cosy familiarity. Their careless, but comforting use means their worth as communicators of ideas has become seriously devalued.

C.S. Lewis, in an essay in 1961, warned that "before we can communicate, what we need to be particularly on our guard against are precisely the vogue words, the incantatory words, of our own circle.... They are like family language or a school slang, and our private language may delude ourselves as well as mystifying outsiders. Enchanted words seem so full of meaning, so illuminating. But we may be deceived. What we derive from them may sometimes be not so much a clear conception as a heart-warming sense of being at home and among our own sort. 'We understand one another' often means 'we are in sympathy' ".

In social work, the definition of supervision lies somewhere between superman's eyesight and the dictionary's offering of : "oversee, superintend execution or performance of (thing) or actions or work of (person);"[1]. Many definitions have been offered, and many of the more recent ones have referred to the developmental requirements of the supervisee. Thus Fred Berl, reporting on the work of an eight-person seminar in America ("an attempt to construct a conceptual framework for supervision" in *"Supervision and Staff Development"* 1966) concluded with the commendably brief statement that "the chief aim of supervision is to help workers gain the capacity to perform adequately".

---

[1] Concise Oxford Dictionary.

Dorothy E. Pettes used as her opening definition of supervision the following : "Supervision is a process by which one social work practitioner enables another social work practitioner *who is accountable to him* to practice to the best of his ability". (The italics are in the original, but are rightly emphasised with regard to this case because of the lack of appreciation of accountability within the relationship between Mr. Ruddock and Mr. Neill and between Miss Reader and Mrs. Henlin). We would want to add to these definitions that the social worker's best ability is directed towards providing a service to clients. The purpose of the social work activity, and therefore of the supervision process buttressing it, is to provide as good a service as possible. In child abuse work, this is a service primarily for the child. Most children are best helped within the context of their own families, and most children's interests are not separate from those of their parents. But the focus remains on the child.

A good description of the purpose of supervision and the role of the supervisor in child abuse cases is provided in the report of the Social Services Inspectorate (March 1986): " Because of the complexity and diversity of the social work task in child abuse work it is essential that all social workers must receive regular professional and managerial supervision. The purpose of professional supervision must be to help them provide the most appropriate form of service for the client and to assist workers to maintain their objectivity. The managerial supervision must ensure that the work is being carried out according to the policies of the agency and that they have reasonable resources for the job. With regard to child abuse case supervision, it is particularly important because of the need to protect the child and to ensure that he or she remains the prime focus for the social worker's attention. ..... It is the role of the supervisor to ask searching and pertinent questions which enable the worker to assess the strengths and needs of each family and work to a plan in accordance with these needs".

## Supervision in the Carlile case

Regular planned supervision of the social worker's, or the health visitor's work with the Carlile family was never undertaken. Mr. Ruddock acknowledged that "one of the important things in a child abuse case is having regular structured supervision". But he also agreed that, while he was dealing with the case from January until June, he did not "have any structured supervision of the case". He certainly had a number (the number was in dispute, but is not important) of short conversations or discussions with Mr. Neill, but nothing approaching what Mr. Ruddock said would have been helpful - namely, sitting down quietly and trying to analyse the work each day, with the file in front of the two of them. Likewise Miss Reader talked to Mrs. Henlin, once formally and then only in a cursory manner.

Mr. Ruddock should have ensured that he received the kind of supervision he needed. In the early stages of his handling of this case, he, as a new team manager with Greenwich Social Services Department, was no doubt keen to demonstrate his ability and competence. In the later stages of the case, when Mr. Ruddock's recollection of what had happened was less clear, he might have reached a state of mind in which he no longer recognised what he was missing by way of supervision.

Given the dearth of supervision, there is little useful comment that can be made on its content. Unfortunately, what we can see in this case is a very clear picture of how a social worker or a health visitor, even a comparatively experienced one, will appear without supervision.

Mr. Ruddock often referred to being confused about what was happening in the Carlile family. He was concerned that he might have overlooked something; he was worried that things in the case were not fitting together, and that he might be taking wrong turns; his question marks about the case were getting larger and larger; he did not call a case conference; he did not contact the child abuse consultant until at a late stage (in fact 3 weeks before Kimberley died); his recollections of the later stages of Kimberley's life became sketchy and vague; he allowed patches of time where the case drifted without a clear plan; he lost sight at times of the possibility of child abuse generally, concentrating on behavioural problems of Kimberley as if they were unrelated to indications of child abuse, and of Kimberley specifically; and he was left haunted at the end by incomprehension - why had he not taken steps that seemed so obvious to him in retrospect?

We accept unhesitatingly that Mr. Neill was an experienced, hard working and approachable manager. A number of witnesses testified to his accessibility. There was constant reference to the fact that the door to his office was always open to anyone to consult him. But, as Dorothy Pettes pointed out, "an open door cannot be open all the time. When one worker is inside, others cannot be". Dorothy Pettes continued, "the old fashioned system of simply catching one's superior when possible, and usually only for emergency decisions, is simply not good enough for a modern social work organisation".

While urgent consultations will always be necessary, because Social Services Departments specialise in emergencies, these immediate, unplanned consultations are no substitute for properly organised and planned supervision. The editors of "Understanding Child Abuse" state: "It is of paramount importance that there is a regular and consistent pattern of sessions. Indeed, the supervisor should demonstrate in the organisation of his work how staff should relate to the families they supervise". Mr. Neill accepted that he failed to set a specific timescale for reporting back action on work with the Carlile family. Setting a timescale for reporting back is a start to supervision. We do not accept that the role of the supervisor is a passive one; nor did Mr. Neill. He saw it as his clear responsibility to do more questioning of Mr. Ruddock's assessment, and to "have been more mindful of the child abuse indicators". So often it is the supervisor who is in the best position to recognise that a case is being left to wander without purpose. Mr. Neill candidly admitted that he considered he had failed to ensure that definite tasks were being established, with definite time targets.

Caught up in a difficult and complex case, it is all to easy to lose sight of procedures, and Mr. Neill also acknowledged that he failed to adhere strictly to Greenwich Social Services Department's child abuse procedure. He told us that a case conference should have been called, at least by the end of April or the beginning of May: "An active child protection line should have been followed". Such an approach would have ensured a medical examination of Kimberley.

## Consultation

There is a respectable body of opinion of some antiquity that supervision may in the course of time be transformed into consultation, as the practitioner becomes more experienced. Florence Hollis expressed this in her book *"Case Work: Psycho-social Therapy"* in 1966: "There is no question but that, ideally, workers should reach a point at which "consultation" can be substituted for supervision. In consultation the worker himself decides which cases he needs to discuss, how frequently and so on ..... It usually takes from four to six years of experience to reach self-dependent practice. During this time there should be a gradual transition from supervision to consultation".

We consider, however, this view to be based on a mistaken conception of workers in large organisations being able to move towards becoming independent practitioners. It also ignores the requirements of the agency and the contents of managerial supervision. Also, we believe that, however experienced the practitioner might be, child abuse work is sufficiently complex and demanding as to require, invariably, good supervision. In this case, both the Team Manager and the Health Visitor were experienced.

We are aware of few people working in the field of child abuse who would express sufficient confidence in their abilities, knowledge and experience, to say that they do not need supervision. We consider there should be no confusion over the position of level III social workers, as was uncovered by the Social Services Inspectorate. We would want to support the proposals, contained in the opening quotation on "supervision and consultation" in *"Understanding Child Abuse"*: "Because of the complexity and diversity of the social work task in child abuse work it is essential that *all* social workers *must* receive regular professional and managerial supervision" (emphasis supplied). **We recommend that local authorities' child abuse procedures should contain some such requirement**. Consultation may conveniently be used to supplement, but never to replace supervision. (see Chapter 21).

## Good supervision

Supervision enables practitioners to know themselves. We all have some areas of our work we find more difficult than others; we all have weaknesses as well as strengths. Social workers have a clear duty to know their weaknesses and to be able to capitalise on their strengths. It will be other children as well as Lear's daughters who will suffer if the social worker, like the King, "hath ever but slenderly known himself". (King Lear, Act One, Scene One). As *"Understanding Child Abuse"* states, "it is important to be alert to personal feelings and reactions. There is considerable evidence from all disciplines of workers struggling to contain feelings of anger and denial and also focusing on one part of the family to the detriment or exclusion of another".

No-one who has undertaken a child abuse investigation will deny that it is a stressful and demanding responsibility. A child's safety may depend upon the investigating officer's professional competence and very best ability. Anything that reduces this competence is dangerous. The Inquiry heard evidence which suggested that Mr. Ruddock was under considerable stress, particularly in the months immediately preceeding Kimberley's death. He accepted that he should have been able to recognise the effect this had on his performance, but unhappily he did not. Good supervision would have recognised this. We also heard evidence suggesting that Mr. Neill himself was under considerable pressure and there might well come a point when a certain level of stressful dysfunctioning becomes institutionalised within an organisation. That is why the capacity to sit back and have a cool and objective assessment of performance is not a luxury but essential, however busy a department might be.

The second function of supervision we wish to draw attention to is its need to help the social worker recognise the effect achieved by the emotions being beamed out from the family. Many emotions and reactions are contagious. Mrs. Carlile was described as an able manipulator and was a veteran when it came to dealing with social workers. Mr. Hall was an assertive, determined and domineering character. To deal with this family any worker would have had to be clear-sighted and aware of the manipulation practised by abusing parents. It is well known that such parents are adept at fobbing off the attempts of public authorities. Likewise, the social worker must be determined and assertive. To achieve this it might well have been necessary for the workers to recognise the psychopathology of the Carlile family. A social worker needs to have his antennae in working order to pick up the signals of child abuse.

While supervision is a skilful and subtle process, supervisors need to be hard-headed and business-like in their approach. Effective work in child abuse cases requires tangible planning. **We recommend that supervision should make sure that certain action is taken, in a way capable of being evaluated within a specified timescale.** The BASW guidelines describe how this plan should include "a regular pattern of visiting children at risk of abuse", and "a duty to monitor that the agreed pattern is being followed, that the child is seen, and that the outcome of visits is properly recorded". In any such complex activity it is remarkably easy to lose sight of the wood for the trees. The supervisor's position, and view point, should make it possible for him or her to stand back from the forest of information and conflicting interests and note the salient features of effective work.

The supervisor also offers evaluation. It is useful to know how we are doing in our jobs and to identify areas for improvement. In addition to general evaluation related to professional development, a supervisor can also offer assessment of work on a particular case. However experienced a worker, it is possible to get stuck, confused, frightened or bored. The task of supervision is to be watchful for these signs, and even contemplate re-allocating the case if the case is overwhelming the social worker. Health visitors, and social workers in Social Services Departments, do not work in specialised agencies. The range of clients and problems that they are expected to deal with is considerable. Whether we like it or not, the statutory and practical framework in which workers operate is becoming more comprehensive and detailed. Given the knowledge that is needed to keep up with these developments, it sometimes seems like our expectations of these workers puts us in the position of the rustics as they gazed at the village schoolmaster:

> "And still they gaz'd, and still the wonder grew,
> That one small head could carry all he knew".
>
> (Oliver Goldsmith, The Deserted Village).

The supervisor can make sure that two small heads are better at storing knowledge than one. The DHSS in its consultative document "*Child Abuse—Working Together*" stated that: "The supervisor's first task is to ensure that the practitioner is familiar not only with any internal practice and procedural guidelines but also with the legal framework relevant to child abuse work and with the local handbook of inter-agency procedures". We heard during the course of the Inquiry that Mr. Ruddock did not feel entirely comfortable with the extent of his legal knowledge; and Mr. Neill acknowledged that the requirements of the child abuse procedures in Greenwich were not followed. Supervision in child abuse cases must be the bedrock which supplies the safeguard that ensures the relevant knowledge is possessed by the practitioner.

Supervision also provides a second opinion. The decisions in child abuse cases are often so fundamental that no one person should be left with the final responsibility for making them. (We recognise however that in urgent situations the person investigating sometimes has to take responsibility for making an immediate decision to protect a child). In "*Understanding Child Abuse*" it is stated that "direct involvement of the supervisor will also give the social worker the reassurance of a second opinion based on direct knowledge of the family". This reassurance will be relevant only if the supervisor does have a thorough knowledge of the family through regular discussions with the social worker and with a thorough knowledge of the material on the case file.

In the light of the findings by the Social Services Inspectorate, we would like to express our view that it is crucial that the supervisor does see, and is familiar with the case file, since the results of effective supervision should be evident in the recording on the file.

We are aware that we may be accused of making too big a claim for supervision, but our emphasis is supported by the report of the Social Services Inspectorate: "Social Services Departments should have a written policy on supervision which makes clear the importance of scheduled and systematic supervision of work with children in care and their families" and "Social services departments should provide written guidance to supervisors about their managerial and professional supervision of workers, and this guidance should cover the specific aspects which are important in child abuse cases".

No supervision, let alone good supervision, was operative in Mr. Ruddock's handling of the Carlile case. We cannot say that the absence of supervision was a cause of the failure to prevent Kimberley Carlile's death. What we do

194

conclude is that both Mr. Ruddock and Mr. Neill should reasonably have foreseen that, without effective supervision, the protection to which Kimberley Carlile was entitled to receive from Social Services would be put at risk. Put that way, the two of them were in breach of their duty to protect Kimberley Carlile.

# CHAPTER 31

# VIOLENCE AND STRESS IN SOCIAL WORK

## Violence to Social Workers

At the outset of the Inquiry we expected the issue of violence to social workers would have to be a major consideration, for two reasons. First, it was rightly receiving considerable attention within the social work profession at the time of the Inquiry; and, second, we knew that Mrs. Carlile had a penchant for violent men and that Kimberley had been treated with extreme violence. In the event we found that violence, or the threat of violence, towards those having contact with the Carlile family, apparently had little bearing on the way the case was handled.

Mr. Stanley Bute reminded us that in the last 3 years four social workers have died in the course of their work: Isobel Schwarz was killed in her office on 5 July 1984 at Bexley Psychiatric Hospital; Norma Morris died in April 1985, while visiting a youth who had tried to commit suicide; Francis Bettridge was killed on 5 September 1986, while visiting the house of a client in Birmingham; and Richard Kirkman, a residential social worker, was stabbed to death at a hostel for single homeless people in May 1987 in Stockport. Many more staff have been assaulted, and even more threatened with violence, although the actual incidence cannot be stated confidently, despite a growing number of studies on the subject. What has been revealed is that most employers do not know what is happening to their staff, and many staff who have suffered at the hands of violent clients have kept quiet about it. We were pleased that the Association of Directors of Social Services (ADSS) and the DHSS have started an initiative on the subject of violence. The ADSS has made a clear statement that "the safety of employees ..... is a management responsibility. Managers must structure policies, procedures and back-up support in such a manner that they are not influenced primarily by resource availability, but rather by their effectiveness". The employee has responsibility too, especially in identifying situations where violence or the risk of such is a potential problem, and in identifying any particular areas where they have problems of their own connected with violence. (Occasionally, clients are the victims rather than the villains). The first step must be for employers and employees to co-operate so that good information exists concerning the incidence of, and the circumstances surrounding, violence to staff. After that, we would commend for consideration the subjects put to us by Stanley Bute in his written evidence:

"1.   The need for a policy statement,

2.   Support for the employee,

3.   Guidelines for the management and prevention of violence,

4.   Anticipation skills,

5.   Communication techniques,

6.   Employees and their appointment,

7. Employees and their work environment,

8. Resources,

9. Monitoring procedures, and

10. Training".

Unfortunately, violence is a fact of professional life that social workers, like members of other occupations, have to live with. What is required is that the practice of social work is made as safe from violence as possible, and that social workers are supported and protected by their colleagues and managers.

The effects of the fear of violence are likely to be very hard to identify. We suspect, however, that these effects are far more widespread and influential than suspected at present. If, as is the case, some social workers are too ashamed after being attacked to report the incident, and are even then inclined to blame themselves, how much more unlikely it must be that they will admit to a feeling of uneasiness before any violence has occurred. It is not easy to admit to being afraid; social workers must, for their own sake and for their clients' sake. For their own sake, so that they do not try to tackle in isolation problems that should be shared; for their clients' sake, so that they are protected from being violent. Clients' interests are also served if their social workers' judgments are not impaired by fear. It is only too easy to find other reasons for doing something, or not doing something, when the real reason is we are afraid to do it. One Member of the Commission (who would like to remain anonymous, but is male and not a Q.C.) can recall being sent out as a social work student to visit "a problem family", but on being greeted at the gate by a mighty alsatian with drooling jowls, returned to the office to record "visited, no response", only to be challenged by an incredulous supervisor who knew that the house contained 8 children who never went to school, and 2 parents who never went to work and probably suffered from agoraphobia into the bargain. Sometimes our efforts at concealment are identified by others or admitted to by ourselves. All too easily, however, we can deny our feelings so effectively that we cease to have the capacity to recognise our rationalisations for what they are.

What research there is on violence to social workers has suggested that violent incidents are more likely to occur when a client's freedom is threatened in some way. Thus, predictably, when compulsory measures apply to the elderly, the mentally ill or children, the risk of violence is at its highest. Here we have another area where every effort must be made to make sure that a social worker's assessment, on which might hinge the safety of a child, is not disarmed by the possibility of violence or the fear of its possibility. We encourage social workers to be straight, open and frank with their clients when investigating possible cases of child abuse; we should also encourage social workers to be straight, open and frank with themselves and to speak out if they are fearful for their own safety or if they consider their performance as a social worker is being handicapped by fear of violence, either generally or in relation to a particular case. In recommending that social workers deal with their own fear we are recommending the very action that many abusing parents have been unable to take for, as James Anthony Froude observed, "fear is the parent of cruelty".

Of those who had contact with the Carlile family it was only the health visitor who considered she had been intimidated, by Mr. Hall during a telephone conversation, and admitted that this might have made her more reluctant to visit the family. Mrs. Swinburne wanted to make sure she did a joint visit, initially proposing to go with a health visitor but then, in the event, being accompanied by the duty senior, Ms Streeter. Mr. Ruddock, on the other hand, was happy to visit the family on his own. Mr. Moorhouse, who visited the family during their short stay in Kensington & Chelsea, did not find Mr. Hall aggressive or intimidating, instead he was described as "quite likeable", and when Mr. Hall pushed forcefully for the return of the children from care, Mr. Moorhouse thought the level of aggression was "probably quite appropriate". Miss Gregory, recording a meeting held at Wingfield School on 23 April 1986, wrote that Mr. Hayter expressed concern about X and about "step-father who appears very aggressive when he is at school". Yet Mr. Cox, the deputy head, and Miss Rouse, X's school teacher, did not find Mr. Hall especially aggressive; they told us there were many more threatening parents with children at the school. Dr. Spencer, who saw Mr. Hall at the clinic on 4 June 1986, when Z was taken for a measles injection, found that her questions caused him "to be ill at ease". Therefore she "decided not to ask any more questions".

Putting these descriptions together, no clear portrait emerges of Mrs. Carlile or Mr. Hall. He undoubtedly set the scene with his visit to the Social Services Neighbourhood Office in Ebdon Way in October 1985, when he announced that he wanted nothing to do with Social Services and suggested "that social workers were the worst people that ever walked the earth". After that we have little direct evidence that threats of violence played a part in the handling of the case, except the admission by the health visitor that she had been intimidated. We remain uneasy, however, about what prevented Mrs. Swinburne and Ms Streeter from resisting the persistent determination of Mrs. Carlile and Mr. Hall during their visit, and what made Mr. Ruddock willing to accept the most fleeting of glimpses of two children during his last visit to the home. It is hard not to conclude that possibly Mrs. Carlile, but more probably Mr. Hall, conveyed messages at some level which suggested that it could be risky to push them too far. His threshold tolerance was probably not all that high.

The last place we want to reach is an environment where high levels of violence have become acceptable. **We recommend that all employers take whatever steps are necessary to make the practice of social work as safe from violence as possible; and we also recommend that all social workers should speak up if they are subjected to any form of violence, or if they are in fear of violence.**

## Stress in Social Work

The Inquiry was faced with a gap between the failures in practice of those trying to work with Kimberley and the high standard of their oral and written evidence. Indeed, given that the staff principally involved set as high standards for themselves as the Commission could wish, we often witnessed them puzzling over the reasons for their falling from their own standards. Faced with such a gap, it is tempting to fill it up with some one thing, even though the discrepancy is caused by many factors. One of the "fillers" offered for our consideration was the effects of stress.

Mr. Ron Baker, who held the Chair in Social Work Practice at the University of New South Wales in the late 1970s, advised us that from his own experience, and "from all the published research" it is clear "that the problem of stress among social workers is now so widespread that it is seriously affecting the quality of sensitive and effective caring that can be provided". Mr. Baker described for us a "typical pattern of an ascending progression of stress", rising to a threshold where healthy anxiety can lead to "enhanced functioning". "Beyond the threshold however, optimal stress gives way to dysfunctional stress which is evidenced by a number of different behavioural reactions including a sense of failure, feelings of anger, resentment, guilt and blame, a sense of isolation and withdrawal leading to discouragement and indifference. As many as 28 different behavioural reactions have been identified as being typical of dysfunctional stress in recent research".

Stress, like hunger and thirst, is an inescapable part of life. It is difficult to judge when it goes beyond;

"... the monotonous moils of strained, hard run
Humanity,"

("In death divided" by Thomas Hardy)

Stress is not the prerogative of any one profession or occupation. Many people will probably want to insist that their job is especially stressful. Research suggests that stress affects people in various walks of life, ranging from Swedish Government officials to British airline pilots. Its sheer ubiquity makes it awkward to employ as an explanation for particular sets of circumstances.

It is not an easy word to define. Donald Norfolk (in *"The Stress Factor"*) noted that: "Attempts to define it invariably fail. A search of the medical literature shows that there are over 300 different definitions of anxiety and none of these can be considered wholly satisfactory .......Although stress is an integral part of our everyday lives, it remains remarkably little understood".

Consequently, we approach the subject with some caution. Coming at it from the direction of good health, what we can say is that those working in the child protection system will have a demanding job, and the life of a child could depend on their decisions. Thus, anything that stops those workers from being in as good shape as possible is dangerous. Elizabeth Ash found, in her study, that "only a few courses.....prepared students for the often stressful experience of decision-making in child care".

A variety of pressures were weighing down heavily on a number of the key personnel working with the Carlile family. Miss Reader had a period "acting up" when her workload would have been particularly heavy, and during this time she received little support or supervision. She then had to start a new relationship on Mrs. Henlin's appointment. Mrs. Henlin herself, with a broad managerial span, had a tough start to her new job. Mr. Neill had a busy area to manage, with 3 new team managers appointed in a short space of time. Mr. Ruddock had to succeed a well-liked and idiosyncratic team manager, had to deal with a number of conflicts affecting his new team, lost two of his most experienced social workers at the beginning of 1986, and had the unfortunate experience of coping with the death of one of his clients involved in an allegation of child sexual abuse, during the time he was responsible for work with the Carlile family. All these staff may have had many other problems at work, and at home, of which we were unaware. These pressures must have had some impact on the confidence and competence of the workers concerned, but it is not possible to define the impact precisely.

Despite the difficulties we have already described,two points can be made about stress. One is that it is the duty of professional people to have sufficient insight into their own condition to recognise if stress, in whatever form, is impairing their judgment and threatening their capacity to achieve a high standard of practice in their work. It is the employer's responsibility to create an environment that does not in itself cause stress, and to offer help when staff are under pressure. Good supervision is central to this responsibility, and we have dealt with that subject in a separate chapter. Dealing with stress can best be seen as part of a general responsibility that employers have in relation to their staff welfare. We were pleased to see that BASW had started an initiative on this front, reported in issues of Social Work Today. **We recommend that all employers make explicit arrangements for dealing with their staff welfare and that these should take into account the effects of stress.**

# CHAPTER 32

# REPORTING BY THE PUBLIC

The Inquiry heard that one anonymous telephone call was received by Area 4 concerning Kimberley. The message was taken efficiently and passed on promptly. The duty senior and duty social worker treated the call with the importance it deserved, and made an urgent visit to Kimberley's home. It is to be regretted that Kimberley was not seen, but that does not detract from the significance of the call. The fact that a neighbour had been prepared to express concern could, and should have saved Kimberley's life. Because of the importance of that call, we want to consider the public's responsibility in cases of suspected child abuse.

We doubt if major advances will be possible in the service we provide to children at risk unless protecting children is accepted as a responsibility we all share. There might well be a tendency to see child protection as somebody else's worry, a job for professionals; in this report we have even suggested that among professional people themselves there might be a tendency to see it as somebody else's worry, a job for the Social Services. Wishing that child abuse did not happen is understandable, but futile: It does. One of the advantages of the recent publicity given to this subject is that public awareness has been raised to a point where it is reasonable to speak of a communal concern. The DHSS draft guide, "Child Abuse - Working Together", stated that: "The community as a whole has a responsibility for the well-being of its children".

In our culture we expect the family, in all its varied forms, to take care of our children, backed-up by the health, social and educational services. The vast majority of children are brought up satisfactorily within families. Many families cope on their own, while others manage perfectly well with a little bit of help from their friends and local services. However, any responsible society must have arrangements prepared for dealing with failures in the usual system. We talk about the nature of this system elsewhere, but in this chapter we want to concentrate on the part the public can play.

When we know of a child at risk (and here we mean a child at risk of physical, emotional or sexual abuse, or neglect), rather than rush to criticise or to gossip, our effort will be best directed towards trying to help. This could be through a personal approach. Passing on a problem to a welfare organisation should not be used as an alternative to giving the kind of support any healthy community should provide for each other, but there will always be circumstances when the offer of a neighbourly, helping hand is not appropriate either because of the nature of the relationships involved, or because of the seriousness of the problem.

If any of us comes to have fears concerning the safety of a child we know it is inexcusable to do nothing, but the decision what action to take is likely to be one of the most difficult we will ever face. Attitudes prevalent in our culture make the decision harder. Many of us have left over from childhood days a distaste for squealing or being a sneak. A deep respect for other people's privacy is usually a virtue. We speak opprobriously of people who spy on their neighbours or poke their noses into other people's affairs; we still talk disparagingly of the copper's nark. It was Robert Frost's neighbour who suggested : "...Good fences make good neighbours". We have already seen how Mr. Hall used the view that an Englishman's home is his castle as a way of keeping Kimberley out of sight. We might well be right to value these views in many circumstances, but they are not of such a high order as a child's safety, well-being and security. We doubt even if the needs of children and the needs of parents are in conflict. We are hardly serving the interests of parents themselves if, by respecting their privacy, we allow them to persist in abusing a child. Such behaviour damages the abuser as well as the child.

In case the priority we give to protecting children is disputed, we want to argue the primacy of meeting a child's needs for the following reasons. First, the worth of any human being means that measures to save us from avoidable harm and pain are pre-eminent, compared with the good manners governing our relationships. If we are on our own at home, totally immobilized by an increasing pain, most of us would prefer the neighbour who forced an entry to see what was up, to the neighbour who minded his or her own business and passed by. Second, caring for our children is the present day's duty to the future. In taking care of today's children we are making our contribution towards what is to come. Finally, children experience a prolonged state of dependency. They cannot look after themselves but have to trust that adults will meet their needs. To betray that trust is to fail one of the basic requirements of life. For these reasons we have no doubt in saying that in most conflicts of opinions, values, or emotions, the needs of children should come first. We also have no hesitation is saying that it is a positive duty of all members of the public to report any instances where they believe a child is at risk.

We see the difficulties concerning this duty. How is a member of the public to judge the degree of risk for a child? We all have different views about child-rearing, and there are is multitude of ways of bringing up children happily. How can anyone judge when a way of treating a child we simply do not like tips over into a form of behaviour that might harm a child? Professional agencies, like the NSPCC, are beginning to produce booklets and to offer guidance to the public over questions such as these. Probably the most helpful advice that can be offered to members of the public is to tell them to trust their instincts and back their own judgment. If we are satisfied that we are not influenced by any malicious motive and if our worries persist concerning the welfare of a child, then we should act. If in doubt, speak out. Such action, even if it subsequently proves to have been mistaken or unnecessary, is justifiable if based on concern for a child. Inaction, and a child suffering unnecessarily as a result, cannot be justified.

How is the public's duty to be discharged? What should they do? Once satisfied concerning the severity of the problem, a child protection agency, such as the local Social Services Department, the NSPCC or the police, should be contacted. This contact might require persistence in a number of ways. To start with, it might require some research to track down an appropriate address or telephone number. The DHSS guide noted that "the size and complexity of Social Services Departments can make it difficult for members of the public to know how to go about" contacting them. Persistence might also be required to make sure that the information has been correctly received and its importance understood. Lastly, where necessary, we would recommend persistence in following-up the initial contact to make sure that appropriate action has been taken.

So far we have been directing our comments at members of the public, but what are the responsibilities of the child protection agencies? To start with they must cultivate an attitude which welcomes contact from the public. After all, as the DHSS guide suggested, "relatives, friends, and neighbours with children are particularly well placed" for bringing cases to the attention of the statutory authorities. Malicious and mistaken calls are bound to occur, but are the price to be paid for the calls that might lead to a child being helped. (We heard evidence that suggested the proportion of "genuine" calls is high enough for this not to be a serious problem). Organisations concerned about the adequacy of the resources at their disposal will be worried about generating demand for their services, but this should not be translated into wanting to turn off referrals unless we are prepared to remain ignorant generally of the level of demand, and ignorant specifically of the needs of an individual child.

The agencies receiving referrals from the public should be clear how to respond. Addressing Social Services Departments, the DHSS guide said that they "should ensure that they have effective arrangements to allow members of the public to refer to them concern about individual children". Any letter should be answered. Referrals made in person, either by a visit to the office or, far more likely, by telephone, should be dealt with in such a way that the people making the referral are made to feel welcome and are put at their ease. The call will often follow a process during which referrers have had to screw up their courage to do something. Any staff likely to deal with these calls must have training in how to handle them. The callers may be nervous and uncertain. The message communicated might be muddled and hesitant. Considerable skill may be required to elicit the kind of information that will enable further action to be taken.

All agencies must have a policy to take such referrals seriously and must make certain they are followed up to the point that a decision can be made concerning the welfare of the child referred.

Ideally, referrers will give their name and address, but this will not always happen. When it does, consideration must be given to interviewing them, and they should be contacted at a later stage and advised what action has been taken, without disclosing confidential information. Where necessary, callers' anonymity must be protected. They could themselves be at risk if their names became generally known. The DHSS guide suggests that the public "must also be confident, because of the difficult and sensitive nature of the situation, that any information they provide will be treated in a confidential way and used only to protect the interest of the child". We believe that what the public need is less that the information they pass on be treated as confidential, for after all it is to be followed up, and more that their identity will not be disclosed. We have heard of some Departments, but certainly not Greenwich Social Services Department, that refuse to accept referrals unless callers agree to give their name and address and allow these to be passed on to the members of the family being investigated. While we wholeheartedly endorse the objective of being as open, straight and frank as possible with the family, we consider this policy to be incompatible with the interests of children and to place too heavy a burden on members of the public.

In order to protect anonymity, staff following up referrals will also have to avoid a clumsy handling of the introduction to the family. Statements such as "your neighbour has called us" can easily lead to identification. Mr. Hall was said by one neighbour to have made serious threats about what he would do if he discovered the identity of the person who called on behalf of Kimberley. Nothing could be more designed to shake the confidence of the public or more to discourage them from playing their part, than an inability to trust they will be taken care of appropriately by the agencies they contact.

We do not think it is sufficient for agencies concerned with child protection to adopt a passive role in their relationship with the public. The DHSS guide cites evidence that the public experience frustration in the difficulties they have in making contact. The guide goes on to suggest that "suitable arrangements" be made including "the use of a special telephone number on posters displayed in public libraries, health clinics, community centres, family doctors' waiting rooms or other suitable local premises". We believe that a variety of opportunities should be sought to educate the public so that they can be helped to know how and when to act on behalf of children at risk.

A CHILD IN MIND:
PROTECTION OF CHILDREN IN A
RESPONSIBLE SOCIETY

# PART V

## CONCLUSIONS AND RECOMMENDATIONS

# CHAPTER 33

# CONCLUSIONS

An anonymous telephone call was received at the Area 4 office of Greenwich Social Services Department in the early afternoon of Friday, 7 March 1986. The caller stated that several neighbours of the Carlile household on the Ferrier Estate were expressing deep concern about the children of the family, in particular a little girl, aged about 4. The neighbours thought that she was, according to a contemporaneous note of the call taken down by a team clerk in Area 4's office and logged on a referral form, "being beaten, cries very pitifully". From that moment, and for the next five days social workers and personnel from other public authorities went into action, although without the degree of urgency or direction which the case warranted. There was neither reference to the Social Services' standby duty officer, nor any contact with the police over that weekend. Few, if any of the social workers and others could have doubted that he or she was engaged in the process appropriate to a case of suspected child abuse, so seriously was the anonymous call treated - and rightly so. Social Services, of course, were acting in accordance with their exclusive statutory duty to investigate whether there were grounds for bringing care proceedings in respect of the child. For the other agencies there was the ostensible acceptance of the duty to aid and assist Social Services.

Two social workers from Area 4 visited the Carlile household in the late afternoon of Friday, 7 March 1986. They were not denied access to the house, but they failed to see the four-year old girl, Kimberley Carlile, or her younger sister. They reported back on the Monday morning to Mr. Martin Ruddock, a team manager in Area 4, who had had previous knowledge of the family.

On that Monday, 10 March, Mr. Ruddock rang the Court Welfare Service at the High Court which indicated that a report on the Carlile household was being requested from Wigan County Court in connection with proceedings for access to the youngest child. Mr. Ruddock was also in touch with Miss Marilyn Reader, the health visitor, who had been in contact with the family and had expressed her own separate concern. Mr. Ruddock spoke to the headteacher of Wingfield Primary School where staff had, two months earlier, been worried by an incident involving Kimberley's older brother (who, with his younger sister, was a pupil at the school) and their step-father, Mr. Nigel Hall. Following the report on the Monday of the social workers' visit, Mr. Ruddock discussed the case with his Area Manager, Mr. Don Neill. Their joint view was that the two younger children needed to be seen. This was because, in part, the visit on the Friday afternoon had not met its prime objective.

Mr. Ruddock went on his own that Monday morning to the Ferrier Estate, but no one in the Carlile household answered the door. He delivered a handwritten letter, pointing out to Mrs. Carlile how imperative it was for both Kimberley and her baby sister to be seen by "a G.P. or health visitor by Wednesday evening". He added: "If you have not done this, I will discuss the situation with the Police Juvenile Bureau with view to considering further action". (This letter is reproduced in Chapter 18). Stung into action, no doubt, by this threat of police involvement (a threat which unhappily was never carried out at any time), Mr. Hall telephoned Social Services the next day, 11 March, and indicated something that led to his being put through to the Child Abuse Section. What Mr. Hall had to tell was significant.

This call was taken by Mrs. Doreen Armstrong, a senior social worker in the Family Finding Unit (a unit for arranging adoption and fostering). Her note of an hour-long conversation gave credence to the worries of the anonymous caller. Mr. Hall described Kimberley, whom he admitted he had shaken and smacked, as unaccepting of him, adding that she was "fouling, wetting, eating faeces, refusing to eat and making herself sick". He also told Mrs. Armstrong that Kimberley had some bruises "due to playing and falling on stairs", but he was insistent that the children were not at risk from abuse. She immediately recorded the substance of the conversation and passed it on to Mr. Ruddock that day. Mr. Hall's call was eloquent testimony to the generally recognised ambivalence of an abusing parent - disarming the audience and yet seeking to rescue the child from anticipated harm. Later that day Mr. Ruddock contacted Mr. Hall, through Mrs. Armstrong, and arranged to visit the Carlile family at 4 o'clock on 12 March.

On the following day, Wednesday, 12 March, the duty social worker at Area 4 rang the clinic and learned from another health visitor that she believed that Miss Reader was intending to visit that day. (That visit, however, did not materialise). A telephone call to the surgery of the general practitioners on the Ferrier Estate revealed that the four children were registered there, and that Kimberley had last been seen on 11 November 1985. (On that occasion Dr. Mahesh, one of the GPs, without examining the child, had written out for Mrs. Carlile a referral note to the Brook Hospital for Kimberley to undergo "speech therapy", a fact unknown to anyone else throughout the handling of this case. The referral was not followed up by Mrs. Carlile who, a week later, on 18 November 1985, went on her own to the health clinic and was seen by Miss Reader).

The arranged visit on 12 March was forestalled by the whole family (parents and four children) unexpectedly turning up at Area 4 offices at about 10 a.m. on that day. The meeting took place in the incommodious conditions of an interview room. Mr. Ruddock's initial impression of Kimberley was of a child "withdrawn, sallow, pasty and still". By the end of a lengthy and amicable discussion he formed the impression of "a happy family", but that Kimberley clearly had behavioural problems that required attention. This was a faulty assessment. Mr. Ruddock should have realised that Kimberley was seriously at risk, if only because her behaviour, as described by her parents, was profoundly disturbing. Far from being reassured, Mr. Ruddock should have doubled his concern.

After the meeting, and having arranged with the Carliles to discuss the case of Kimberley further with them on 3 April, Mr. Ruddock telephoned the headteacher at Wingfield school, requesting that a nursery place be made available to Kimberley. He spoke to the education welfare officer, asking for "ongoing monitoring" of the two older children. And he spoke to Miss

Reader. Both thought it important that Kimberley should be medically examined. He wrote the following day to Mr. Hall and Mrs. Carlile, telling them that he had requested the health visitor - he was in no position to order - to "consider arranging a medical examination" and that a school nursery placement at Wingfield school had been requested. There was nothing at all to prevent Mr. Ruddock himself arranging for a medical examination of Kimberley, by calling the general practitioner or the hospital and accompanying Mrs. Carlile and Kimberley to the doctors. He was in fact in breach of Greenwich's Child Abuse Procedures Guide (para 4) which states that assurances by the parents that a medical examination will be arranged are insufficient. Mr. Ruddock compounded that constant failure to have Kimberley medically examined, by not even managing to see Kimberley for himself; when he visited the Carlile home on 14 April he allowed himself to be manipulated egregiously by Mr. Hall. During the weeks of April, May and June Kimberley was never seen by any of the personnel of the agencies in the management of the child abuse system, other than, on the one occasion, by Mr. Ruddock, uncertainly and only fleetingly through a glass panel above a door at the Carlile home.

Three months later, on 8 June 1986, Kimberley died as a result of a fatal blow inflicted on her head by her step-father. From the post-mortem report and from Dr. Heath's evidence to us, it was obvious that Kimberley had been tortured and starved for many weeks before her death.

* * * * * * * * * * *

Mr. Ruddock failed in a number of respects and on a number of occasions to protect a child manifestly at risk of abuse. But did the multi-disciplinary child abuse system, developed over the last fifteen years, in some sense fail Mr. Ruddock?

This inquiry, to our knowledge, is the twenty-seventh major child abuse inquiry under local government auspices in the last fifteen years - there have also been seven such inquiries set up by a Secretary of State (see Appendix H). In many, if not all of those inquiries, the reports have pinpointed deficiencies in the multi-disciplinary system. All those who have conducted such inquiries, as we have, would have had the like ambition to ensure, so far as possible, the protection of children. We have asked ourselves why it is that inquiry after inquiry has come up with similar recommendations refining the multi-disciplinary system. We think that the time is now ripe for a fundamental questioning of the system which is structured to protect children.

All those who manage and operate the child abuse system can do so effectively and efficiently only so long as that system is itself well constructed and fully operable at the instance of all those involved. Systems, of course, are constructed to facilitate and promote, but never to act as a substitute for, good practice. Kimberley Carlile's death was not averted, because of the failure of Mr. Ruddock to operate the existing child abuse system by calling a case conference. But we discern in the system that there is no reliable mechanism whereby the oversight of a social worker can be compensated for by action on the part of the other agencies in the system. At various points in the management of the Kimberley Carlile case the system spluttered and malfunctioned, because those other agencies did not act fully in accepting responsibility alongside Mr. Ruddock. In short, in this case, the system permitted too much reliance being placed on one person.

This inherently defective system was made even less fully functional by the special circumstances in Greenwich during 1985/86, of recurring resource restraints of a rate-capped London Borough, of reduced staffing levels due to key members leaving, of disarray of the community health services, and of a sudden increase in reported cases of children at risk, which was the common experience across the country.

These factors in turn bore down upon those daily trying to cope with a difficult situation, and produced stress in individuals, hardly conducive to good work which requires planning, assessing and thinking about the problems of child care in an atmosphere of quiet contemplation and studied action within the framework of a well-equipped team. Those who undermine the confidence and morale of the people that society is sending out in its name to protect our children should realise that what they are thereby doing is, unwittingly, to put at risk the children whom they wish devoutly to protect. (Accordingly, we have recommended in Chapter 24 a review of the existing child protection system).

The present system, which is a fudge of the divided responsibilities - Social Services in respect of child care, and the health and educational authorities for the physical and developmental health of children - should not be allowed to continue. We have developed the argument for a reconstructed child protection service in Chapter 24. We do not repeat it here. We would simply re-iterate our firm view that if the main individuals involved in the management of the Kimberley Carlile case are properly to be criticised for their bad practices and persistent failure to protect Kimberley (as indeed they should be, and as they themselves have commendably acknowledged) such criticism must be tempered by acknowledging that the system they are asked to operate is insufficiently supportive of individual workers.

\* \* \* \* \* \* \* \* \* \* \*

The failure in the child abuse system, as it applied to Kimberley Carlile, was precisely traceable to the period before the three Carlile children arrived in Greenwich on 4 October 1985, when they were discharged from voluntary care by Wirral Social Services. In two major respects Greenwich Social Services were handicapped by the failure of Wirral Social Services.

The three older children had been in voluntary care for the previous fourteen months and had been placed with foster-parents. (Z had remained with her mother since birth in November 1984). At the time of receiving the children into care, the Wallasey office of Wirral Social Services held two case conferences (which were not strictly child abuse conferences, although so titled) on 3 May and 15 August 1984. From our reading of the minutes of the first of the two case conferences, the health visitor failed to draw attention to the fact that Kimberley in November 1983, at her 24-month developmental assessment, was showing distinct signs of failure to thrive, and there was a question mark over her progression in expressive language. No further mention was provided at the second case conference; and no developmental assessment at 36 months (i.e., November 1984) was arranged by Wirral Social Services which had Kimberley in their trust. But the prime responsibility rested with Wirral Health Authority to have arranged for that developmental assessment to take place. And nothing other than a routine medical check (the equivalent of a "free from infection" inspection) took place on 4 October 1985. Yet within a month of transfer, Mrs. Carlile was visiting the general practitioners on the Ferrier Estate, seeking "speech therapy" for Kimberley.

Little of the information that was in the possession of Wirral Social Services - neither the case files, nor a summary of the case file, nor any of the details of Kimberley's development - came south to Greenwich. Any continuity in the care of the three children was instantly broken. Some of the information (including the summary of the two case conferences) did percolate down to Greenwich Health Authority, but not until 16 February 1986, and there was no onward transmission to Greenwich Social Services.

The health visiting records, including the result of the developmental assessment of November 1983 arrived in Greenwich only after Kimberley's death. Had there been a case conference in Greenwich at any time after March 1986, the minutes - and not just the summaries - of those earlier case conferences would surely have surfaced: a failure in communication between the disciplines of child care and child health. Whatever the flaws in the flow of information from Wirral - there is, sad to relate, no national system of information exchange - the reception and distribution of health records by Greenwich Health Authority was inadequate. This defect was a reflection of general maladministration within the Authority. We heard a good deal of evidence however, which strongly suggests that the shortcomings have been recognised, and major changes in the management of child health services in Greenwich are, we understand, well in hand.

The second failure was the absence of proper communication between the Social Services Departments of two local authorities: There were three major pieces of information that were not passed on. (1) Greenwich Social Services were unaware of the extent of the domestic violence of the Carlile household; (2) there was no mention of the two case conferences, let alone their content; and (3) there was no reference to the intention in August 1984 (to be abandoned by April 1985) on the part of Wirral Borough Council to assume parental rights in respect of the three children under Section 3, Child Care Act 1980. Furthermore, Wirral had made no plan of rehabilitation, phased or direct, of the three children into the reconstructed family in Greenwich. In fact, the hand-over at Edgehill Family Group Home on 4 October 1985 was, to say the least, perfunctory. The absence of any such plan, compounded by the nature of the hand-over, was inexcusable.

In a letter sent that day, Wirral Social Services merely requested Greenwich Social Services to engage in "some sort of monitoring .... while the children settle back with their mother". It is, therefore, hardly surprising that Greenwich offered their services to the Carlile family only on a take-it-or-leave-it basis.

Indeed the summary provided to Greenwich of what Wirral thought was relevant for purposes of future "monitoring" of the Carlile family shows only too clearly how poor Wirral's assessment was of Mrs. Carlile's ability to provide proper parental care. But that is no excuse for not having taken steps to get further information from Wirral about the reunion of the Carlile family.

Prime responsibility for a formal hand-over of the case lies with Wirral Social Services. Had the full results of the background to the family's reunion been communicated to Greenwich there would, however, have been a clear duty on Greenwich to be vigilant over the welfare of the three children, and Kimberley in particular, in view of her lack of development in the past. That the duty of protection never arose is attributable mainly to a failure on the part of the Wirral Social Services and Health Services, to acknowledge their responsibility to ensure proper procedures were adopted for the transfer out of a local authority's area of children who had been in their trust for an appreciable length of time. This too was inexcusable. Wirral Social Services appeared to have no idea what kind of life the children would be experiencing in this reconstituted family. They appear not even to have made any proper assessment of Mrs. Carlile as a parent, with or without a new, unknown co-habitee. In the event the response to the offer of help from Greenwich Social Services was the calculated snub from Mr. Hall.

We think that Mr. Ruddock was fully entitled to say, as he did in submissions to us, that if he had been in possession of the full history of the Carlile family "the case would have been handled differently, possibly decisively differently". Greenwich Social Services and Greenwich Health Authority were not helped by Wirral in their initial involvement with the Carlile family; the same allowance cannot be so readily be made for their handling of the case thereafter.

\* \* \* \* \* \* \* \* \* \* \* \*

The first alert came via Wingfield School in mid-January 1986 when the eldest child aroused the concern of the school staff when he announced, with not a little bravado, that he had been "thrown across" (or "around", according to some records) the room at home by his step-father. We have described the response of the school staff and the educational welfare officers in an earlier chapter. It does not call for repetition. Only two matters deserve to be noted.

First, there is evidence of something less than wholehearted commitment to the multi-disciplinary process. The headteacher at Wingfield School, Mr. Hayter, might usefully have communicated more information to the health authorities about the continued surveillance of the two older Carlile children at the school and the fact of their removal to Henwick School at the end of April. His liaison with Social Services, on the other hand, was excellent.

That apart (which we do not regard as seriously detracting from the caring attitude and approach adopted by Mr. Hayter and all his staff), the incident of mid-January was handled sensitively and sensibly. The teacher, Miss Rouse, in particular, acted in a responsible and professional manner in first taking an early opportunity to examine the Carlile boy physically, and then continuing to watch out for any signs of child abuse in the Carlile family. What came out of the incident within the educational setting was an aspect of the behaviour of Mr. Hall to one at least of his four step-children. It was an incident that would have acquired an importance had it been considered at a case conference.

Second, the concentration by the educational personnel on the two children at school deflected from the worry that ought to have been directed towards the one child for whom a nursery school place was offered, and significantly rejected. That rejection, with its instant avoidance of daily monitoring of the child, ought to have been treated with urgent concern. Coupled with the repeated failure by Social and Health Services to have Kimberley Carlile medically examined, it should have prompted immediate action. It was not so perceived, because the focus was on the two older children - particularly X - and not primarily, if at all, on Kimberley Carlile. This educational distraction can be seen clearly enough now, but only in hindsight. We stress, however, that the case conference model is designed precisely to subject one discipline's perception of its work to the objective scrutiny of another discipline's expertise and experience.

\* \* \* \* \* \* \* \* \* \* \*

Our Inquiry has thus been narrowed down to a series of questions: why was Kimberley not taken by a social worker to the clinic for a medical examination, or even visited in the home by the health visitor, Miss Reader? The primary responsibility for seeing that the child was seen by a doctor lay with the parents - strictly speaking, they did not need to be prompted, but in fact they were frequently urged to have the child examined. Should their persistently evasive behaviour, and refusal to comply with the need for Kimberley Carlile to be medically examined, have been properly appreciated for what it was, the active concealment of child abuse? It was not as if the relevant agencies did not alert themselves to the need for such an examination, and for the examination to take place promptly.

Mr. Ruddock's letter to Mrs. Carlile of 10 March 1986 is explicit on that score, although it could have been more demanding. The actual sense of urgency and the threat of enforcement that did exist then was, however, forestalled by the visit of the whole Carlile family to the Area Office on 12 March 1986, and Mr. Ruddock's ill-judged assessment that all that needed attention were the "serious behavioural problems" of Kimberley. Long before April 14, when Mr. Ruddock was permitted by Mr. Hall only to catch, at most, a guarded glimpse of Kimberley, there was ample justification to intervene in order to assess the risk of abuse and to protect Kimberley from further harm.

But what action? Judging the situation as it presented itself to Mr. Ruddock in mid-March 1986, we conclude that it was as if Mr. Ruddock was going round and round the Mulberry bush but not taking the crucial step into the bush to pluck out the helpless child. Why did he not take that step of moving the child from the Carlile home? Was his omission to take it an error of judgment, or was it a more serious failure?

We remind ourselves at the outset what statutory powers Mr. Ruddock had at his command. Kimberley was not the subject of a Care Order. Greenwich Borough Council, through its Social Services Committee and Social Services Department, had not vested in it any parental rights and duties. It had no Supervision Order, which would have required constant monitoring of the child's welfare. Further still, the child was not on the child abuse register; that would have committed the Social Services Department to appropriate some of its stretched resources to watching the development of the child. The case would have been allocated to a member of the Ferrier team in Area 4.

In the absence of any such statutory power or obligation to apply some input from Social Services, the sole relevant statutory duty on the part of Social Services was to investigate the case as a result of what Mr. Ruddock and others had seen, plus the information communicated by the anonymous neighbour. This year's White Paper, *The Law on Child Care and Family Services* (Cm.62) indicates (para 42) that the existing statutory duty to investigate should be widened by substituting a more active duty to investigate in any case where it is suspected that the child is suffering harm or is likely to do so. Mr. Ruddock appears to us, wisely, to have interpreted his investigative duty in that more ample sense.

The question is, did his investigations go far enough, and if so, did he act appropriately? It is clear that Mr. Ruddock was trying to have the child medically examined, or to see for himself what her physical condition was like. In neither, however, did he succeed. Should he then have resorted to other means of achieving that objective?

It is as well if at this point we interject our view that there is no basis for the allegation that welfare services - and Mr. Ruddock in particular - ever abandoned Kimberley to the fate she suffered, other than in a loose, colloquial sense that Kimberley might have been killed at any time during the "investigation" of a suspected case of child abuse. Even on 12 May Mr. Ruddock had discussed the case with the Child Abuse Co-ordinator, Mrs. Gabbott (we think that this was far too late, but better late than never). Mr. Ruddock records Mrs. Gabbott's view that if Kimberley was not seen by early June "we should consider further action to ensure her safety". And only 4 days before her death Miss Reader rang to say Mr. Hall and the baby, Z, had been seen at the clinic but there was, according to Miss Reader's note of her conversation with Mr. Ruddock, "no mention of Kimberley".

There are other indicators of continuing concern during April and May 1986. The fact is that Kimberley's welfare was never far from their thoughts, even though this attitude was not translated into action. Mr. Ruddock did have a concern for Kimberley, and had not foresaken her, or given up trying to protect her. It was simply that his attempts fell far short of what could be expected of a social worker. He failed to provide *continuous* case-work. In short, the case was allowed to drift. Procrastination is the parent of drift, and drift is the enemy of protection.

The drifting question that continued throughout the weeks and months was how could they get Kimberley medically examined so as to satisfy themselves that they would be justified in interfering with parental rights

214

and powers. Should Mr. Ruddock in mid-March, and certainly after 14 April, have applied for a Place of Safety Order, particularly since that Order does no more than suspend parental rights and powers for the period of the Order, potentially for a maximum of 28 days, but probably for some substantially less period? It has always been assumed that such an Order carries with it the power in the person applying for the Order to have the child medically examined. We think that there is much confused thinking among social workers and magistrates about the precise legal effect of a Place of Safety Order. (We have discussed this at length in an earlier chapter). It is interesting to note that Mr. Ruddock's form of sanction for the Carliles' failure to get Kimberley medically examined was, in the letter of 10 March, to invoke the aid of the "Police Juvenile Bureau". By Section 40 of the Children and Young Persons Act 1933, any person who has reasonable cause to suspect that a child is being maltreated, in a manner likely to cause unnecessary suffering or injury to health, may apply to a magistrate on information on oath for a warrant.

Such warrant authorises a police officer to search for the child and, if found to be maltreated, to remove the child to a place of safety. Additionally, by Section 17(1)(e), Police and Criminal Evidence Act 1984, the police may enter premises if risk to life and limb is suspected.

Given hindsight and the practice of these disparate provisions in child care legislation, which is hopelessly piecemeal and incomplete, we do not think Mr. Ruddock or his supervisor can be blamed for refraining from using these powers, although they should not have needed to resort to them at that stage if, as they perceived, the parents were co-operating. Having heard evidence from a senior Justices' Clerk on behalf of the Magistrates' Association, and other witnesses, we are confident that few, if any, juvenile justices would have declined to grant a Place of Safety Order in respect of Kimberley Carlile at any time after 11 March. But, since legal opinion within Greenwich Borough Council was that the Place of Safety Order conferred no power in anyone to examine the child medically without the parent's consent, we do not criticise Mr. Ruddock on that account.

Even if Mr. Ruddock is not to be criticised for failing to apply for a Place of Safety Order, it does not follow that he and his Area Manager, Mr. Neill, cannot be criticised for failing to initiate protective action. It is likely that any decision would have been preceded by a case conference. We do think, however, that some positive action was strongly indicated after April 14, when there was an unreasonable refusal by the Carlile parents - in particular, Mr. Hall - to concede access to the home sufficient for an examination of Kimberley.

Where we think Mr. Ruddock did err in his assessment of the case - and in this he should share the responsibility jointly with his Area Manager, Mr. Neill, who was involved in the decision-making process at least by March - was to do no more than display a passive watchfulness over Kimberley's welfare. For Miss Reader and her supervisor, Mrs. Henlin, we describe their failure to provide health surveillance and to arrange for Kimberley to be medically examined as seriously misguided inactivism.

A meeting of the various disciplines, all pooling their expert knowledge and collectively recommending to the Social Services what immediate steps were to be taken by them, by the health services, GP or even the police, should have taken place at some time after mid-March, and in any event after April 14. Had there been a case conference we are confident that, seized of all the relevant information, *plus* crucially the social and medical history of the whole family which ought to have been supplied by Wirral Social Services, or garnered by Greenwich Social Services, the conference would have decided - this (and the selection of the key worker) is the only thing that it can decide, as opposed to recommend - that Kimberley should immediately be put on the Child Abuse Register. That alone would have activated Social Services and the other agencies. We think it was the only sensible action that would have produced a chain reaction, leading to the medical examination of Kimberley Carlile.

Both Mr. Ruddock and Miss Reader have accepted in advance the criticism that they, jointly or separately, should have initiated the calling of a case conference, once it was apparent that they had been unable by any other available means to achieve the immediate objective of having Kimberley Carlile medically examined.

Their acknowledgement that in that respect they fell below the standards they expected of themselves does them great credit. Our considered opinion, now that they are to be criticised, should not be taken as meaning anything other than criticism of their respective conduct in this case, with all the qualifications which we have mentioned at the beginning of this chapter.

The same can be said about their immediate seniors in line management. Neither Mr. Neill nor Mrs. Henlin can avoid sharing the blame. Their respective failure to do no more than to make themselves readily available - that is, not to provide active supervision - contributed to the drift that occurred in the management of the Carlile case in the three months before Kimberley's death. Neither fulfilled the essential role - particularly in a troublesome case of child protection - of bringing to bear an objective assessment of the case, and in that process engaging in questioning of the fieldworker. In Mr. Neill's case there was the dislocating effect of Mr. Ruddock, a team manager, acting in the capacity of a field social worker. The fact that Mr. Ruddock was acting down from team manager should not have altered one iota the constant need for supervision of him as a social worker holding a case. In the result the case was allowed to drift further into aimless inaction.

In the case of Mrs. Henlin's responsibility to supervise Miss Reader, there is the partial excuse that she was new in post, was overwhelmed with her workload and was too reliant upon a health visitor of considerable experience. But these factors are no excuse for derogating from the vital role of supervision.

We think that the absence of supervision of the two field workers was a crucial feature of the mishandling of the case.

* * * * * * * * * * * *

We conclude that Kimberley Carlile's death was avoidable through the

216

intervention of the welfare agencies. Given that Social Services and Health Services were operating under an imperfect system in the management of child abuse cases, there was nevertheless a number of occasions between mid-March and early June 1986 when appropriate action should have been taken, which would have almost certainly led to the rescue of Kimberley from the Carlile household.

Our finding is that each of the four of them failed in a number of serious respects to apply the standard of skill, judgment and care that could objectively be expected from a social worker or health visitor of their respective grades and experience.[1]

$$\star \quad \star \quad \star \quad \star \quad \star \quad \star \quad \star \quad \star \quad \star \quad \star \quad \star \quad \star$$

This has been an unusual inquiry into a case of child abuse. We have been greatly assisted by all those who have appeared before us under the brooding cloud of potential criticism, with all the attendant consequences to future employment and careers. Mr. Philip Gaisford, on behalf of Dr. Hooper, began his submissions thus:

"Against the stark fact of the violent end of another unfulfilled young life, attempts by lawyers to protect the interests of their own clients risk the opprobrium of the merely shabby".

There has been nothing shabby about the legal representation of the parties before us, whose written and oral submissions were uniformly of a very high quality. Even less could it be said of the lawyers' clients. Everyone who came before us accepted the overriding interest of the inquiry - to promote in every possible way the optimum methods in child protection. We think that their unstinting efforts overall to relegate personal interests to a secondary place has helped us to make recommendations which we hope will keep the incidence of death and serious harm to children from abuse by their parents to an irreducible minimum, a goal not yet achieved.

We have not had to reach any conclusions about the conduct of the main participants in this tragedy beyond what they have reached about themselves. There has been no disagreement about the requirement of good professional practice. The central participants' recognition that they fell below the standards they set themselves is more eloquent than any adverse finding that we have made[2]. We have taken this opportunity to look beyond the particular, and to examine some general issues pertaining to a child protection service in a responsible society.

We are fully alive to the fact that there have been vast improvements in child protection, from Maria Colwell in 1973 to Kimberley Carlile in 1987. And we remind ourselves that for every death from child abuse thousands of

---

[1] We have adapted the formula used by Mr. Justice Hodgson in his judgment in *Dietmann v Brent London Borough Council* [1987] I.C.R. 737, 749A, an action for wrongful dismissal arising out of the child abuse inquiry into the Beckford case.
[2] We think that this applies as much to Mrs. Henlin as to the other three, although Mr. Roger Titheridge QC on her behalf did not accept that Miss Reader was right to accept any failures on her part, and for which Mrs. Henlin would be responsible as Miss Reader's supervisor. Since we would have made findings adverse to Miss Reader, unprompted by any concession from her, we have concluded from Mrs. Henlin's helpful testimony that she would not allow Miss Reader to take any blame exclusively on her own account.

children have been rescued from a similar fate. That has been due in no small measure to the dedicated work of those operating within the system.

Yet, while we are critical of the present structure in the management of the child abuse system, and would wish to see it replaced, we do not wish to be interpreted as in any way condoning the poor practices that we have found. Bad practices are bad practices under whatever circumstances pertaining at the time. At most, the bad practitioners may plead mitigation of their culpability. That is how we view the criticisms of the four main participants, as indeed it is how they presented their own practices to us.

We cannot end this report without making one final observation. Those whom we have necessarily had to criticise for their bad practices or lack of professionalism subjected themselves to the total scrutiny of the Inquiry. They were fully engaged in a case of child protection, and failed. Others who, by declining to come forward and render themselves accountable for their possible failures, thereby escape criticism that might likewise justifiably be made of them. There were a few others who avoided becoming engaged in child protection and shuffled off their responsibilities. The result is an inequality in the distribution of fairness.

# RECOMMENDATIONS

The recommendations made in this report are listed below. The recommendations are not in the order they appear in the report, but are classified under appropriate headings, to assist readers. The chapter in which each recommendation appears is given in brackets.

## Recommendations to specific authorities arising out of this case

### Delay in bringing criminal proceedings

We recommend that the Director of Public Prosecutions should set up an internal inquiry as to why the prosecution of Mr. Hall and Mrs. Carlile was so long delayed. *(Chapter 1.)*

### Greenwich Child Abuse Procedures

We recommend that this [the role of the police as outlined in the Greenwich child abuse procedures guide] should be amplified to include police involvement, where and when appropriate, in the investigative stages. *(Chapter 17.)*

We recommend that when the revised [Greenwich child abuse] procedures guide is published in the near future (as we are assured it will be) the Area Review Committee should take steps to ensure its efficient dissemination among all relevant personnel. *(Chapter 27.)*

We recommend that the [Greenwich and Bexley] Family Practitioner Committee should ensure that all child abuse procedures are currently available to all general practitioners in its area. *(Chapter 28.)*

### Collaboration between agencies

We recommend that urgent consideration be given to closer collaboration between the health visitors on the Ferrier Estate and the general practitioners at Telemann Square. *(Chapter 28.)*

We recommend that both services [Greenwich Social Services and the Inner London Probation Service] should give consideration to ensuring that even closer contact, both formally and informally, should be continually developed and improved. *(Chapter 28.)*

### Social Services staffing and facilities

We recommend that consideration be given to seeing if action can be taken to manage the turn-round of staff more efficiently. We recommend specific consideration be given whether the departure of a member of staff can become a longer process, so that proper planning can take place. *(Chapter 11.)*

We recommend that urgent consideration be given by Greenwich Borough Council to providing its Social Services Department with proper facilities for interviewing members of the public. *(Chapter 19.)*

We recommend that he [Mr. Ruddock] should not in the future perform any of the statutory functions in relation to child protection. *(Chapter 3.)*

### Training

Our recommendation [is] that Greenwich Borough Council, Mr. Ruddock's employing authority, should make the document [Mr. Ruddock's written statement to the Commission] available as an educational tool for the training of social workers generally, and for those involved in child abuse particularly. *(Chapter 3.)*

# Recommendations regarding the child protection system generally

### Framework of the child protection service

It is this review [of the fundamental structure of the child protection service] we seek to inspire, and recommend should take place. *(Chapter 24.)*

Subject to what we said in Chapter 24, we recommend that any such legislative provision [for co-operation between statutory and voluntary agencies in the investigation of harm, and protection of children at risk] should include a specific duty on the Health Authorities in this context to promote the welfare of children, in terms similar to Section 1, Child Care Act 1980. *(Chapter 23.)*

Given the national explosion in reported cases of child abuse, we recommend that all Social Services Departments fundamentally review the organisation of their services, and the distribution of their resources, to make sure that they are as well-equipped as possible to respond to this trend. *(Chapter 11.)*

We recommend that employing authorities take on board the need to ensure [health visiting] staff have adequate knowledge of the subject [of child abuse] and of the importance of inter-agency co-operation, possibly by shared learning. *(Chapter 28.)*

We recommend that Health Authorities and Social Services should include in their budgets an item appropriating sufficient funds for the Area Review Committee to carry out its functions. *(Chapter 27.)*

We recommend that all authorities with, or in the process of producing formal child care policies, make sure that child protection has the prominence it deserves. *(Chapter 12.)*

### Exchange of information

We recommend that urgent consideration be given to the establishment of a child protection information system as between Social Services Departments of all local authorities in England and Wales. *(Chapter 26.)*

We recommend that each Area Review Committee undertakes forthwith, under the auspices of the DHSS, a study of the needs in its area, with a view to establishing an information system. *(Chapter 26.)*

## Powers available for the investigation of cases of suspected child abuse

In summary we recommend in ascending order of interference with rights, a bunch of Orders relating both to the investigation of cases of child abuse and to immediate action where child abuse is suspected :

(*a*)  A Power to enter and inspect premises (including a right to interview and examine the child) where a child is living and is thought to be at risk, coupled with a right to see the child.

(*b*)  A Child Assessment Order for the production of the child at a clinic for medical examination.

(*c*)  A warrant to search for or remove a child - a re-enactment, with amendment, of Section 40, Children and Young Persons Act 1933.

(*d*)  An Emergency Protection Order, to replace, with modifications, the Place of Safety Order.

(*e*)  A police officer's right of entry and search without warrant under Section 17(1)(e), Police and Criminal Evidence Act 1984 to save life or limb. *(Chapter 25.)*

We recommend that there is a process of consultation before legislation [confering a right of access to a child suspected of being abused] is proposed. *(Chapter 25.)*

We recommend also that the Secretary of State should, in any future legislation, be given the power to extend the right of access [to a child suspected of being abused] to officers of the NSPCC. *(Chapter 25.)*

We recommend that the Secretary of State should authorise, by regulations under the Statute, the classes of persons who could apply [for a Child Assessment Order]. *(Chapter 25).*

We recommend that the [Child Assessment] Order should be specific as to the time and place of examination. *(Chapter 25.)*

We recommend that the law should provide that when issuing the warrant [to search for or remove a child or young person] a magistrate should be empowered to authorise a medical practitioner to conduct a medical examination. *(Chapter 25.)*

We recommend accordingly, that the new provisions for an Emergency Protection Order should contain a requirement that on obtaining the Order the applicant must forthwith give notice of the Order to the parent (and child, where appropriate) and indicate the right to ask the court to review the grounds of the application. *(Chapter 25.)*

## Procedures relating to applications for Orders

We positively do not recommend a replication of the Tyneside experiment [of informing parents when an application for a Place of Safety Order is to be heard]. Our recommendation is that the legislation should provide redress to the parents only *after* the Place of Safety Order has been made. *(Chapter 25.)*

It will, we think, be sensible if the decision in the Bristol Justices case [that the police are entitled to be notified of an application for the release of a detained child, and to give evidence] is statutorily declared. We so recommend. *(Chapter 28.)*

### Child care policy

We recommend that all Health Authorities ensure that there is a ready supply of appropriate percentile charts and that they are used for all children up to the age of 2, and for other children whose development gives rise to concern. *(Chapter 5.)*

We recommend that no such distinction [by Social Services Departments, between statutory and non-statutory work] be made in child protection. *(Chapter 12.)*

We recommend that any Social Services Department accommodating unallocated cases must establish the appropriate criteria whenever a case remains unallocated, and policies to determine what happens next, including a clear definition of accountability for each case. *(Chapter 11.)*

### Child abuse procedures

We recommend that any child abuse procedure should state that a response must be made immediately to any referral suggestive of child abuse, and that in any event the action must be taken within 24 hours. *(Chapter 17.)*

We recommend that the procedure for following up any referral of suspected child abuse should insist that all the children in the family be seen. *(Chapter 17.)*

It is our recommendation that if a social worker has any difficulty in obtaining access to a child in pursuit of the statutory duty to investigate cases where information is received which suggests that there are grounds for care proceedings, the police must be informed. *(Chapter 28.)*

We recommend that team managers should not carry child abuse cases. *(Chapter 30.)*

We recommend that local authorities' child abuse procedures should contain some such requirement [that *all* social workers *must* receive regular professional and managerial supervision]. *(Chapter 30.)*

We recommend that supervision should make sure that certain action is taken, in a way capable of being evaluated within a specified timescale. *(Chapter 30.)*

We recommend the section on Child Abuse Consultants at pp.27-29 of the BASW publication, *The Management of Child Abuse*, should be revised to take account of the matters [relating to manner of consultation] to which we have alluded. *(Chapter 21.)*

We also recommend that Social Services and Health Authorities should take note of what we have said about the proper function and role of child abuse co-ordinators or consultants. *(Chapter 21.)*

### Social work training

We recommend that child care in general, and child abuse specifically, should be a compulsory part of all courses offering basic training to social workers. *(Chapter 29.)*

222

All social work courses should provide their students with a thorough grasp of the legal framework within which they will work, and all students should be assessed as to the adequacy of their knowledge of the relevant legal provisions. *(Chapter 29.)*

We recommend that agreement is reached concerning the minimum expectations of the social worker at the point of qualification. *(Chapter 29.)*

We recommend that CCETSW, in considering the minimum expectations of social workers at the point of qualification makes sure that proper weight has been given to training social workers for taking up their statutory responsibilities. *(Chapter 29.)*

We also recommend that teachers on these [basic social work training] courses must be sufficiently up-to-date in their own knowledge and practice [with regard to child care and child abuse] to be able to prepare students adequately. *(Chapter 29.)*

We recommend that CCETSW should oversee continuing discussions, between those organising courses and employers, to dovetail their respective responsibilities for the standard of service provided to clients. *(Chapter 29.)*

We recommend that the DHSS and CCETSW come speedily to a decision on the minimum period of basic training for social workers and that central government makes the necessary resources available. *(Chapter 29.)*

We recommend that [Social Services] Departments should allocate to training a set proportion of their expenditure on staffing. *(Chapter 29.)*

### Health Visitor training

We recommend that all health visitor training courses provide students with training in child protection as a separate subject. *(Chapter 28.)*

### Management training

We recommend that all new first line managers are provided with an appropriate induction programme and management training. *(Chapter 29.)*

### Violence and staff welfare

We recommend that all employers take whatever steps are necessary to make the practice of social work as safe from violence as possible. *(Chapter 31.)*

We also recommend that all social workers should speak up if they are subjected to any form of violence or if they are in fear of violence. *(Chapter 31.)*

We recommend that all employers make explicit arrangements for dealing with their staff welfare and that these should take into account the effects of stress. *(Chapter 31.)*

### Action in cases where child abuse has occurred

We recommend that the Secretary of State for Home Affairs should consider exercising that power [to impose a time limit on a criminal trial, under the Prosecution of Offenders Act 1985] in relation to child abuse cases. *(Chapter 1.)*

We make the like recommendation [that the criminal trial should take place within 3-4 months of the homicidal event] in respect of child abuse prosecutions where there is no statutory responsibility towards the child, but Social Services (as in this case) or other agencies have been working with the family in circumstances where child abuse is suspected. *(Chapter 1.)*

We recommend that active consideration be given to the systematic recording and publication of cases of child abuse. *(Part IV: Introduction)*

## Child abuse inquiries

We recommend that in its forthcoming circular on procedures for child abuse inquiries, the Department of Health and Social Security should include a paragraph indicating that local authorities and health authorities will not be in breach of confidence if they decide to disclose the relevant records to an independent review body. *(Chapter 2.)*

We recommend that there should be a statutory power in the Secretary of State, on application by the inquiring body, to authorise the disclosure of probation records by the relevant Probation Committee. *(Chapter 2.)*

We recommend that consideration should be given to enlarging the scope of Order 38, Rule 19 [concerning the power to issue subpoenas, to include non-statutory child abuse inquiries]. *(Chapter 3.)*

We recommend that the precaution of protecting the identity of vulnerable individuals (particularly children) should be adopted in all future child abuse inquiries. *(Chapter 2.)*

# A CHILD IN MIND:
## PROTECTION OF CHILDREN IN A
## RESPONSIBLE SOCIETY

# APPENDICES

## A – H

# Representation of Parties

| | |
|---|---|
| COUNSEL TO THE COMMISSION | Miss Presiley Baxendale and Miss Monica Carss-Frisk, instructed by Mr. Colin Roberts, Solicitor to Greenwich Borough Council |

| PARTIES BEFORE THE INQUIRY | REPRESENTATIVE |
|---|---|
| London Borough of Greenwich | Mr. Richard Drabble, instructed by Mr. Colin Roberts, Solicitor to Greenwich Borough Council |
| Greenwich Health Authority | Mr. Alan Hannah, Solicitor, of Bracher Son & Miskin |
| Metropolitan Borough of Wirral | Mr. David Park, Solicitor, Wirral Borough Council |
| London Borough of Kensington and Chelsea | Mr. Alan Muir, Solicitor, Royal Borough of Kensington and Chelsea |
| Inner London Education Authority | Miss Patricia Scotland and Miss Brenda Roller, instructed by ILEA Legal Services Department |
| British Association of Social Workers, Mr. Martin Manby and Mr. Manny Devaux | *Mr. John Trotter, Solicitor, of Bates, Wells and Braithwaite |
| Health Visitors' Association and Miss Marilyn Reader | Mr. Nigel Pitt, instructed by Kershaw, Gassman & Matthews, Solicitors |
| Royal College of Nursing and Mrs. Ruby Henlin | †Mr. Roger Titheridge Q.C. and Mr. Steven Coles, instructed by Legal Department, Royal College of Nursing |
| Transport and General Workers Union, Mrs. Beryl Fitzgerald and Mrs. Olive Swinburne | Mr. David Richardson, instructed and assisted by Miss Niamh O'Brady, Solicitor, of Pattinson & Brewer |
| National Association of Local Government Officers | ‡Ms Denise Kingsmill, Solicitor |
| Inner London Probation Service and Mrs. Deborah Carrigan | Mr. Jonathan Fisher, instructed by Oppenheimers, Solicitors |

* Miss Rita James of BASW acted in the absence of Mr. Trotter.

† Mr. Roger Titheridge Q.C. appeared on 1 and 3 September 1987 only to make oral submissions.

‡ On several occasions Mrs. Pauline Hendy appeared on behalf of the National Association of Local Government Officers.

| | |
|---|---|
| Commissioner for the Metropolitan Police | Miss Jean Craig, of Solicitor's Department, Metropolitan Police |
| Mr. Martin Ruddock | Ms Joanna Dodson, with and instructed by Mr. Brian Raymond, Solicitor, Bindman & Partners |
| Mr. Don Neill | Miss Anna Worrall, instructed by Hodge, Jones and Allen, Solicitors |
| Dr. Anita Hooper | Mr. Philip Gaisford, instructed by Le Brasseur & Bury, Solicitors |
| Mrs. Doreen Armstrong, Mrs. Jean Gabbott, Ms Carol Roper, Ms Barbara Peacock and Ms Marilyn Streeter | Mr. Stephen Bellamy, instructed by Wilford McBain, Solicitors |

# Witnesses
## (In Alphabetical Order)

\* Denotes witnesses who gave expert evidence.

| | |
|---|---|
| Mrs. Linda Allen | Clerical Officer (School Health Section), Greenwich Health Authority. |
| *Mrs. Susan Amphlett, S.R.N. | Director, Parents Against Injustice (PAIN). |
| Mrs. Doreen Armstrong, C.Q.S.W. | Social Worker (Family Finding Unit), Greenwich Social Services. |
| *Ms. Celia Atherton | Social Worker, Family Rights Group. |
| Miss Camilla Bacon | Neighbour of the Carliles on the Ferrier Estate. |
| *Mr. Ron Baker, M.A., A.P.S.W., Dip. Soc. Stud., S.R.N., R.M.N. | Head of College & Assistant Director (Training), The Richmond Fellowship. Professor of Social Work Practice, University of New South Wales, 1977–81. |
| *Mrs. Caroline Ball, J.P., LL.B.(Hons.) | Lecturer in Social Work Law, University of East Anglia. |
| *Mr. Stanley Bute, S.R.N., R.M.N., C.Q.S.W. | Area Manager, Hampshire Social Services. |
| Mrs. Pauline Carlile | Kimberley's mother. |
| Mrs. Deborah Carrigan, M.A. (Exeter), Dip. S.A. (LSE), M.Social Work (Nottingham) | Court Welfare Officer, Royal Courts of Justice. |
| Mrs. Christine Chapman | Administration Assistant, (School Health), Greenwich Health Authority. |
| Mr. John Collins | Unit Administrator (Community), Greenwich Health Authority. |
| Mrs. Barbara Coker, S.R.N. | School Nurse, Wingfield School. |
| Mr. Derek Cox | Deputy Headteacher, Wingfield School. |
| Mr. J. Emmanuel Devaux, C.S.W. | Assistant Director (Fieldwork), Greenwich Social Services. |
| Councillor Christopher Fay | Member, Greenwich Borough Council. |
| Mrs. Beryl Fitzgerald | Team Clerk, Ferrier Social Work Team, Greenwich Social Services. |
| Mrs. Jean Gabbott, C.Q.S.W., C.M.S. | Child Abuse Co-ordinator, Greenwich Social Services, 1983–1987. |
| *Ms. Katherine Gieve | Solicitor, Family Rights Group. |

| | |
|---|---|
| Miss Patricia Metcalfe | Records Clerk, Greenwich Health Authority. |
| Mr. Richard Moorhouse, C.Q.S.W. | Social Worker, Royal Borough of Kensington & Chelsea. |
| Mr. Don Neill, M.A. (Cantab), C.S.S.A. (LSE), Cert. P.S.W. (Liverpool) | Area Manager, (Area 4), Greenwich Social Services. |
| Ms. Christine Nuaimi, B.A. (London) | Senior Education Welfare Officer, ILEA. |
| Mrs. Pamela O'Connor, R.G.N., H.V.Cert., F.W.T. | Director of Nursing Services (Community), Greenwich Health Authority. |
| *Mr. John Pickett, Cert. P.S.W. (Leeds) | Regional Child Care Director, NSPCC. |
| Ms. Marilyn Reader, R.G.N., H.V.Cert., R.M. | Health Visitor, Greenwich Health Authority. |
| *Mr. Dennis Reed | Assistant Organising Officer, NALGO. |
| Ms. Carol Roper, B.Sc.(Econ.) (Cardiff), Cert.Ed., C.Q.S.W. | Social Worker (Area 4), Greenwich Social Services. |
| Ms. Susan Rouse, B.Ed. | Teacher, Wingfield School. |
| Mr. Martin Ruddock, C.Q.S.W., Cert.Ed. | Team Manager (Area 4), Greenwich Social Services. |
| Mrs. Rosemary Sharpe, C.Q.S.W. | Deputy Area Officer, Royal Borough of Kensington & Chelsea. |
| Dr. Mary Spencer, MB.B.S., D.Obst., R.C.O.G., D.C.H. | Clinical Medical Officer, (Pre-school Health), Greenwich Health Authority. |
| Ms. Marilyn Streeter, B.Ed. (Hons.), C.Q.S.W. | Social Work Team Manager (Area 4), Greenwich Social Services. |
| Mrs. Olive Swinburne, C.Q.S.W. | Social Worker (Area 4), Greenwich Social Services. |
| Ms. Sheila Thomas | Clerical Officer, Greenwich Health Authority. |
| WPS Shirley Tullock | Youth & Community Office, Metropolitan Police. |
| Mrs. Sylvia Walton | Clerical Officer, Greenwich Health Authority. |
| *Ms. Sally Watling, C.Q.S.W. | Senior Training Officer (Child Abuse), Wandsworth Social Services. |
| *Mr. C. Paton Webb, LL.B. | Justices Clerk, North Tyneside Magistrates. |
| Mr. Gordon Whiteley | Foster Parent of Y and Kimberley, 1984–85. |
| PC Steven Williams | Eltham Police Station. |

| | |
|---|---|
| *Ms. Susan Willis, B.A. | Assistant General Secretary, Health Visitors Association. |
| Miss Rose Wong | Principal Housing Advisor, Royal Borough of Kensington & Chelsea. |
| Chief Inspector Barry Wright | Community Liaison Officer, Greenwich and Bexley Division, Metropolitan Police. |

The Commission also considered written statements from the following:—

| | |
|---|---|
| Mr. R. J. Christopherson, M.A., Dip. App. Soc. Stud. | Lecturer in Social Work, University of Nottingham. |
| Councillor J. Draper | Member, Greenwich Borough Council. |
| Ms. Ruth Howard, B.A. | Deputy Divisional Education Officer, ILEA. |
| Ms. Barbara Peacock | Social Worker (Area 4), Greenwich Social Services. |
| Miss Jean Rowlands, R.G.N., R.M., R.H.B., R.D.N., D.H.S.A. (Aston) | Director of Nursing Services, Wirral Health Authority. |
| Mr. Ian Scott | Social Worker (Area 4), Greenwich Social Services. |
| Chief Inspector A. Wisdom | Greenwich & Bexley Division, Metropolitan Police. |

The Commission also made use of material provided by the British Association of Social Workers and the National Council for the Prevention of Cruelty to Children.

APPENDIX C

# Chronology of Events

|  |  |
|---|---|
| 3 November 1981 | Kimberley Carlile born. |
| 26 May 1982 | First known contact with the family by Wirral Social Services, following an assault on Pauline Carlile by her husband. About this time the health visitor had expressed concern about possible abuse of the children. |
| 6 August 1982 | Pauline Carlile's husband died. She suffered depression. |
| 3 March 1983 | Kimberley started at day nursery. Day nursery reported "a bruise on her forehead ....scars of ulcers at the top of her legs". |
| 13 April 1983 | Following concerns by Wirral Social Services about all three children, the case was referred to the Intensive Family Case Work Team. |
| 29 June 1983 | The case of the Carlile family was declared "dormant" by Wirral Social Services. |
| 2 September 1983 | Pauline Carlile married David Carlile, who was known to authorities as being a violent man. |
| 3 November 1983 | Wirral Social Services became aware of the marriage and alerted other agencies about the possibility of violence in the household. |
| 17 November 1983 | Kimberley was given a 24-month developmental assessment, and was found to be "below 3rd centile for weight". |
| February - April 1984 | Between these dates there were a series of incidents of violence by Mr Carlile on Pauline Carlile. Although there were some problems with the children, there were no reports of violence towards them. |
| 25 April 1984 | The case was discussed by Wirral Social Services, and it was decided to terminate continuing involvement with the Carlile family, but to deal with incidents as and when they arose. |
| 1 May 1984 | Pauline Carlile and David Carlile were arrested for fraud. Place of Safety Orders were made by the Police on the three Carlile children. |
| 3 May 1984 | A case conference was held. The participants were concerned about the level of domestic violence, although there was no evidence of physical harm to the children. Wirral Social Services offered voluntary care for the children and decided to monitor. |

| | |
|---|---|
| 4 May 1984 | The children were taken into voluntary care. |
| 16 May 1984 | David Carlile was taken into custody. He remained in prison until 2 July 1984. |
| 25 May 1984 | The children were discharged from voluntary care by Pauline Carlile. Kimberley was medically examined and weighed. |
| 3 July 1984 | The day after David Carlile's release from prison Pauline Carlile suffered a broken jaw (serious fracture) and was admitted to hospital. The children were admitted to voluntary care and were placed with foster-parents (Kimberley and her older sister with Mr and Mrs Whiteley.) |
| 13 July 1984 | The children were discharged from voluntary care. Pauline Carlile was told by Wirral Social Services that consideration would be given to taking care proceedings on the children if she returned to David Carlile. |
| 3 August 1984 | Pauline Carlile and David Carlile were convicted of fraud and both were sentenced to six months' imprisonment. The children were initially cared for by a relative. |
| 13 August 1984 | The children were admitted to voluntary care. Kimberley and her sister returned to the Whiteleys and remained with them until 4 October 1985. |
| 15 August 1984 | A case conference was held. A decision was made to start the procedure for a local authority resolution under Section 3, Child Care Act 1980, and to consider the long-term placement of the children. |
| 5 November 1984 | A child (Z) was born to Pauline Carlile in prison. Wirral Social Services decided not to proceed with a Section 3 resolution in respect of the 3 eldest children and instead considered wardship proceedings. David Carlile was released from prison. |
| 3 December 1984 | Pauline Carlile was released from prison; her release had been delayed because of the birth of the child. |
| 13 December 1984 | Pauline Carlile left David Carlile (the two never co-habited again) and, with Z, went to York. |
| 20 December 1984 | Pauline Carlile and Z living in Wigan. She met Nigel Hall, whom she had known as a friend of her first husband. An application for divorce proceedings was made before Wigan County Court. |
| 8 February 1985 | Pauline Carlile arrived in London, with Z. |
| 23 February 1985 | Pauline Carlile visited the three children in the Wirral. |
| 9 March 1985 | Pauline Carlile visited the children in the Wirral. |

| | |
|---|---|
| 1 April 1985 | The case was reviewed by Wirral Social Services, who were considering re-uniting the children with their mother. |
| 2 April 1985 | Wirral Social Services asked Kensington and Chelsea Social Services to check out Pauline Carlile's present situation. |
| 6 April 1985 | Pauline Carlile visited the children in the Wirral. |
| 22 May 1985 | Richard Moorhouse of Kensington and Chelsea Social Services Department telephoned Wirral Social Services Department and discussed Pauline Carlile's intention to take the children out of voluntary care. Wirral Social Services requested a check on Nigel Hall, who was then co-habiting with Pauline Carlile. |
| 15 June 1985 | Pauline Carlile visited the children in the Wirral. |
| 4 July 1985 | Richard Moorhouse submitted a written report to Wirral Social Services on Pauline Carlile's situation, and on an interview he had had with Nigel Hall. |
| 12 July 1985 | Wirral Social Services indicated to Kensington and Chelsea Social Services Department that they were willing to discharge the children from voluntary care once Pauline Carlile obtained suitable (3 bedroomed) accommodation. |
| 16 August 1985 | Pauline Carlile and Nigel Hall were offered Council accommodation in the London Borough of Greenwich. |
| 28 August 1985 | Richard Moorhouse submitted a referral report on the family to Greenwich Social Services. |
| 2 September 1985 | The tenancy of 49 Cambert Way was granted to Pauline Carlile and Nigel Hall. Pauline Carlile asked Wirral Social Services to return the three children in voluntary care. |
| 30 September 1985 | Wirral Social Services telephoned Greenwich Social Services Department and informed the Duty Officer that Mrs. Carlile would be collecting the children on 4 October. |
| 3 October 1985 | Martin Ruddock, Team Manager, Area 4 Greenwich Social Services, wrote to Pauline Carlile offering assistance to the family. |
| 4 October 1985 | Kimberley was medically examined by the foster-parents' G.P., who described her as "well and healthy". Pauline Carlile and Nigel Hall travelled to the Wirral to collect the 3 children on their discharge from voluntary care. The hand-over of the children to Pauline Carlile was made at Edgehill |

|  | Family Group Home in the Wirral. Wirral Social Services Area Manager, wrote to Greenwich Social Services asking that they undertake "some sort of monitoring..... while the children settle back with their mother". |
|---|---|
| 10 October 1985 | Nigel Hall called at the Social Services office on the Ferrier Estate and rudely rejected the offer of assistance. |
| 28 October 1985 | Kimberley's older brother and sister (X and Y) started at Wingfield Primary School. |
| 11 November 1985 | Dr Mahesh, G.P. on the Ferrier Estate, was consulted by Pauline Carlile about Kimberley's speech. He made a referral to the Brook Hospital "for speech therapy". |
| 18 November 1985 | Pauline Carlile called in on her own at the Health Clinic on the Ferrier Estate and gave brief details about the family. Marilyn Reader, Health Visitor, Greenwich Health Authority, asked that health records on the Carlile family be obtained from Wirral Health Authority. |
| 5 December 1985 | Marilyn Reader repeated her request for records. |
| 15 December 1985 | The School Nurse requested the school health records of X and Y. |
| 16 December 1985 | Marilyn Reader again requested records. |
| 9 January 1986 | The eldest Carlile child (X) reported to a teacher at Wingfield Primary School that he had been thrown across the room by Nigel Hall. The teacher looked for any marks during a P.E. lesson that day. The school decided to monitor. |
| 15 January 1986 | Carol Roper, Greenwich Social Services, was told by the school staff of the allegation against Nigel Hall. She alerted Marilyn Reader, and asked her to visit the family. |
| 16 January 1986 | Marilyn Reader visited the Carlile household. Of the four children, she saw only the baby Z. |
| 17 January 1986 | Martin Ruddock, Ferrier Social Work Team Manager, discussed the information from the school with his Area Manager, Don Neill, and they decided to monitor the family. Marilyn Reader and the School Headteacher were contacted and asked to communicate any worries that arose in their contacts with the family. |
| 20 January 1986 | Martin Ruddock asked the Education Welfare Officer at Wingfield Primary School to monitor the situation with regard to the eldest Carlile child (X). |

| | |
|---|---|
| 3 February 1986 | X and Y were routinely examined by Dr. Kamalan-athan, the School Medical Officer. |
| 4 February 1986 | Greenwich Health Authority received from Wirral Health Authority school medical records on X, Y and Kimberley together with the summaries of the two Wirral case conferences. |
| 7 March 1986 | Greenwich Social Services received an anonymous telephone call about the Carlile family, in particular "a little girl about 4" whom the caller thought was "being beaten, cries very pitifully". The Duty Officer, Olive Swinburne, asked Marilyn Reader to accompany her on a visit to the family, but this was declined. A joint visit was carried out on late Friday afternoon by Olive Swinburne and the Duty Team Manager, Marilyn Streeter. They were allowed into the Carliles' home but were refused sight of the two younger children (Kimberley and Z). |
| 10 March 1986 | Marilyn Reader discussed the case with her supervisor, Mrs Henlin. Olive Swinburne reported in writing and orally to Martin Ruddock, who discussed the case with Don Neill and then visited the family. As they were not at home, Martin Ruddock left a letter saying that Kimberley and Z had to be seen by a G.P. or Health Visitor within the next two days, or the matter would be discussed with the Police Juvenile Bureau. |
| 11 March 1986 | Nigel Hall telephoned Social Services, and was put through to the child abuse section. He talked to Doreen Armstrong of the Family Finding Unit and described to her difficulties with a "4 year old". Doreen Armstrong made an extensive note of the discussion and arranged a meeting between the Carlile family and Martin Ruddock at their home at 4 p.m. the next day. |
| 12 March 1986 | The Carlile family unexpectedly visited Area 4 Office in advance of the appointment for Martin Ruddock to visit them. Martin Ruddock was concerned about Kimberley. He described the baby as very lively and demanding, "whilst Kimberley appeared withdrawn, sallow, pasty and still". Mrs Carlile and Mr Hall agreed to accept a nursery school place for Kimberley, and agreed to a further meeting with Martin Ruddock in early April. Martin Ruddock informed the health visitor, the School Headteacher and the Education Welfare Service of his meeting with the family. |

| | |
|---|---|
| 13 March 1986 | Martin Ruddock wrote in friendly terms to Pauline Carlile and Nigel Hall thanking them for the visit and telling them that he had asked the health visitor to consider arranging a medical examination of Kimberley, and had also asked Wingfield School to consider offering a nursery school place for her. |
| 19 March 1986 | The Headteacher of Wingfield School informed the Social Services Department that a nursery school place for Kimberley had been offered, but that the family had not responded. |
| 24 March 1986 | Marilyn Gregory (Education Welfare Officer) telephoned the Social Services Department to say that Kimberley had not attended nursery school. |
| 25 March 1986 | Marilyn Reader informed the Social Services Department that the children had not attended the clinic. |
| 1 April 1986 | Marilyn Reader spoke on the telephone to Pauline Carlile to arrange to see the family. She was told that the family would be going away for Easter. The Social Services Department received two telephone calls from the family cancelling the appointment for Martin Ruddock to visit them the following day. |
| 14 April 1986 | Marilyn Reader telephoned the family to arrange an appointment to see them. She spoke to Nigel Hall who was abusive and made it clear that he did not want her to visit. Martin Ruddock visited the Carlile home, but saw only Nigel Hall. He was allowed only a brief glimpse of Kimberley and Z through a glass panel above a door. |
| 16 April, 1986 | Marilyn Reader discussed the case with her Senior Nurse, Mrs Henlin. |
| 24 April 1986 | Martin Ruddock telephoned Marilyn Reader and the School Headteacher and asked them to maintain a watch over the family. He also spoke to the Court Welfare Officer (who had been asked to prepare a report in connection with the divorce proceedings between Pauline and David Carlile) who informed him that she would be visiting the family on 9 May. |
| 28 April 1986 | The Wingfield Primary School Headteacher informed the Social Services Department that Nigel Hall had asked for X and Y to be transferred to Henwick Primary School. |
| Early May 1986 | Martin Ruddock informed the Headteacher of Henwick Primary School of the situation and asked that the children, X and Y, be monitored. |

| | |
|---|---|
| 12 May 1986 | Martin Ruddock discussed the case with the Child Abuse Co-ordinator, Jean Gabbott. They agreed to consider convening a case conference if Kimberley had not been seen by late May/early June. |
| 13 May 1986 | A letter was received by Greenwich Social Services from the Court Welfare Officer saying that she had been unable to see the family on 9 May. |
| 29 May 1986 | Marilyn Reader telephoned Mrs Carlile to arrange a home visit. This was declined, but it was agreed that Nigel Hall would bring both Kimberley and Z to the clinic the following week. |
| 4 June 1986 | Nigel Hall brought Z to the clinic for an immunization. He did not bring Kimberley. After Nigel Hall left the Clinic, the Clinical Medical Officer, Dr. Spencer, and Marilyn Reader discussed Kimberley. |
| 8 June 1986 | Kimberley died. Place of Safety Orders were taken by the Police on X, Y and Z. |
| 9 June 1986 | A case conference was held. |
| 15 June 1986 | Wirral health visiting records relating to Kimberley were received by Greenwich Health Authority. |

* * * * * * * * * * *

| | |
|---|---|
| 5-15 May 1987 | Nigel Hall and Pauline Carlile were tried at the Central Criminal Court. Nigel Hall was convicted of the murder of Kimberley and was sentenced to life imprisonment. Pauline Carlile was convicted of grevious bodily harm and sentenced to 12 years' imprisonment. |
| 28 May 1987 | Greenwich Borough Council and Greenwich Health Authority set up an Independent Commission of Inquiry into the circumstances surrounding the death of Kimberley Carlile. |

# Dramatis Personae

## The Carlile Family

### Kimberley Carlile

Kimberley Carlile was born on 3 November 1981 in the Wirral. She died on 8 June 1986. Kimberley was the third child of Pauline Carlile and her first husband who died of a brain haemorrhage when Kimberley was 9 months old. When Kimberley was 22 months old, her mother married David Carlile, but the relationship frequently involved violence by Mr. Carlile towards Mrs. Carlile. In May 1984 Kimberley, along with her older brother and sister, was admitted into voluntary care with Wirral Borough Council and discharged 3 weeks later. The 3 children were re-admitted to voluntary care for a further period of a week in July 1984. In August 1984 the three children were again received into voluntary care by Wirral Borough Council when Mr. and Mrs. Carlile were imprisoned for fraud. Kimberley and her sister were placed with foster-parents (Mr.and Mrs. Whiteley) and remained with them in the Wirral until re-united with their mother in London on 4 October 1985.

### Kimberley's siblings (referred to as X, Y and Z)

Kimberley's brother (referred to as X) was born on 28 February 1978. Kimberley's elder sister (Y) was born on 6 October 1979. Z was born on 5 November 1984 while Mrs. Carlile was in prison. After discharge from prison in December 1984, Mrs. Carlile and Z at first lived in the Wirral with Mr. Carlile, but after a few days moved away, staying for short periods in Women's Refuges in York and Wigan. In February 1985, Mrs. Carlile and Z moved to London where they lived, mostly, in bed and breakfast accommodation, until moving into Council accommodation on the Ferrier Estate on 27 September 1985.

### Pauline Carlile

Pauline Carlile was born on 16 February 1959, one of six children. She had three children by her first marriage, of which Kimberley was the youngest. She suffered depression when her first husband, a heavy drinker, died of a brain haemorrhage in August 1982. She and David Carlile co-habited during 1983 and married in September 1983. Mrs. Carlile suffered from violence at the hands of Mr. Carlile, including in July 1984, a broken jaw and ribs, at which time she was four months pregnant.

In August 1984, Mrs. Carlile received a six month prison sentence for fraud. She gave birth to her fourth child in November 1984, while in prison. On her release from prison in December 1984, Mrs. Carlile initially returned to Mr. Carlile. Following further violence towards her, however, she left him and stayed for short periods in Women's Refuges before moving to London where she began co-habiting with Nigel Hall, a friend of her first husband.

They lived together in hotel bed and breakfast accommodation in the Royal Borough of Kensington & Chelsea, before moving in September 1985 to Council accommodation on the Ferrier Estate.

In August 1986, two months after Kimberley's death, Pauline Carlile gave birth in prison to a son by Nigel Hall.

In May 1987, Pauline Carlile was found guilty of causing Kimberley grievous bodily harm, and received a sentence of 12 years' imprisonment.

*Nigel Hall*

Nigel Hall was born on 25 May 1962; the youngest of four children. On leaving school he trained as an engineer but was made redundant before completing his apprenticeship. Following this, he was employed on a number of casual jobs, such as building work, in Liverpool and in Algeria. In 1983, Nigel Hall moved to London where he gained employment as a washing machine engineer, but he lost this job a year later when his driving licence was revoked for a drinking and driving offence. Whilst living with Mrs. Carlile, initially in hotel accommodation in the Royal Borough of Kensington and Chelsea and then in Council accommodation in Greenwich, Nigel Hall worked as a self-employed repair man.

He was convicted on 15 May 1987 of the murder of Kimberley Carlile, and sentenced to life imprisonment.

# Kensington & Chelsea Social Services Personnel

*Richard Moorhouse, Dip. A.S.S., C.Q.S.W.*

Social worker with Kensington & Chelsea Social Services Department between July 1985 and September 1986. Now employed by Bromley Social Services.

Mr. Moorhouse came into contact with the Carlile family in April 1985, when working in the Homelessness Team of Kensington & Chelsea Social Services Department. Following a request by Wirral Social Services Department for a report on Pauline Carlile's present situation, Mr. Moorhouse interviewed Mrs. Carlile and Mr. Hall. Following Mr. Moorhouse's report, Wirral Borough Council informed Mrs. Carlile that it would discharge the 3 children in its care to her once she received adequate accommodation.

*Rosemary Sharpe C.Q.S.W.*

Deputy Area Officer, Royal Borough of Kensington & Chelsea Social Services Department. Possesses Certificate of Qualification in Social Work (1974), and Advanced Certificate in Child Family Protection Service. Previously worked as Senior Social Worker, Kensington & Chelsea Social Services Department, with special responsibility for cases of Non-accidental Injury.

Mrs. Sharpe was responsible for supervising the work of Richard Moorhouse, and discussed with him the report in July 1985 to Wirral Council, and the referral report in September 1985 to Greenwich Council.

# Greenwich Social Services Personnel

*Martin Manby, M.A. (Oxon), Dip. S.A., Dip.A.S.S., C.Q.S.W.*

Director of Social Services, Greenwich Borough Council, since 1982. Obtained MA in Modern History at Oxford University in 1966, Diploma in Social Administration at Manchester University in 1967, and the Certificate of Qualification in Social Work at Sheffield University in 1969. Also possesses Diploma in Applied Social Studies and Home Office Letter of Recognition in Child Care. Previous posts: Social Welfare Officer, Sheffield (1967-68); Child Care Officer and subsequently Senior Child Care Officer and Senior Social Worker, Bradford Children's Department/Social Services Department (1968-73); Co-ordinating Officer, Fieldwork Division, Islington Borough Council (1973-74); Assistant Director (Fieldwork), Islington Borough Council (1974-79); Assistant Director (Fieldwork), Lothian Social Work Department (1980-82).

Responsible for a Department with a £35.2 million revenue budget, a £0.8 million capital budget (1987/88); a total staff of 2,700; 32 residential establishments.

Mr. Manby was not directly involved in the case, and had no knowledge of the family until he was informed of Kimberley's death.

*Jacques Emmanuel Devaux, C.S.W.*

Assistant Director of Social Services (Fieldwork,) Greenwich Borough Council, since 1974, and Chair of Greenwich Area Review Committtee from 1981 to 1987. Responsible for approximately 1,100 members of staff. Possesses Certificate in Social Work (1970). Previous posts : Mental Health Social Worker (1965-68 and 1970-72), Social Work Team Manager (1972), Acting Area Manager (1972-74), Haringey Borough Council; Area Manager (1974), Greenwich Borough Council.

Mr. Devaux had been made aware, prior to Kimberley's death, by the Team Manager and the Area Manager, of unallocated cases and pressure of work in the Ferrier Social Work Team.

*Don Neill, M.A. (Cantab), C.S.S.A., Cert.P.S.W.*

Area Manager, Area 4, Greenwich Social Services, since 1972. Obtained M.A. degree in Geography and History at St. John's College, Cambridge in 1957; Certificate in Social Service and Administration at the London School of Economics in 1958; and Certificate in Psychiatric Social Work at Liverpool University in 1965. He previously worked as an Assistant Mental Welfare Officer, London County Council (1960-62); Mental Welfare Officer (1962-66), Mental Health Social Worker (1966-69); Assistant Team Leader (1969-72).

Mr. Neill's first involvement with the Carlile case was in January 1986, when Martin Ruddock (the Team Manager), discussed with him an incident concerning Kimberley's brother, reported by the school. Mr. Ruddock again consulted Don Neill in March 1986, following the visit to the family by Duty

Social Work staff; and in May 1986, following Mr. Ruddock's unsuccessful visit to the family in April.

## Martin Ruddock, Cert. Ed., C.Q.S.W.

Team Manager, Area 4, Greenwich Social Services, since October 1985. Obtained Certificate of Education at Brighton College in 1971, and Certificate of Qualification in Social Work in 1979. Previous jobs: Secondary School Teacher (1971-72); Community Worker/Adventure Play Leader (1972-73); Manager of a Youth Centre (1973-75); Detached Youth Worker (1975); Group Work Organiser, East London Family Service Unit (1976-79); Social Worker, Hackney Borough Council (1980-83); Senior Social Worker, Thamesmead Family Service Unit (1983-1985).

Mr. Ruddock was Team Manager of the patch-based Social Work Team covering the Ferrier Estate, where the Carlile Family lived while in Greenwich. As the Carlile case was not allocated to a specific social worker, Mr. Ruddock oversaw the case and was the main social services contact with the family in the months prior to Kimberley's death.

## Marilyn Streeter, B.Ed (Hons.), C.Q.S.W.

Team Manager, Team B, Area 4, Greenwich Social Services, since 1985. Obtained her degree in 1974 from Goldsmiths College, and the Certificate of Qualification in Social Work in 1978 at Southampton University. Previous posts: Generic Social Worker, London Borough of Bromley (1978-1983), Generic Social Worker, London Borough of Greenwich (1983-1985). As Duty Team Manager on the day that the anonymous telephone call concerning Kimberley was received by the Social Services Department in March 1986, Ms Streeter accompanied the Duty Officer on the visit to the Carlile family.

## Olive Swinburne, C.Q.S.W.

Social Worker, Area 4, Greenwich Social Services, 1982-1986. Obtained Certificate of Qualification in Social Work in 1982 at North East London Polytechnic. Previous posts: Trainee Maternity and Child Welfare Officer (1946-49), Almoner, Deptford and Woolwich chest clinics (1949-52), employed by Greenwich Social Services as an unqualified social worker working with physically handicapped people (1972-74), Residential Child Care Officer (1976-78), Family Aide (1978-1980). Left employment with Greenwich in March 1986, to take up an appointment as Fostering Social Worker on a research project.

Mrs. Swinburne was Duty Social Worker on 7 March 1986, (a Friday) when the anonymous telephone call was received by Greenwich Social Services Department. She made a home visit that day (with Ms Streeter) to the Carlile family. Access to Kimberley and her younger sister was refused. Mrs. Swinburne informed her Team Manager, Mr. Ruddock, of the telephone call and the visit on the following Monday.

## Carol Roper, B.Sc(Econ), Cert.Ed., C.Q.S.W.

Social Worker, Area 4, Greenwich Social Services, since 1983. Obtained degree in Sociology from University College Cardiff in 1974; Post-Graduate

Certificate in Education from Goldsmiths College, University of London, in 1975; then worked for several years as a teacher before attending Newcastle University where she obtained the Certificate of Qualification in Social Work.

Ms Roper was Duty Officer on 3 occasions when the Social Services Department received information about the Carlile family. She was also responsible for attending regular meetings with staff at the local primary school, and received information through this liaison arrangement about possible ill-treatment of Kimberley's older brother in January 1986.

### Jean Gabbott, C.Q.S.W., C.M.S.

Child Abuse Co-ordinator, Greenwich Social Services, 1983-1987. Responsible for maintaining the Greenwich Child Abuse Register, and for giving guidance on child abuse. Obtained Certificate of Qualification in Social Work in 1978 at North East London Polytechnic and Certificate in Management Studies in 1978. Previous posts: Social Worker (1978-80), and subsequently Senior Social Worker specialising in child care (1981-83), Bexley Social Services. Now employed as Child Abuse Consultant and Co-ordinator, Tower Hamlets Social Services.

Mrs. Gabbott was consulted by Martin Ruddock on 12 May 1986, on his concerns about Kimberley.

### Doreen Armstrong, C.Q.S.W.

Social Worker, Family Finding Unit, Greenwich Social Services, since 1980. After qualifying as a probation officer (CQSW), Mrs. Armstrong worked between 1965 and 1976 initially in Essex and then for the Inner London Probation Service.

Mrs. Armstrong spoke to Nigel Hall and Pauline Carlile in March 1986, during the week after the visit to the family by social work staff following up the anonymous telephone call.

### Beryl Fitzgerald

Team Clerk, Ferrier Social Work Team, Greenwich Social Services, since 1980. Previously worked as a personal assistant to a publicity officer in an insurance company, and as a personal assistant to the managing director of an advertising agency.

Mrs. Fitzgerald acted as receptionist at the Social Services Neighbourhood Centre on the Ferrier Estate, and it was to her that Mr. Hall strongly objected to Social Services involvement with the family in October 1985. She also took the anonymous telephone call on 7 March 1986, and managed to identify the family concerned from the information given as that of Mrs. Carlile.

## Greenwich Health Authority Personnel

### Dr. Jeevaruthnum Govender, MB. B.S.

Senior Clinical Medical Officer (Child Health, Pre-school), Greenwich Health Authority since 1975. Dr. Govender had responsibility for all children under five, not at nursery school, within the Health Authority's boundaries, but was unaware of Kimberley's existence.

*Dr. Anita Hooper, MB.B.S, F.R.C.S., M.R.C.O.G.,*

Senior Medical Officer (School Health), Greenwich Health Authority, since 1982.

Dr. Hooper was responsible for dealing with the school health records on Kimberley and her older brother and sister, when these records were received on 16 February 1986, by Greenwich Health Authority.

*Dr. Selladurai Kamalanathan, MB.B.S., M.R.C.P., D.C.H.*

School Medical Officer, Greenwich Health Authority, since 1984.

Dr. Kamalanathan carried out routine medical examinations on Kimberley's older brother and sister at Wingfield School on 3 February 1986. He was unaware that the school and the health visiting service had been asked to monitor the family following the suggestion of possible ill-treatment to X in January 1986.

*Dr. Mary Spencer, MB.B.S., D.Obst., R.C.O.G., D.C.H.*

Clinical Medical Officer, Greenwich Health Authority, dealing in child health and family planning. Dr. Spencer saw Mr. Hall on 4 June 1986, when he brought Kimberley's younger sister, Z, to the health clinic for a measles injection.

*Mrs. Pamela O'Connor, R.G.N., H.V.Cert., F.W.T.*

Director of Nursing Services (Community), Greenwich Health Authority, since October 1986. Responsible for Community Nursing Services (district nursing, family planning, health visiting, school nursing, and the terminal support team), which has a budget of £2,861,253 (1987/88) and a staff of 224.

*Mrs. Ruby Henlin, S.R.N., B.T.A. Cert., S.C.M., H.V. Cert., F.W.T., R.N.T.*

Senior Nurse (Health Visiting), Greenwich Health Authority, since September, 1985. Previous appointments: Staff Nurse (general nursing) 1958-59, District Nursing 1961-65, Community Midwifery 1965-72, Health Visiting 1973-80, Nurse Tutor 1981-85.

Mrs. Henlin was responsibile for health visiting, clinic nursing and family planning services in the area of Greenwich in which Mrs. Carlile and Mr. Hall lived. She was consulted by Miss Reader, the Health Visitor dealing with the family, on two occasions: in March 1986, about the anonymous telephone call to the Social Services Department; and in April 1986, about Mr. Hall's refusal to allow Miss Reader to see Mrs. Carlile and the children.

*Marilyn Reader, R.G.N., H.V.Cert., R.M.*

Health Visitor, Greenwich Health Authority, between September 1982 and December 1986. Now employed by Bromley Health Authority.

Miss Reader was the Health Visitor dealing with the Carlile family. She visited the Carlile home in January 1986 (at the request of the Social Services Department, after the report from the primary school about the possible ill-treatment of Kimberley's elder brother), and saw Mrs. Carlile and Kimberley's younger sister.

In March 1986, Miss Reader refused a request by the Social Services Duty Officer to accompany her on a joint visit to the family to investigate an anonymous telephone call. Miss Reader had further contacts by telephone with the family in April and May 1986, but did not see Kimberley on any occasion or manage to have her medically examined.

## Inner London Education Authority Personnel

*Christine Nuaimi, B.A.*

Senior Education Welfare Officer (Team Leader), ILEA Division 6 (Greenwich), 1983-86. Obtained degree in English, History and Philosophy in 1973 at London University, and in 1975 was awarded Proficiency as a Qualified Teacher. Currently studying for the Certificate of Qualification in Social Work. Previous appointments: Secondary School Teacher of English (1973-80); Education Welfare Officer, ILEA Division 7 (1981-83).

Ms Nuaimi was Team Leader for the Education Welfare Team covering the area which included Wingfield School. She agreed to a request from the Social Services Department in January 1986, to monitor the children at Wingfield School. No concerns arose as a result of this monitoring although the nursery place made available by Wingfield School for Kimberley was not taken up.

*Marilyn Gregory, B.A.*

Education Welfare Officer, ILEA Division 6 (Greenwich) since 1985. Obtained degree in Sociology and Community Work at Simmons College, Boston, Mass., U.S.A. in 1967. Previous appointments: Social Worker (Mass., USA) 1967-69; Child Care Officer (1970-72), and Adoption Social Worker (1974-75), London Borough of Greenwich; Post-natal Counsellor, National Childbirth Trust (1979-82); Advice Worker, Citizen's Advice Bureau (1985).

Ms Gregory was allocated the case of the Carlile family in January 1986 (following the suggestion of ill-treatment to Kimberley's older brother), and was asked to monitor the children in the school. Nothing of major concern came to her attention, however. Her responsibility in respect of the family ended in May, 1986, when X and Y were transferred, at Mr. Hall's request, to Henwick Primary School.

*Edward Hayter*

Headteacher, Wingfield Primary School, since 1980. Possesses Teachers' Certificate and Academic Diploma in Education (Institute of London). Teacher since 1955, and a Headteacher since 1966.

Mr. Hayter received information from one of his staff in January 1986, that Kimberley's older brother had claimed to have been thrown across the room by Mr. Hall. He arranged for this information to be passed informally to Social Services Department staff.

Mr. Hayter was not aware that Kimberley's brother and sister were to be medically examined by the school doctor in February 1986 and information about the concerns and monitoring of the children was not conveyed to the school nurse or doctor. There was a discusssion in March 1986 between Mr. Hayter and the school doctor about the children.

*Susan Rouse, B.Ed.*

Teacher, Wingfield Primary School, since 1976. Bachelor of Education and Holder of a Teaching Certificate.

In 1985/86 Miss Rouse's class included Kimberley's older brother. In January, 1986, he told her that he had been thrown across the room by Mr. Hall. Miss Rouse checked for any signs of bruising during a P.E. lesson that day but saw no marks. She informed the Deputy Headteacher of the incident, and checked with the boy the following day whether he had had any further punishment.

## General Practitioner

*Dr. Mahesh, MB.B.S., D.C.H.*

General Practitioner, Ferrier Estate, SE3, since 1977. Dr Mahesh qualified as a Bachelor of Medicine and a Batchelor of Surgery in Varanasi, India in 1966, and obtained a Diploma in Child Health in 1970 in London. Prior to starting general practice in 1977, he worked in children's hospitals. He also had 3 years work in psychiatry.

Dr. Mahesh was consulted by Pauline Carlile about Kimberley once whilst she lived on the Ferrier Estate - in November, 1985 - on concerns about Kimberley's speech. Dr. Mahesh referred Kimberley to the Speech Therapy Department of a local hospital, but there is no record that Mrs. Carlile ever made an appointment.

## Court Welfare Officer

*Mrs. Deborah Carrigan, M.A., Dip.S.A., M.Social Work.*

Court Welfare Officer attached to the Royal Courts of Justice in The Strand, since 1985. Previously worked as a Probation Officer (1979-85). Obtained a degree in English in 1976 at Exeter University, a Diploma in Social Administration from the London School at Economics in 1977, and a Master's Degree in Social Work from Nottingham University in 1978.

Mrs. Carrigan had the task of preparing a Court Welfare Report in connection with the divorce proceedings between Mr. and Mrs. Carlile. She attempted to see Mrs. Carlile on three occasions between March and May 1986 on the Ferrier Estate, but without success.

# Correspondence with Wirral Social Services

## 1. Correspondence between the Commission and solicitors for the Wirral social workers

L Blom-Cooper Esq Q.C.
The Chairman,
Commission of Inquiry
Shrewsbury House Community Centre
Bushmoor Crescent
Shooters Hill
London SE18                                                6th July 1987

Dear Sir,

**Re: Commission of Inquiry into the death of Kimberley Carlile**

I was instructed at the beginning of last week to act on behalf of three members of the Wirral Borough Council Social Services Department, Mrs. N. Madeley, Mr. R. Ewbank, and Mrs. D. Stuart, who had been requested to attend the Commission of Inquiry into the death of Kimberley Carlile. In view of the fact that the Inquiry had already commenced, I travelled down to London on Wednesday of last week so that I could ascertain the progress of the Inquiry, the issues that were to be covered by the Inquiry and to obtain copies of the relevant documentation. I had the opportunity of meeting with both Counsel to the Inquiry and I am grateful to them for the assistance which they gave to me and also to the Secretary to the Inquiry for providing me with copies of much of the documentation.

However, I have to advise you that my clients, after having given very careful consideration to the nature and format of the Inquiry, have indicated that they decline the request for them to attend at the Inquiry to give evidence.

As a result it is not my intention to attend any of the hearings of the Commission nor to make any submissions at the close. I have also written to the Secretary to the Commission to request that the statements made by Mr. Ewbank and Mrs. Stuart in answer to specific questions put to them be withdrawn and returned to me.

It is not felt appropriate that the present form of Inquiry which has been established by the Greenwich Borough Council and the Greenwich District Health Authority should be enabled under its terms of reference to investigate the involvement of the Wirral Borough Council Social Services Department and its officers with the family. In particular there are the following areas of concern:

1.  My clients have been in the unfortunate position of not knowing, until after the Inquiry had started, who would be responsible for paying for the costs of their representation at the Inquiry, and therefore they had no opportunity of making representations about the nature of the Inquiry and the way in which it was to proceed. I appreciate that a Solicitor from Wirral Borough Council was present at the preliminary

248

meeting, but he of course was appearing on behalf of the Wirral Borough Council and not on behalf of individual members or employees of the Council.

If Inquiries of this nature are to be held in the future, then any persons who have been involved at some stage with the family and whose actions are likely to be subjected to critical scrutiny must be assured at the earliest opportunity who is to pay for their legal costs. This has not happened in this case.

2. The Greenwich Borough Council is one of the agencies that has set up this Inquiry, and yet it is clear that some of the members of that Authority intend to make criticisms of some at least of my clients. Furthermore the administration of the Inquiry is being dealt with by the Greenwich Borough Council and I would submit that it is of fundamental importance that if there is to be more than simply an internal Inquiry into the facts of this case (and my clients do not accept the necessity for this in so far as their involvement is concerned) where a report is ultimately to be made public,then it must be seen to be fair and impartial. The only way in which this can be effected is if the Inquiry is administered by the D.H.S.S. Furthermore there is the practical problem in this case that many of the personnel involved reside in the Merseyside area, making it difficult for an exhaustive investigation to be carried out from Greenwich into matters which occurred on the Wirral and into the witnesses involved. It is already apparent that many witnesses who have had involvement with the children are not to be called to the Inquiry and I would have expected that a decision should have been made before the start of the Inquiry as to exactly which witnesses were to be called, although there are always bound to be some witnesses whose involvement only becomes apparent after the commencement of the Inquiry.

3. My clients have been greatly concerned, rightly or wrongly, about the unfortunate publicity that was given to the Inquiry by the Guardian Newspaper at the beginning of last week, and which has left fears on their part that the Inquiry could develop into recriminations between the Greenwich Social Services Department in particular and the Wirral Borough Council Social Services Department, and they are understandably reluctant to become embroiled in such a conflict.

In recent years most of such cases have resulted not only in an internal Inquiry being conducted within the relevant agency, but have also led to some form of independent panel of Inquiry. My firm has in the past been instructed by the National and Local Government Officers Association to represent its members in the independent inquiries set up to examine the deaths of Darren Clarke (in Liverpool) and Paul Brown (in the Wirral) The Darren Clarke Inquiry was a statutory Inquiry set up by the D.H.S.S.

With regard to the Paul Brown case, there were in fact two main inquiries; the first was a non-statutory inquiry which was set up jointly by the Wirral Borough Council Social Services Department and the Wirral Area Health Authority. This inquiry was held in private and the Report, although made public, did not identify the names of the representatives of the Social Services Department and the Health Authority who had been involved in the case. This inquiry suffered both from the fact that it was not a statutory inquiry and therefore had no powers to compel people to attend the inquiry and also from the fact that an exhaustive investigation of the facts was not carried out and a number of key personnel were not invited to attend.

Subsequently a further inquiry was held into the death of Paul Brown, which was set up by the D.H.S.S. under statutory powers under the chairmanship of Michael Morland Q.C.

In the two statutory inquiries in which my firm was involved, the Treasury Solicitors Department was instructed by the D.H.S.S. to carry out all the work in tracing witnesses and the preparation of witness statements, under the guidance of Counsel to the Inquiry. After the preliminary meeting to discuss the format of the inquiry and representation of witnesses, the Treasury Solicitors' representatives spent several weeks in collating all the statements and they went to great lengths to obtain statements from every person or organization that had been concerned in some way with the children of the particular family. I believe that they were greatly assisted in this task by the fact that witnesses realized that they could be compelled to attend such an inquiry.

It is my view that if the Department of Health and Social Security decide that an external inquiry should be held, then such an inquiry should be held in private and the only persons who should be entitled to be present whilst a particular witness is giving evidence to that inquiry are the members of the panel, the Counsel to the Inquiry and the witness' legal representative. It should be left to the Counsel to the Inquiry to be able to cross-examine the witness, with the assistance of the statements which should already have been provided to the inquiry, rather than to have a witness facing the ordeal of cross-examination by a number of different legal representatives.

I do not feel that that form of inquiry would in any way inhibit the search for the facts of the case, or prevent the making of recommendations where appropriate, or of making critical observations of certain of the witnesses. It seems to me that such a form of inquiry, if one has to be held, would be particularly suitable in this case because the Commission of Inquiry could sit for part of the time in Greenwich and for part of the time in Wirral.

I hope that these views may be of some value, both with regard to the conduct of any future inquiries into cases of child abuse, and also to show the reasons for my clients' anxiety in this case and for their decision to decline to give evidence before your Commission of Inquiry. I hope that the members of your Commission of Inquiry will appreciate and respect the decision which my clients have reached. They have no wish to avoid a critical appraisal of their role in the case, and indeed an internal review has already been carried out by the Wirral Social Services Department, and my clients are confident that the various decisions which they took with regard to the family were correct and in accordance with procedures established by their Authority.

I would finally express my clients' regret to the members of the Commission of Inquiry at any inconvenience which may have been caused by the decision not to give evidence and I would respectfully trust that no adverse inferences will be drawn against any of my clients for their non-attendance at the Inquiry.

Yours faithfully,

R H Dawson

R H Dawson Esq,
Morecroft, Dawson and Garnetts,
Queen Building,
8 Dale Street,
Liverpool, L2 4TQ                                               7 July 1987

Dear Mr Dawson

**Re: Commission of Inquiry into the circumstances surrounding the death of Kimberley Carlile.**

Your letter to Mr Blom-Cooper of 6 July sent by Fax made depressing reading, if only because for over three weeks until last Friday, the Commission had every reason to suppose that your three clients were, as everyone else has been, keen to assist the Inquiry. The Commission is still hopeful that your clients may see the wisdom of changing their minds, and if they were to do so the Commission would certainly consider seriously the idea of taking their evidence at a venue in the Wirral.

From this you will gather that the Commission fully intends to complete its Inquiry. You specifically request that the Commission should draw no adverse inferences against any of your clients for their absence from the Inquiry. The Commission will certainly not draw any adverse inference; indeed it will be scrupulous to avoid being affected by the decision of your clients. However, it must be made clear that the Commission in its report may wish: a. to make findings on the basis of the substantial documentation supplied by Wirral Borough Council, and b. to allude to the fact of your clients' non-assistance and the manner in which they indicated their willingness to assist, and then suddenly at the end of the first week's hearings withheld any further assistance.

This is not the occasion for us to deal with the various reasons you advance for your clients' decision, but we are concerned that your clients should understand that their objection to the Inquiry and to its procedure do not in our view provide valid grounds for their withdrawal from the Inquiry. We would also emphasise that we do not think your clients are serving the best interests of children for whose benefit this Inquiry is being conducted.

Also, all these matters could have been aired at the preliminary hearing which the Commission held on 8 June, and again on 15 June when the Commission handed down its reasoned decision to hold the Inquiry in private. All the other parties made their submissions and have very helpfully assisted the Inquiry in every way possible, and in particular made submissions about the procedure the Commission should adopt.

Yours sincerely,

Mr. L. Blom-Cooper, Mr. J. Harding, Miss E. Milton.

The Independent Commission of Inquiry
Shrewsbury House Community Centre
Bushmoor Crescent
Shooters Hill
London SE18                                                    13th July 1987

Dear Sirs and Madam,

**Re: Kimberley Carlile Inquiry**

I am writing to acknowledge receipt of your leter of 7th July which I have discussed with my clients.

I do not propose to reply in detail to the letter but I think that it is important to clarify the position of my clients in the light of some of the comments made in your letter.

Prior to the preliminary meeting on 8th June Mr. Ewbank and Mrs. Madeley received letters from the Director of Social Services of Wirral Borough Council indicating that they may be required to attend before the Commission of Inquiry. The letter indicated that no decision had yet been made by the Commission of Inquiry as to which witnesses were to be called.

Mr Ewbank applied to his Union, Nalgo, for assistance and Nalgo's Head Office made a request to Greenwich Borough Council to ask that the Greenwich Borough Council should agree to meet the legal costs of individual members who may be called to give evidence before the Inquiry. I understand that although Greenwich agreed to pay for the costs of its own employees it refused to meet the costs of employees of the Wirral Borough Council and it was then that an application was made by Nalgo to the Wirral Borough Council.

Mrs Madeley requested representation from B.A.S.W.A. and she had thought that she would be represented by BASWA's solicitors at the Inquiry. On 18th June she received an indication that she was not going to be required to attend the Inquiry and it was not until her return from holiday on 29th June that she was told after all that her attendance was being requested. She then contacted BASWA's solicitors, only to be told that they were no longer able to represent her at the Inquiry because they had been retained by one of the representatives from Greenwich Social Services Department. She then made a request for assistance from Nalgo of which she is also a member.

With regard to Mrs. Stuart, she received no notification that she may be involved in this Inquiry until some time after the preliminary meeting on 8th June and she also then applied for assistance from Nalgo.

The point remains that my clients were not given sufficient time and opportunity to arrange for legal representation because of the time scale that was laid down by the Commission of Inquiry and I feel that the preliminary meeting ought not to have been held until the Commission of Inquiry had had an opportunity to consider which witnesses they wished to attend. You state that all the other parties made submissions to the preliminary hearing but I suspect that it had been known for a long time which of the employees of Greenwich Borough Council and Greenwich Area Health Authority were likely to be called to give evidence and of course the preliminary meeting was held on their doorstep.

Although my clients accept that they did attend meetings with the Solicitor from the Wirral Borough Council who was dealing with the matter on behalf of the Council and were involved in preparation of statements for the Inquiry nevertheless none of my clients had any direct communication with the Commission of Inquiry; it was not until they had had the opportunity of discussing matters with their own solicitor and of considering the form of the Inquiry and recent developments that they took the decision to decline to appear.

It is noted that you may wish to make findings on the basis of documentation supplied by the Wirral Borough Council and to refer in your report to the fact that certain witnesses from the Wirral Borough Council Social Services Department had been invited to attend but declined to do so, but I would suggest that it would be most unreasonable for you to make any further comment with regard to my clients' non-attendance at the Inquiry.

I endeavoured to set out in detail my clients' reasons for not attending the Inquiry and I regret that the Commission did not appear to accept my clients' views. I should make it clear that my clients have not had any change of heart about their decision not to attend the Inquiry.

Yours faithfully,

R H Dawson.

R H Dawson Esq
Morecroft, Dawson and Garnetts
Queen Building
8 Dale Street
Liverpool
L2 4TQ                                                    15 July 1987

Dear Mr Dawson,

**Re: Kimberley Carlile Commission of Inquiry**

Thank you for your letter of 13 July. We have much sympathy with your clients' difficulties over funding their legal representation. But, as we understand the position, that was finally resolved on the evening of 29 June when Wirral Borough Council decided to pay for limited costs of your clients' legal representation. It was following that decision that you came to London and liaised with our Counsel. We were under the impression that there was then no obstacle to your clients coming before the Inquiry; the only question was one of timing their appearance to give evidence. We appreciate that it was only then that your clients had had the opportunity of taking advice from their legal representative on the Salmon letters written to them, to which incidentally you make no reference.

Assuming for present purposes that by the first days of July your clients had insufficient or inadequate opportunity to arrange for legal representation and preparation of their statments preparatory to appearing before the Inquiry (an assumption that we do not think is in fact warranted), the position now is that we are hereby renewing our invitation to your clients to come and give evidence in the week commencing 27 July. This will give them another fortnight in which to prepare their cases. If they still decline to attend there could be no conceivable complaint, therefore, if the Commission of Inquiry makes findings on the basis of the full documentation and the evidence it may hear. In this latter respect we should inform you that we shall be taking evidence from workers of Kensington and Chelsea, and Greenwich, who had direct dealings with Mr Robert Ewbank in the summer and autumn of 1985.

Yours sincerely,

Mr. L. Blom-Cooper, Mr. J. Harding, Miss E. Milton

The Independent Commission of Inquiry
Shrewsbury House Community Centre
Bushmoor Crescent
Shooters Hill
London SE18                                        21 July 1987

Dear Sirs and Madam

**Re: Kimberley Carlile Inquiry**

I write to acknowledge receipt of your letter of 15 July. I have to advise you that my clients have re-affirmed their decision not to attend the Inquiry's hearings.

I accept that at the time that I met with Counsel to the Inquiry on Wednesday 1 July no indication was given that my clients would not be attending the Inquiry. However, I had only been instructed within the previous 24 hours and I had not then considered the matter in detail with my clients. I was made aware by Counsel to the Inquiry that Salmon letters were being sent but my clients' decision not to attend the Inquiry had nothing to do with the Salmon letters.

My clients further appreciate that the Commission of Inquiry may wish to make findings on the basis of the documentation presented to it and the evidence it hears, but any such findings must of course be subject to the qualification that oral evidence was not given by some of the parties involved.

I also have to advise you that Mr Surridge spoke with me last week and requested me to write on his behalf to notify you that he also would not be attending the Inquiry.

Yours faithfully,

R H Dawson.

R H Dawson, Esq.,
Morecroft, Dawson & Garnetts,
Solicitors,
Queen Building,
8 Dale Street,
Liverpool. L2 4TQ                                              28 July 1987

Dear Mr. Dawson,

**Re: Kimberley Carlile Inquiry**

Thank you for your letter of 21st July, 1987, explaining further why your clients remain unwilling to attend the Inquiry and give evidence.

We write once more urging your clients to co-operate with the Inquiry, because an issue has emerged during the course of the evidence which your clients may not be aware of, and with which they may feel compelled to deal.

It appears from a reconstruction of the percentile chart for Kimberley that from the age of 5 months she failed to thrive. When the 24-month developmental assessment was made in November, 1983, her weight was below the 3rd centile and her height had not maintained a normal increase. She was last weighed on 24th May, 1984: this date was the moment of discharge from the three week voluntary care. From the documentation at present in the possession of the Commission of Inquiry, that weighing was never plotted on a percentile chart. No developmental assessment took place at the 36th month of life. Nor was there any weighing, let alone a developmental assessment of Kimberley when she was discharged from voluntary care on 4th October, 1985. (We enclose a copy of the constructed percentile chart). Indeed, the "hand over" of the three Carlile children on that day to their mother and new step-father appears not to have been part of any planned rehabilitation of the Carlile family in the newly constituted household.

We are writing simultaneously to the Director of Social Services, Mr. Rickard, and to the legal adviser of the Mersey Regional Health Authority, advising them of the emergence of the above-mentioned facts. In the circumstances, we confidently expect a positive response from your clients, the Director and the Health Authority, to our earnest request that the Inquiry should be fully assisted in its desire to conduct a thorough investigation of the facts surrounding Kimberley Carlile's death. We feel we can best serve the interests of all children if we can report comprehensively in this case.

Yours sincerely,

Mr. L. Blom-Cooper, Mr. J. Harding, Miss E. Milton

Independent Commission of Inquiry
Shrewsbury House Community Centre
Bushmoor Crescent
Shooters Hill
London SE18                                          3 August 1987

Dear Sirs and Madam,

**Re: Kimberley Carlile Inquiry**

I am writing to acknowledge receipt of your letter of 28 July 1987, which
was only received this morning, bearing the post mark dated 30 July, although
I had been telephoned by a Journalist from The Times Newspaper on 29
July about such a letter.

The matter is receiving attention and I will reply to you in due course.

Yours faithfully,

R H Dawson


Independent Commission of Inquiry
Shrewsbury House Community Centre
Bushmoor Cresent
Shooters Hill
London SE18                                          12 August 1987

Dear Sirs and Madam,

**Re: Kimberley Carlile Inquiry**

I have now been able to take instructions with regard to your letter of 28
July.

I am not sure as to how the issue which you describe in your letter of 28
July has emerged but my clients have instructed me that they do not feel
that they are able to assist the Inquiry with regard to the particular issue that
you mention, and confirm that they are not prepared to attend to give evidence
before the Inquiry.

So far as my clients are concerned no mention or reference was made at any
case conference (or otherwise) of the percentile chart relating to Kimberley.
Moreover the Commission of Inquiry appears to have overlooked the fact
that the records from the Social Services Department contains a medical
report at the time of Kimberley's admission into voluntary care on 24 August
1984 and also a medical report dated 4 October 1985 on Kimberley's discharge
from care. In addition your Inquiry has already received evidence from Mr
Gordon Whiteley about Kimberley's condition in July 1984.

My clients are fully aware of their professional obligations and would have
been willing to attend an Inquiry properly administered and organised.
However, I made it clear in my letter to the Commission of Inquiry of 6 July
1987 why my clients were not prepared to attend the inquiry and your letter
of 28 July only serves to reinforce the concern which my clients expressed.
As a result my clients do not have confidence that the present Inquiry would

be able to produce a comprehensive and accurate report, particularly so far as the period when the family resided in the Wirral is concerned.

I should be obliged if you would kindly let me know whether the Commission of Inquiry is able to assist as to how the Guardian Newspaper was able to acquire information about the identity of my clients and also about the position of Mr Surridge.

Yours faithfully,

R H Dawson


Mr R Dawson
Morecroft, Dawson and Garnetts
Solicitors
Queen Building
8 Dale Street
Liverpool L2 4TQ                                             18 August 1987

Dear Mr Dawson,

### Re: Kimberley Carlile Inquiry

The Members of the Commission have asked me to reply to your letter of 12th August 1987.

The Members of the Commission have certainly not overlooked the medical reports on Kimberley Carlile of 24 August 1984 and 4 October 1985. Neither of these medical reports were developmental assessments of Kimberley; nor did the doctors weigh the child, who was known in November 1983 to be below the 3rd centile. It is precisely because there was no proper surveillance of Kimberley's physical and psychological development in 1984 or 1985 that the Commission expressed the wish to hear from your clients an explanation of these facts.

It is not accurate to suggest that this Inquiry is not properly administered or organised. As an Independent Commission of Inquiry established by Greenwich Borough Council and Greenwich Health Authority (and with Wirral Borough Council also given the opportunity to sponsor it), it has been welcomed and supported by the DHSS. I understand that the DHSS has no intention of setting up a statutory inquiry. It has expressed complete confidence that the Members of the Commission will present a full and impartial report.

The reluctance of your clients to assist the Inquiry is disappointing. However the Members of the Commission nevertheless feel entirely satisfied that they can present a complete and accurate report from the statements and documentation made available to the Inquiry, together with some highly pertinent oral evidence from the personnel of Kensington and Chelsea Social Services Department who had direct dealings with Mr. Ewbank.

The Commissioners' letter of 28 July set out what this evidence indicates with regard to the action taken (or lack of action) to monitor the development of Kimberley whilst she was in voluntary care, and to plan for the return of the three children to their mother and to a reconsitituted family in another part of the country. The Commissioners' letter gave your clients the opportunity to comment on those specific issues, and that opportunity is still available to them. The Commission will be sitting for 3 days in early September, after which the opportunity to give oral evidence may no longer be available. The fact that your clients do not have confidence that the Inquiry can produce a comprehensive report with regard to the period the family resided in the Wirral, is of course, entirely due to your clients' refusal to attend.

With regard to the final paragraph of your letter, I have no knowledge as to how the Guardian Newspaper obtained the names of your clients, or the position of Mr Surridge. On all occasions I have received any requests for specific information about, or comments from, your clients (and I can recall only two such occasions) I have referred the journalists concerned to you. You will appreciate that your clients' names appear frequently on the documentation supplied to the Inquiry by Wirral Borough Council, and this documentation has been copied and distributed to all the parties represented before the Inquiry. Also Mr Ewbank's name has been mentioned in the course of oral evidence before the Inquiry.

I am sure you will appreciate that the Report of the Commission will include the names of the main people involved in the matters under the Inquiry, including those of your clients. The Commission has further asked me to let you know that it intends publishing in full the correspondence between you and the Commission in an Appendix to its Report. The letter to you of 7th July, 1987 from the Members of the Commission also indicated their intention to comment on your clients' absence from the Inquiry.

Yours sincerely,

Peter Bailey,
Secretary to the Commission.

P. Bailey Esq.,
Independent Commission of Inquiry,
Shrewsbury House Community Centre,
Bushmoor Crescent,
Shooters Hill,
London SE18                                        24th September, 1987

Dear Mr. Bailey,

I am writing to acknowledge receipt of your letter of 18th August. I apologise for the delay in replying.

The present form of Inquiry may well have the support of the DHSS. It was however established not by the DHSS but by the Greenwich Borough Council and the Greenwich Area Health Authority.

I have already made it clear in previous correspondence the deficiencies in the present form of Inquiry, particularly because of the involvement of agencies from different parts of the country, and the factors which caused my clients to decide not to attend the Inquiry, compounded by the quite inadequate length of time which the Commission of Inquiry allowed before commencing its hearings.

If the DHSS feel that it was necessary for there to be a full Inquiry into this case to include a detailed examination of the period when the children were within the Wirral area, then they ought to have been prepared to set up the Inquiry themselves with staff from the Treasury Solicitors Department dealing with the organisation and the preparation for the Inquiry.

Indeed it is noteworthy that on 28th July 1987 a number of advocates appearing at the Inquiry had occasion to write a lengthy letter to the Commission of Inquiry criticising its organisation and conduct.

I would also wish to add this. Since Mrs. Carlile's release from prison on 3rd December 1984, she had not lived in the Wirral area; she moved to London in February 1985 and then later on, during 1985, she moved into the Greenwich Borough Council District. Her children were discharged from voluntary care and collected by her on 4th October 1985 and thereafter remained within the district of the Greenwich Borough Council. It is appreciated that when Mr. Ewbank wrote to both Kensington Social Services and Greenwich Social Services, his letter did not include all the background information about the family, but it is clear from the documents which the Commission of Inquiry has received from the Wirral Borough Council that the principal area of concern had revolved around Mrs. Carlile's relationship with Mr. David Carlile and its consequences, and Mrs. Carlile was by then no longer living with Mr. Carlile.

There are no set procedures (either locally or nationally) for the transmission of files or indeed of the type of information to be transmitted from one area to another. Certainly Mr. Ewbank's letter made reference amongst other matters to Mrs. Carlile's recent release from imprisonment and the fact that her husband Mr. Carlile was violent towards her and requested that the family be monitored, and Mr. Ewbank and Mrs. Madeley both consider that Kensington and Greenwich had sufficient information to enable them to deal with the case.

Yours sincerely,

R. H. Dawson.

Mr. R. Dawson,
Morecroft Dawson and Garnetts,
Solicitors,
Queen Building,
8 Dale Street,
Liverpool L2 4TQ                                    30th September, 1987

Dear Mr. Dawson,

The Members of the Commission of Inquiry have asked me to thank you for your letter of 24th September 1987. They think you have stated very clearly all the points that led to your clients declining to assist the Inquiry, but they do not agree that there were sound reasons for them declining to appear. Had the Commission possessed the statutory power to subpoena witnesses, it would undoubtedly have issued subpoenas to your clients. In the absence of any such statutory power the Commission felt, nevertheless that your clients would have considered it a public duty to respond positively to the request to assist in an important child abuse inquiry. The Commission Members are naturally very disappointed in your clients' decision.

As you were previously informed, the Commission will be publishing in an Appendix to its report this recent exchange of letters as well as the earlier correspondence.

Yours sincerely,

Peter Bailey,
Secretary to the Commission

# 2. Correspondence between the Commission and the Director of Social Services, Wirral Borough Council

Mr D Rickard
Director of Social Services
Metropolitan Borough of Wirral
Social Services Centre
Cleveland Street
Birkenhead
Wirral
L41 6BL                                                                    15 July 1987

Dear Mr Rickard,

**Re: Kimberley Carlile Commission of Inquiry**

During the last few weeks we have been much concerned about the position of three members of staff in your Department who have been invited to give evidence to the Commission of Inquiry. We need not rehearse here the steps taken, except to say that those members were due to come to the Inquiry but withdrew shortly before the arranged attendance. Although, we have been in correspondence with their solicitor, Mr R H Dawson, urging his clients to come to the Inquiry, they are still declining to give evidence.

In these circumstances we are inviting you to come and give evidence to the Commission of Inquiry to speak to the work of your Department in respect of the Carlile family.

Yours sincerely,

Mr. L. Blom-Cooper, Mr. J. Harding, Miss E. Milton

The Independent Commission of Inquiry
into the death of Kimberley Carlile
Shrewsbury House Community Centre
Bushmoor Crescent
Shooters Hill
London SE18                                                              21 July 1987

Dear Sirs and Madam,

**Kimberley Carlile Commission of Inquiry**

With reference to your letter dated 15 July 1987 in which you invite me to give evidence and speak to the work of my Department, this is a matter on which I feel I need to take instructions from members of this Authority.

I am sure it would help them in deciding on this matter if you could expand on exactly what evidence you think I am able to provide, given that I have had no personal involvement in the case, and exactly what aspects of the work of this Department you are interested in.

Yours faithfully,

D Rickard,
Director of Social Services.

Mr D Rickard
Director of Social Services
Metropolitan Borough of Wirral
Social Services Centre
Cleveland Street
Birkenhead
Wirral L41 6BL                                      23 July 1987

Dear Mr Rickard,

**Re: Kimberley Carlile Commission of Inquiry**

In response to your letter, the contents of which we have been informed, the Commission of Inquiry would think that there are two aspects to the request that you should come and give evidence.

Firstly, the Commission would anticipate that there are aspects of the work of the Social Services Department with the Carlile family upon which you, the Director, would wish to make observations.

Secondly, the Commission of Inquiry is interested among other things in the following:-

1. What attention was paid, during the period that Kimberley was in voluntary care, to the fact that she had been failing to thrive.
2. What prompted the decision of the Department not to seek a Section 3 resolution, or alternatively to make the children Wards of Court.
3. What was the Department's plan for the rehabilitation of the Carlile family in the Autumn and Summer of 1985.

We enclose herewith the 'Salmon' letters which were sent to Mr Ewbank and Mrs Madeley on 9th July, which it may be helpful for you to see.

We understand that you wish to consult with Members of your Authority. We would only urge that we could have a reply by tomorrow evening, as the Commission is expecting to finish hearing oral evidence by the end of next week.

Yours sincerely,

Mr. L. J. Blom-Cooper, Mr. J. Harding, Miss E. Milton

## Enclosures

Copies of two letters, both dated 9th July, 1987, from the Secretary to the Commission to Mrs Madeley and Mr Ewbank, which both contained the following statement:-

"I am writing on the instructions of the Commission of Inquiry into the circumstances surrounding the death of Kimberley Carlile.

I have been asked to notify you that the following criticism may be made of your practice as set out herein below:

1. You failed to ensure that Greenwich Social Services Department was supplied with sufficient information on the Carlile family having regard to the documentation available in Wirral Social Services Department.
2. You failed to ensure that there was an adequate programme for the proper development of the children on their return to their mother on 4th October 1985, and their discharge from voluntary care".

Mr D Rickard
Director of Social Services,
Metropolitan Borough of Wirral
Social Services Centre
Cleveland Street
Birkenhead
Wirral L41 6BL

28 July 1987

Dear Mr Rickard,

**Kimberley Carlile Inquiry**

We have today written to the Solicitor for the three members of your Department whom we wish to call to give evidence, and to the Legal Adviser to the Mersey Regional Health Authority about an aspect of the Inquiry that has emerged from the evidence. (We enclose copies of those two letters). You will appreciate that the fact of Kimberley's failure to thrive since she was 5 months old appears to us to raise a serious issue about her discharge from voluntary care on 4th October, 1985, which we think calls for a thorough investigation. To that end, it is imperative that personnel from your Department and from the Health Authority should come and give evidence to the Inquiry.

Yours sincerely,

Mr. L. J. Blom-Cooper, Mr. J. Harding, Miss E. Milton,

Independent Commission of Inquiry
into the death of Kimberley Carlile,
Shrewsbury House Community Centre
Bushmoor Crescent,
Shooters Hill
London SE18                                              29 July 1987

Dear Sirs and Madam,

**Kimberley Carlile Commission of Inquiry**

Thank you for your further letter dated 23rd July 1987. Having consulted Members of this Authority it is their view that it would not be appropriate for me to attend the Inquiry. I regret I have not been able to advise you on this matter earlier.

Yours faithfully,

D Rickard,
Director of Social Services.


Independent Commission of Inquiry
into the death of Kimberley Carlile
Shrewsbury House Community Centre
Bushmoor Crescent
Shooters Hill
London SE18                                           10 August 1987

Dear Sirs and Madam,

**Kimberley Carlile Inquiry**

Thank you for your letter dated 28 July to which was attached copy letters to Morecroft, Dawson & Garnetts, and the Mersey Regional Health Authority. This is my first day back from sick leave, so I apologise if you feel that any delay has taken place in replying.

Perhaps I have not made my position clear enough for the Members of the Commission, but as Director I am under instructions from Members of my Committee. It is their view, as previously explained, that it would not be appropriate for me to attend in the present circumstances. Furthermore, I am in no position to direct my staff to attend, and even less staff from the Health Authority. Mr Dawson has informed me that it is his intention to respond to your letter on behalf of the staff he advises.

Yours faithfully,

D Rickard
Director of Social Services.

Mr D Rickard
Director of Social Services
Metropolitan Borough of Wirral
Social Services Centre
Birkenhead
Wirral L41 6BL                                                    18 August 1987

Dear Mr Rickard,

**Re: Kimberley Carlile Inquiry**

The Members of the Commission have asked me to reply to your letter of 10th August 1987.

The Members of the Commission would be grateful for some clarification on the reasons why you decline to attend the Inquiry. It was thought that Wirral Borough Council had decided from the outset that it would assist the Commission, and indeed the Inquiry has been much helped by the presence throughout of Mr David Park on behalf of the Authority. However, this appears inconsistent with your comments that you are under the instructions of the Members of your Committee that it would be inappropriate for you to attend.

The Commissioners' letter of 28th July explained that a serious issue has been raised about the manner of Kimberley's discharge from voluntary care on 4th October 1985, and the Members of the Commission confidently expected that your Authority would wish this issue to be fully examined. In the continued absence of the Social Workers concerned, the Commission would feel that you, as Director, should account for their actions in 1984 and 1985.

I am instructed to inform you that the correspondence between yourself and the Commission will appear as an Appendix to the Commission's Report.

Yours sincerely,

Peter Bailey
Secretary to the Commission.

Mr. P. Bailey
Secretary to the Commission of Inquiry
into the Death of Kimberley Carlile
Shrewsbury House Community Centre
Bushmoor Crescent Shooters Hill
London SE18                                            18 September 1987

Dear Mr. Bailey

**Kimberley Carlile Inquiry**

Thank you for your letter of 18 August concerning this matter. I apologise for the delay in replying which has been due to a number of factors including the need to consult appropriate members of the Council during the peak holiday period. Even though the Inquiry has now concluded and it is therefore to some extent academic whether I clarify my position or not I believe it is important to do so in the light of your intention to publish the correspondence between us as an Appendix to the Commission's Report. I would not wish anyone reading the Report to be under any misconception as to the true position.

For the record and by way of further explanation I considered it inappropriate for me to attend the Inquiry for the following reasons:

1. You invited me to attend the Inquiry to give evidence. I have not been personally involved in the case and I do not have any further evidence or information other than that which is contained in the files which have been forwarded to you. Accordingly, I do not consider that I could usefully have assisted you.

2. I was requested to speak on the work of my Department in respect of the Carlile family. It would have been inevitable in my view that I would have been required to comment upon or interpret the actions of those social workers involved in the case which is something which would have been both unfair and improper since they themselves have not given evidence.

3. I have seen the correspondence between the Commission and Mr. Dawson, the solicitor representing Wirral's social workers. I have also read with interest the articles which have appeared in The Guardian and The Times concerning the case. It is clear that a great deal of pressure has been put upon those social workers to try to persuade them to give evidence. It occurs to me that my own appearance would simply add to that pressure, and would have served no other useful purpose for the reasons set out above. I am not in a position to instruct staff to attend the Inquiry when, after consultation with their solicitor, they have decided against that course of action, and when the Council itself has steadfastly refused to consider such an instruction.

4. In agreeing to co-operate with the inquiry the members of this Authority clearly wished to benefit by its deliberations. However, they also wished to have the benefit of their Chief Officer's advice on any recommendations stemming from the Inquiry, once all the facts surrounding the case had been collated. That advice would lack objectivity if the Chief Officer had already become involved in expressing views or opinions at a stage when all the evidence or information was not available.

With regard to the second paragraph of your letter I should perhaps explain that there is in fact no inconsistency in practice. When I received your request I gave it a great deal of thought in personal and professional terms. The matter was discussed by relevant members of the Council, myself and the Borough Secretary and Solicitor. We jointly concluded that it would be inappropriate for me to attend for the reasons given. No specific instruction was given to me by my Members, but having spoken to them again it is clear that they would have been prepared to issue an instruction to me had they thought it necessary. It must be recognised by the Commission that as a Chief Officer employee of the Council I am not a free agent in this sort of situation.

As I said at the outset I trust that the Commission will publish this letter as well as previous correspondence in the Appendix to the Report.

Yours sincerely

D. Rickard
Director of Social Services.


Mr. D. Rickard,
Director of Social Services,
Metropolitan Borough of Wirral,
Social Services Centre.
Birkenhead, Wirral L41 6BL                    /30th September, 1987

Dear Mr. Rickard,

The Members of the Commission of Inquiry have asked me to thank you for your letter of 18th September in which you spell out your reasons for declining to give evidence before the Inquiry. You will appreciate that the Commission does not agree that there were solid grounds for you declining to appear to answer for the work of your Department with the Carlile family over the 3 years, 1982-1985, and more particularly during the period leading up to the discharge of the three children from voluntary care on 4 October 1985. Had the Commission possessed the statutory power to subpoena witnesses it would undoubtedly have issued a subpoena to you irrespective of any subpoena on officers in your Department. In the absence of any such statutory power the Commission felt nevertheless that you would have considered it a public duty to respond positively to the request to assist in an important child abuse inquiry. The Commission Members are naturally very disappointed in your decision.

As you are aware, the Commission reserves the right to comment in its report on your response to its request for your help in this matter. I confirm that all the correspondence passing between yourself and the Commission will appear in an Appendix to the report. It will appear alongside the correspondence which the Commission has had with Mr. Dawson, acting on behalf of three officers in your Department.

Yours sincerely,

Peter Bailey
Secretary to the Commission

# Kimberley Carlile Commission of Inquiry
## Commission's Reasoned Decision on the Mode of Inquiry, 15th June 1987

In framing the terms of reference for the Commission of Inquiry the sponsoring authorities have left to the Commission the question whether the Inquiry should be conducted in public or in private. At the preliminary meeting on 8 June 1987 the Commission heard submissions from a number of parties and persons. At the conclusion of the hearing the Commission indicated that it desired to consider its decision. The Commission promised to give a reasoned decision a week hence. It now gives that decision.

The Commission also indicated that it was willing to receive any further submissions, in writing, before arriving at its decision. The Commission duly received submissions from the following:-

1. Mr. John Trotter, of Bates, Wells & Braithwaite, on behalf of the British Association of Social Workers and of the Director and Assistant Director of Social Services of Greenwich.

2. Mr. Brian Raymond, of Bindman & Partners, on behalf of Mr. Martin Ruddock, Team Manager, Area 4, Greenwich Social Services.

3. Mr. James Gibbons, instructed by Pattinson & Brewer, on behalf of the Transport and General Workers Union, Mr. Don Neill, Area Manager, Area 4, Greenwich Social Services, Mrs. Olive Swinburne, Social Worker, Area 4 and Mrs. Beryl Fitzgerald, Team Clerk, Area 4, Greenwich Social Services.

4. Wilford McBain, Solicitors, on behalf of Mrs. Jean Gabbott, former Child Abuse Co-Ordinator, Greenwich Social Services; also on behalf of Ms Marilyn Streeter and Mrs. Doreen Armstrong.

All these submissions reinforced their separate oral submissions in favour of the Inquiry being held in private. The organisations and personnel in the Health Services likewise favoured hearings in private. But no written submissions were received from anyone involved in the Health Services in the Greenwich Area. None of those who argued in favour of hearings in public were engaged in the Social or Health Services of Greenwich, but were individuals who felt strongly that the tradition of public inquiries should be maintained. An organisation, Parents Against Injustice, made a written submission in support of a public hearing.

## General

Whenever government, be it central or local, considers that a particular event has caused sufficient public disquiet to warrant an independent inquiry to establish what happened, and who (if anyone) was responsible, the instinctive reaction is that such inquisition must be subject to open scrutiny. It would be unthinkable that a disaster such as a Flixborough explosion, a

Brixton riot, a Stafford Hospital outbreak of poisoning, or a Zeebrugge ferry capsizing could be investigated other than under the full glare of publicity. Those whose conduct would inevitably come under scrutiny cannot avoid public accountability (and that includes being accountable in private), the more so if they are professional people whose obligations extend their personal and private practice. Every professional person, as Francis Bacon observed, owes a debt to his profession. The conventional wisdom is that such inquiries must be held in public (subject to exceptional circumstances that dictate occasional withdrawal into private session for a specific reason of confidentiality or privacy), for it is only when the public is present that the public will have complete confidence that everything possible has been done for arriving at the truth. Unless inquiries into major tragedies or disasters are held in public they are unlikely to achieve their main purpose, namely that of restoring or maintaining the confidence of the public in the integrity of public life. On this approach to the problem there must be a presumption that the inquiry will be in public; only special circumstances would lead to an inquiry in private.

A good example of the exception was the Profumo Inquiry of 1963, conducted by Lord Denning wholly in secret. None of the witnesses before Lord Denning heard any of the evidence given against him by others, nor had they any opportunity of testing it. The transcript of the evidence has never been published. Lord Denning was detective-inquisitor, advocate and judge. Such a procedure has never been an accepted model, although there may be exceptional cases in the future when such an extra-judical process might be acceptable. But is the death of a child at the hands of its parent(s) an exception? So long as there are grounds for thinking that some responsibility may rest with Social Services and the allied agencies for the failure to protect the child from abuse, can the inquiry be conducted with thoroughness and scrupulous fairness to those on whom criticism may be placed, if it is in public or private? It is axiomatic that the Commission would indicate fully in its report the evidence upon which it relied; and the sponsoring Authorities have already undertaken to publish the Commission's report.

## Child Abuse Inquiries Generally

Parliament has empowered the Secretary of State to set up an Inquiry in the field of Social Services. Section 98 Children Act 1975 (now Section 26, Child Care Act 1980) empowers the Secretary of State to hold an inquiry in any matter related to the exercise of the functions of the Social Services Committee of a local Authority, in so far as those functions relate to children.[1] The Secretary of State has the power to order that such inquiries, or part of

---

[1] The British Association of Social Workers in its Report, *Child Abuse Inquiries*, noted in Section 1, Paragraph 12:

"Only two public inquiries have been set up by the Secretary of State for Social Services since 1975, these being into the deaths of Darryn Clarke and Paul Brown. In both these instances there had been considerable public disquiet regarding allegations of failure by the police and the welfare services to protect the children. In the latter case there was also suspicion that attempts had been made to mislead the two previous non-statutory inquiries. In these two cases, therefore, a public accounting was considered necessary. For the most part, however, investigating authorities have chosen to hold their inquiries in private. The majority continued to publish reports of their findings, although the practice adopted of referring to participants by designation rather than by name gave some measure of privacy."

such inquiries should be held in private, although if no direction is given, the person holding the inquiry has power to determine whether it shall be in public or private. A similar provision is to be found in Section 84, National Health Service Act 1977, in relation to Health Services.

In its report, *A Child in Trust,* the Panel of Inquiry thought that this was a statutory recognition of the presumption in favour of a public inquiry (Page 25). This may be right, but it must be remembered that the statutory inquiry carries with it the powers to subpoena witnesses and produce documents, a fact that sharply distinguishes it from the non-statutory inquiry set up by a local authority, which does not qualify for the right to apply to the Crown Office for an Order of Subpoena. Since any local authority inquiry will just as much desire to ascertain the truth and to that end need to hear **all** the relevant witnesses, it will need to encourage every person to come forward voluntarily. Public hearings will, if anything, operate as a disincentive on some people to give evidence. Hence the presumption for non-statutory inquiries into child abuse deaths is, we think, a private hearing. The Department of Health and Social Security in its Consultative Paper of 4 July 1985 on Child Abuse Inquiries stated (para 4.2) that "the Inquiry should normally be conducted in private", and advocated a departure from the norm only in rare instances (para 4.3). If held in private, more witnesses will come forward with evidence which they might not be prepared to give in public. Clearly the quantity of evidence will be greater in private hearings. But will the giving of evidence out of sight and hearing of the public debase its quality? It sounds plausible to say that evidence in private is likely to be more candid, and inferentially reveal more nearly the truth, even though the evidence in public is likewise tested for its veracity and credibility. But there is another side to the coinage of testimony. A witness is more likely to be cautious about any allegation that he makes in the forensic arena than he might be in private. He will be less inclined to embellish or elaborate on his testimony and thereby give a distorted version of events. Caution in accusation is, therefore, to be encouraged, and not discouraged. If the inquiry is to be in private, it must, we think, at least replicate the process of confrontation of a witness with those whom he or she accuses or blames.

## Recent Child Abuse Inquiries

The Panel of Inquiry into the circumstances of the death of Jasmine Beckford (The Beckford Inquiry) sat throughout (except on two very minor occasions) in public. It heard every witness that it wanted to call and in the event did not feel it had failed in any respect to conduct a thorough investigation. There were several features about that case which dictated a departure from the norm of a hearing in private. First, Jasmine Beckford had been the subject of a Care Order, which placed the local Authority in the position of the child's parent for nearly 3 years before her death at the hands of her step-father, and had been removed from her foster-parents back to the natural family on trial. Second, there were some allegations that the social workers had snatched the child away from the foster-parents. Third, there was an acute conflict between the members of the local Authority and the Officers of the Social Services Department, together with a public suggestion of a cover-up by the local Authority. Fourth, the case came at a time of maximum public disquiet about the role of social workers in effecting a child protection service. Since the case of Maria Colwell in 1973 there have been major advances towards greater protection of children at risk. Nevertheless there remained considerable public concern in 1985 about the way in which the Beckford case was handled by Social Services and other supportive agencies. The public interest and media preoccupation with cases of child abuse in 1985 was fanned by a widespread feeling of a dire need to reassess the role of social workers in the community. It was also a time of heightened perception of the conflicting claims of natural parenthood and children's rights. For all these reasons we think that a public inquiry in the Beckford case was inescapable.

The immediate response of Brent Borough Council to the publication of the Beckford Report was instant dismissal of three employees of the local Authority's Social Services Department who in varying degrees had been criticised in the Report. Disciplinary proceedings were launched against the three, together with disciplinary action against the Director of Social Services and an Area Manager. This precipitate action embittered the trade union representatives, and has made them reluctant to co-operate in subsequent inquiries. While this is understandable, it is an undesirable and unfortunate aspect of the conduct of inquiries. It is a factor that cannot be ignored in the manner of conducting these inquiries. This was reflected in the Tyra Henry Inquiry by Lambeth Borough Council. That Council made it a part of the terms of reference that the Inquiry be held in public, and so it was. The Panel of Inquiry received very full written statements from the social workers involved and heard submissions from Counsel representing them throughout the Inquiry. The social worker most involved did not give oral evidence. Members of Tyra Henry's family did not give evidence, although they were invited to do so. The Tyra Henry case does not afford any compelling reason for conducting such cases in public. It is better that the Inquiry body should decide the issue, according to the circumstances prevailing. We are grateful to the sponsoring Authorities for having allowed us to determine the issue.

## This Inquiry

We see no special features in this case to depart from the norm of conducting the Inquiry in private. The trial judge in the criminal proceedings at the Central Criminal Court, Mr. Justice Steyn, appeared to envisage an independent inquiry in public. We do not, however, think that we are bound to accept that high judicial opinion, although naturally such opinion could not be other than influential. It is true that the public distress and disquiet about the facts of this case, so far as they have been selectively reported, has been considerable. While the public is naturally disturbed by yet another appalling death of a child at risk who might have been protected by social agencies, the public seems to exhibit confidence in a thorough investigation by this Commission, which has already publicly indicated the possibility of hearings in private.

There is the further fact that, while some fierce criticism has been precipitately levelled by the media at one or more social workers in Greenwich, there have been no individual allegations. Furthermore, unlike the Beckford case, there does not appear to be any over-riding issues of sensitive social policy to be reckoned with. The handling of the Kimberley case does not, for example, involve questions of racial discrimination.

In the course of extensive submissions made during the hearing on 8 June 1987 we were addressed by Mr. R. Roebuck, on behalf of The Daily Mail, Mr. Peter Hildrew, Social Services correspondent of The Guardian, Mr. Tindall, a private citizen who resides in the Borough of Greenwich, and Dr. Howard Baderman, consultant physician at University College Hospital, London, all of whom spoke strongly in favour of public hearings. Mr. Roebuck reminded us that Mr. Justice Steyn had described the case as one of unique wickedness in the annals of cruelty to children. That apart, the submissions were directed to considerations of a general nature. Dr. Baderman who spoke in his professional capacity and with some knowledge of the management of child abuse systems made six points, which individually and cumulatively call for detailed and earnest consideration.

His points were prefaced by the observation that there were distinct advantages of conducting the Inquiry in private. Privacy meant a quiet, unsensationalised unfolding of evidence, thus avoiding the limited and selective press coverage that so often appeared to be ill-motivated towards social workers. But an open inquiry would be seen to be scrupulously thorough and fair, even though the individual actors might find the experience of publicity stressful. Dr. Baderman's point is that the advantages of privacy were all ephemeral, related to the present Inquiry; the long term disadvantages to the traditional approach to inquiries into disasters outweighted the short-term advantages. It is difficult to assess what the impact will be, if the Inquiry is held privately. But whether Dr. Baderman is right in his estimation of the effect, we think he has a point which must be weighed in the balance.

His second point is that individuals actually gain by the experience of explaining their actions and decisions (sometimes admitting their errors of judgment, and even accepting that they acted negligently). There is, he claims, actual protection in the very fact of a public hearing. Again, we acknowlege that theoretically there could well be a valuable outcrop of publicity, although, so far as we are aware, there is no research evidence to support the assertion.

Dr. Baderman's third point is that he does not think that potential witnesses who may be the subject of criticism are deterred in coming forward to assist the Inquiry. We have some doubt about this proposition. It is true that the Panel of Inquiry in the Beckford case managed to attract all the witnesses it wanted to hear, despite the obvious fact that from the outset heavy criticism was likely to be made about quite a few of them.

We think, as Mr. Trotter on behalf of BASW submitted, that that case was exceptional. It worked once, but will it always work, he asked theoretically. And in that case there were exceptional features that made it impossible to keep the public out. There were serious allegations that the two Beckford sisters were snatched, screaming and shouting, from the foster-parents by two social workers. At the outset there appeared to be an issue involving racial discrimination (that it turned out not to be so was not anticipated).

There was, moreover, more than just a hint of a cover-up. None of these features is present in this Inquiry; and we can discern no other special features.

Dr. Baderman's fourth point is, we think, his strongest and deserves a persuasive answer. He asserts that members of a profession are, as we have said earlier, bound in duty to their professional ethics to stand up in public and be counted. There is a natural and understandable tendency, he says (and we agree), for professionals to deal with their public responsibilities within their professional organisations. The public perception is that professionals as a breed indulge far too readily in a closure of ranks. There are, Dr. Baderman adds, grounds for such a perception. *The Guardian*, in its leader of 8 June 1987, put it succinctly: " The social workers, health visitors, doctors and other professionals must be publicly not privately accountable for their actions ". We are inclined to accept this submission, so long as it is related to the generality of professionals who are either self-employed, or who, if employed by a public authority, nevertheless retain a high degree of autonomy, and in any event are personally answerable for their clinical judgment. A doctor in the National Health Service retains exclusive responsibilities for his clinical judgment. This is the very point that the DHSS in its Consultative Document of July 1985 makes in concluding that social workers cannot be in this respect equated to the medical profession. Paragraph 2.2 of the Consultative Paper states: "Each agency is responsible for the review of its own Services as part of its managerial and professional accountability. There are, however, differences in the way that this responsibility applies; for example, local authorities' Elected Members are ultimately responsible for all aspects of Social Services, whereas in the Health Services, while Health Authority members are ultimately responsible for services provided, traditionally clinical responsibility rested with professional staff. The organisational structure within agencies also varies; for instance, there are the different professional groups in hospitals and the line management relationship of nurses, and of staff in Social Services and Education departments and the independent status of general practitioners."

We would make two other points in answer to Dr. Baderman's point. A social worker employed by a local authority is part of line management, up to the Director of Social Services and, through him or her, is accountable, at least as to policy matters, to the members of the local Authority who probably will not possess any professional qualifications and indeed, as elected representatives of the public, may require actions and decisions respectively to be taken and made according to non-professional, political considerations. The position may not be very different in the case of health visitors in relation to their supervisors and to the relevant employing Health Authority. Furthermore, we doubt whether it is correct to treat social workers as professionals in the strict sense of that concept. The mark of the professional is that he is bound by a code of conduct established by a professional organisation that is capable of disciplining him and, if necessary, preventing him from practising his profession. If a lawyer or a doctor breaches his profession's code, his licence to practice may be taken away from him either temporarily or permanently. (It is worth noting that journalists are not professionals. It would be a gross invasion of the freedom of speech if a reporter in the media could be so disciplined). If and when social workers organise themselves under a Council of Social Work, that will be the time to apply the like standards of professional conduct to them. Until then, they must be treated as public servants whose skills and judgment are subject to the dictates of public employers. We would add that social workers who practice say, as guardians ad litem or independent social workers may be more nearly equated with doctors or lawyers.

Dr. Baderman's fifth point is directed to social systems. If they are shown to be weak, under-resourced or imperfect instruments of social policy, those features should be exposed quickly and publicly, for only in those conditions will public authorities respond appropriately. This is true, but we think that the published report of the Inquiry should suffice to induce action. If there is urgency, the Commission can always issue an interim report calling for immediate action.

Dr. Baderman's sixth point is that there is a tradition in this country of openness in matters of public interest, and not simply in matters that interest the public. And long may it remain so. We would heartily endorse this general approach. Were this Inquiry about a major national disaster or an investigation into corruption in high places we would not dissent from the view that it would be unthinkable for the Inquiry to be held in private. But the approach to child abuse inquiries must be different. If we thought that these were serious allegations beyond negligence or gross incompetence, we would consider a departure from the norm. But we think that there are in this instance no such special features. We are confident that we can conduct a thorough and fair inquiry without incurring the expenditure in terms of time and cost that is the inevitable concomitant of public hearings.

During the oral submissions on 8 June and the written submissions sent to the Commission we particularly noted that little mention was made of interests of children, either those within the Carlile household or generally. We find it necessary to remind ouselves that the essence of this Inquiry is to find ways in which children may be protected from abuse by their parents. It is that consideration which finally should determine the mode of inquiry. If the interests of the children would not be best served by an inquiry in public, that would be a powerful indicator to us to conduct our Inquiry in private.

We are strongly of the opinion that only a thorough inquiry will fully reveal the strengths and weaknesses of the present management of child abuse systems. Thoroughness might be in jeopardy if some important evidence was unavailable, due to the fact that the hearing was in public. We cannot afford to take that risk. A private hearing at which we can almost guarantee that a complete picture of the events surrounding the death of Kimberley Carlile will emerge, will be of lasting benefit to all those concerned to protect children at risk, and hence the children themselves. A thorough inquiry will ensure the optimum opportunity for making positive and constructive recommendations towards the reduction, to an irreducible minimum, of the number of children who die or suffer serious harm from child abuse.

# Verdict and Sentences on Nigel Hall and Pauline Carlile at the Central Criminal Court, 15 May 1987.

## A. Charges against Nigel Hall

1. Murder of Kimberley on 8 June 1986

   Plea:     Not guilty
   Verdict:  Guilty

   > Sentence: Life imprisonment (no minimum recommendation was made as to the time to be served)

2. Two counts of causing grievous bodily harm to Kimberley with intent to do grievous bodily harm between 3 October 1985 and 9 June 1986 (counts 2 and 6 of the indictment)

   Plea on both counts: Not guilty
   Verdict on count 2:  Not guilty
   Verdict on count 6:  Guilty

   > Sentence on count 6: 18 years' imprisonment

3. Inflicting grievous bodily harm on Kimberley between 3 October 1985 and 9 June 1986

   Plea:     Not guilty
   Verdict:  Not guilty

4. Wounding Kimberley with intent to do grievous bodily harm between 3 October 1985 and 9 June 1986

   Plea:     Not guilty
   Verdict:  Guilty

   > Sentence: 18 years' imprisonment

5. Assaulting Kimberley occasioning actual bodily harm between 3 October 1985 and 9 June 1986

   Plea:     Not guilty
   Verdict:  Guilty

   > Sentence: 5 years' imprisonment

6. Cruelty to Kimberley, contrary to Section 1(1), Children and Young Persons Act 1933, between 3 October 1985 and 9 June 1986

   Plea:     Not guilty
   Verdict:  Guilty

   > Sentence: 2 years' imprisonment[1]

---

[1] This is the maximum term prescribed by the statute.

Two further charges of unlawful wounding (count 5 of the indictment), and of inflicting grievous bodily harm (count 7) were withdrawn during the course of the trial.

All determinate sentences were made concurrent.

## B. Charges against Pauline Carlile

1. Two counts of causing grievous bodily harm to Kimberley with intent to do grievous bodily harm between 3 October 1985 and 9 June 1986 (counts 2 and 6 of the indictment)

   Plea on both counts: Not guilty
   Verdict on count 2:  Not guilty
   Verdict on count 6:  Guilty

   Sentence on count 6: 12 years' imprisonment

2. Inflicting grievous bodily harm on Kimberley between 3 October 1985 and 9 June 1986

   Plea:     Not guilty
   Verdict:  Not guilty

3. Wounding Kimberley with intent to do grievous bodily harm between 3 October 1985 and 9 June 1986

   Plea:     Not guilty
   Verdict:  Guilty

   Sentence: 12 years' imprisonment

4. Assaulting Kimberley occasioning actual bodily harm between 3 October 1985 and 9 June 1986

   Plea:     Not guilty
   Verdict:  Guilty

   Sentence: 5 years' imprisonment

5. Cruelty to Kimberley, contrary to Section 1(1), Children and Young Persons Act 1933, between 3 October 1985 and 9 June 1986

   Plea:     Not guilty
   Verdict:  Guilty

   Sentence: 2 years' imprisonment[1]

Charges of murder (count 1 of the indictment), unlawful wounding (count 5), and of inflicting grievous bodily harm (count 7) were withdrawn during the course of the trial.

All sentences were made concurrent.

---

[1] This is the maximum term prescribed by the statute.

# Child Abuse Inquiries, 1973–1987

## 1.  Central Government

| NAME OF CHILD | DATE OF INQUIRY | STATUS OF CARE | AUTHORITIES BY WHOM INQUIRY COMMISSIONED |
|---|---|---|---|
| Maria COLWELL | 1974 | No Care Order, Supervision Order | Secretary of State for Social Services (Pre Children Act 1975) |
| John George AUCKLAND | 1975 | No Care Order, voluntary care prior to death | Secretary of State for Social Services |
| Richard CLARK | 1975 | No Care Order | Secretary of State for Scotland |
| Stephen MENHENIOTT | 1978 | No Care Order | Department of Health and Social Security (Non statutory) |
| Darryn James CLARKE | 1979 | No Care Order | Secretary of State for Social Services |
| Paul Steven BROWN | 1980 | No Care Order | Secretary of State for Social Services |
| CLEVELAND Child Abuse Inquiry | (1987) to report | [Not Applicable] | Secretary of State for Social Services |

## 2.  Local

| NAME OF CHILD | DATE OF INQUIRY | STATUS OF CARE | AUTHORITIES BY WHOM INQUIRY COMMISSIONED |
|---|---|---|---|
| Graham BAGNALL | 1973 | No Care Order | Salop County Council |
| Max PIAZZANI | 1974 | No Care Order | Essex County Council and Essex Area Health Authority |
| David Lee NASEBY | 1974 | No Care Order | Staffordshire Area Review Committee |

| NAME OF CHILD | DATE OF INQUIRY | STATUS OF CARE | AUTHORITIES BY WHOM INQUIRY COMMISSIONED |
|---|---|---|---|
| Lisa GODFREY | 1975 | No Care Order | Lambeth, Southwark and Lewisham Area Health Authority (T), Inner London Probation and After Care Committee, and London Borough of Lambeth |
| Steven MEURS | 1975 | No Care Order | Norfolk County Council and Norfolk Area Health Authority |
| Neil HOWLETT | 1976 | Care Order | City of Birmingham District Council and Birmingham Area Health Authority |
| Wayne BREWER | 1977 | No Care Order, 3 year Supervision Order | Somerset Area Review Committee |
| Simon PEACOCK | 1978 | No Care Order | Cambridgeshire and Suffolk County Councils and Area Health Authorities |
| Karen SPENCER | 1978 | Care Order | Derbyshire County Council and Derbyshire Area Health Authority |
| Lester CHAPMAN | 1979 | No Care Order | Berkshire and Hampshire County Councils and Area Health Authorities |
| Carly TAYLOR | 1979/ 1980 | No Care Order | Leicestershire County Council and Area Health Authority (Teaching) |
| Darren COOPER | 1980 | No Care Order | Solihull Metropolitan Borough Council |
| Claire HADDON | 1980 | Supervision Order | City of Birmingham Metropolitan Council |
| Malcolm PAGE | 1980/ 1981 | Care Order | Essex County Council and Area Health Authority |

| NAME OF CHILD | DATE OF INQUIRY | STATUS OF CARE | AUTHORITIES BY WHOM INQUIRY COMMISSIONED |
|---|---|---|---|
| Richard FRASER | 1981 | Care Order | Lambeth, Southwark and Lewisham Area Health Authority (T), London Borough of Lambeth, and ILEA |
| Lucy GATES | 1981 | No Care Order | London Borough of Bexley and Bexley Health Authority |
| Emma HUGHES | 1981 | Care Order | Calderdale Metropolitan Borough Council |
| Maria MEHMEDAGI | 1981 | Care Order | Lambeth, Southwark and Lewisham Area Health Authority (T), London Borough of Southwark and Inner London Probation and After-Care Committee |
| Christopher PINDER Daniel FRANKLAND | 1981 | No Care Order | Bradford Area Review Committee and Bradford Metropolitan Borough Council |
| Jason CAESAR | 1982 | No Care Order | Cambridgeshire County Council |
| Shirley WOODCOCK | 1984 | Care Order | London Borough of Hammersmith and Fulham |
| Jasmine BECKFORD | 1985 | Care Order | London Borough of Brent and Brent Health Authority |
| Reuben CARTHY | 1985 | No Care Order | Nottinghamshire Area Review Committee |
| Heidi KOSEDA | 1985 | No Statutory Order | London Borough of Hillingdon Area Review Committee |
| Charlene SALT | 1986 | Supervision Order | Oldham District Review Committee |
| Tyra HENRY | (1987) to report | Care Order | London Borough of Lambeth |

| NAME OF CHILD | DATE OF INQUIRY | STATUS OF CARE | AUTHORITIES BY WHOM INQUIRY COMMISSIONED |
|---|---|---|---|
| Kimberley CARLILE | 1987 | No Care Order | London Borough of Greenwich and Greenwich Health Authority |

# A CHILD IN MIND:
# THE PROTECTION OF CHILDREN IN A
# RESPONSIBLE SOCIETY

# INDEX

286

290

292